ACT!® 2006 For Dummi...

D1285126

Shortcut Keys

Activity	Press This	Activity	Press This
Add a sales opportunity	Ctrl+F11	Record history	Ctrl+H
Attach a file	Ctrl+I	Refresh	Ctrl+F5
Clear an activity	Ctrl+D	Schedule call	Ctrl+L
Close a menu or dialog box	Esc	Schedule meeting	Ctrl+M
Copy the selected text	Ctrl+C	Schedule to–do	Ctrl+T
Cut the selected text	Ctrl+X	Undo	Ctrl+Z
Delete a contact, group, company, or lookup	Ctrl+Delete	Help	F1
		View Company List	Alt+F10
Display the Timer	Shift+F4	View Contact List	F8
Exit ACT!	Alt+F4	View Contact Detail window	F11
Insert Note	F9	View Group List	F10
New contact, group, or company	Insert	View Monthly Calendar	F5
Paste the last cut or copied text	Ctrl+V	View Task List	F7
Print address books, calendars, reports, labels, or envelopes	Ctrl+P	View Weekly Calendar	F3

User Roles

Function	Administrator	Manager	Standard	Restricted	Browse
Activities					
Create/edit/delete own activities	X	X	X	X	
Edit/delete other users' activities	X	X			
Create/edit events	X	X			
Synchronize Outlook activities	X	X	X	X	
Customize activity types	X	X			
Manage Priorities List	X	X			
Activity Series					
Create, edit and delete my own activity series templates	X	X	X		
Delete or edit activity series of others	X	X			
Schedule activity series	X	X	X	X	
Communications					
Create/edit templates	X	X	X		
E-mail	X	X	X	X	X
Enable a merge	X	X	X	X	
Contact, Companies, and Groups					
Create/edit	X	X	X	X	
Delete my contacts/companies/groups	X	X	X		

For Dummies: Bestselling Book Series for Beginners

ACT!® 2006 For Dummies®

Cheat Sheet

User Roles (cont'd)

Function	Administrator	Manager	Standard	Restricted	Browse
Contact, Companies, and Groups					
Delete other users' contacts/companies/groups	X	X			
Change Record Manager for contacts/companies/groups	X	X			
Customization					
Add fields	X	X			
Access Layout Designer	X	X			
Customize menus/toolbars	X	X	X		
Data Exchange					
Export to Excel from list views	X	X	X		
Export data from File menu	X	X			
Import data	X	X			
Database Management					
Add user	X				
Back up database	X	X			
Define fields and protected drop–down lists	X	X			
Delete database	X				
Lock database	X	X			
Change database preferences	X	X			
Perform maintenance	X				
Restore database	X				
Run ACT! update	X	X	X	X	X
Opportunities					
Create/edit	X	X	X	X	
Delete my opportunities	X	X	X		
Delete other users' opportunities	X	X			
Change Record Manager for opportunities	X	X			
Manage opportunity processes	X	X			
Manage opportunity products	X	X			
Reporting					
Create/edit	X	X	X		
Run reports	X	X	X	X	X
Synchronization					
Enable synchronization	X	X			
Manage Subscription List	X	X	X		
Manage synchronization set–up	X				
Premium Features					
Manage teams	X	X			
Manage resources	X	X			

For Dummies: Bestselling Book Series for Beginners

by Karen S. Fredricks

ACT! Certified Consultant and Premier Trainer

WILEY

Wiley Publishing, Inc.

ACT!® 2006 For Dummies®

Published by
Wiley Publishing, Inc.
111 River Street
Hoboken, NJ 07030-5774

www.wiley.com

Copyright © 2006 by Wiley Publishing, Inc., Indianapolis, Indiana

Published by Wiley Publishing, Inc., Indianapolis, Indiana

Published simultaneously in Canada

For general information on our other products and services, please contact our Customer Care Department within the U.S. at 800-762-2974, outside the U.S. at 317-572-3993, or fax 317-572-4002.

For technical support, please visit www.wiley.com/techsupport.

Wiley also publishes its books in a variety of electronic formats. Some content that appears in print may not be available in electronic books.

Library of Congress Control Number: 2005933552

ISBN-13: 978-0-471-77454-9

ISBN-10: 0-471-77454-5

Manufactured in the United States of America

10 9 8 7 6 5 4 3 2 1

1O/SR/RR/QV/IN

WILEY

About the Author

Karen S. Fredricks began her life rather non-technically growing up in Kenya. She attended high school in Beirut, Lebanon, where she developed her sense of humor while dodging bombs. After traveling all over the world, Karen ended up at the University of Florida and has been an ardent Gator fan ever since. In addition to undergraduate studies in English and accounting, Karen has a Master's degree in psycholinguistics. Beginning her career teaching high school English and theatre, Karen switched to working with the PC during its inception in the early '80s and has worked as a full-time computer consultant and trainer ever since.

Karen is an ACT! Certified Consultant, an ACT! Premier Trainer, a Microsoft Office User Specialist, and a QuickBooks Pro Certified Advisor. She is the author of both the *ACT! 6 For Dummies* and *ACT! 2005 For Dummies* books, many copywrited training manuals, and the editor of *ACT! Extra,* a monthly newsletter. She is a frequent guest on the several syndicated radio talk shows and has frequent public speaking engagements. A true ACT! FanACTic, she founded the ACT! Users Group of South Florida and served as the official host for the ACT! 6 Launch Tour in Florida.

Karen resides in Boca Raton, Florida. Her company, Tech Benders, provides computer consulting, support, and training services. In her spare time, Karen loves to spend time with family and friends, play tennis, practice Yoga, and write schlocky poetry.

Feel free to send your comments about the book to www.dummies@techbenders.com.

Dedication

To my Mother, Frances Conn, in recognition of her ninetieth birthday. You've always been there for me when I've needed you. You're a smart, independent lady who has been able to conquer just about anything — including driving a stickshift in an RHD car. I love you!

Author's Acknowledgments

I like to start each day reflecting on the many things for which I am thankful. Here are a few of the people who have made my life a truly wonderful one.

The people at Wiley Publishing are fantastic to work with and have made writing this book a pleasure! My acquisitions editor, Terri Varveris, has become my friend as well as my editor. Thanks, Terri, and congratulations on the new baby! My project editor, Blair Pottenger, was a true delight to work with; thanks, Blair — and best wishes on your upcoming marriage! Teresa Artman, my copy editor, had the unenviable task of making me look good; Teresa, your edits were always right on!

I started my company, Tech Benders, just a few years ago and have come to think of it as my third child. All the members of the ACT! Users Group are the greatest; they remind me what using ACT! is all about. Thanks also to my many wonderful clients who have become my friends along the way and have helped to make my baby so successful! There have been many changes within the ACT! organization during the course of the last year. This year saw the departure of Ted Cooper after many years with ACT!. Fortunately, Melissa Lorch, Paul Selby, and Beth Kohler are but a few of the great people who continue to make ACT! better and better, year after year. Joe Bergera and Larry Ritter have recently joined the organization — their ideas and leadership will ensure that ACT! continues to thrive. Richard McMakin — thanks for all your help; like me, you never give up until you find the answer! Rich Carey — we make an awesome team!

If you've ever worked with an ACT! Certified Consultant, I know you've found them to be incredibly knowledgeable, conscientious, and professional. My thanks go out to the entire ACT! CC Community for their willingness to share anything and everything ACT!. Special thanks go out to some of the top gurus — and my good friends — Susan Clark, Stan Smith, John Kaufman, Elaine Wirth, and Gay Chambers. Roy Laudenslager worked as an ACT! Support Specialist for over 12 years before taking the plunge to come work with me. He also let me coerce him into being the technical editor for this book. He approached that job with the same thoroughness and cheerfulness that he dedicates to any task. His incredible knowledge and experience make him a joy to work with. Thanks, Royel!

As George Carlin once said, "Keep only cheerful friends. The grouches pull you down." I'm lucky to be able to say that I've got a lot of cheerful friends! The names you see throughout this book are not fictional; they are the names of all the special people in my life. Greetings go out to my Wednesday, Saturday, and Sunday tennis games (Kalle, Nancy, Susan, Sue, Joanne, Jo, and Linda) and to the whole gang at the Swim and Racquet Center of Boca Raton. You guys rock!

Words can't describe how special my daughters are to me. They have brought such joy to my life and are a constant source of pride and support. All my love goes out to the two most special people in my life: Andrea and Alyssa Fredricks. You come from a family of strong women and will see your hard work and efforts come to fruition. May you both continue to aim for the stars! And finally to Gary Kahn, my wonderful friend, who came to me with questions and ended up by supplying me with answers. All I can say is "Thank you" — and pass the licorice, Teriyaki Boy!

Publisher's Acknowledgments

We're proud of this book; please send us your comments through our online registration form located at www.dummies.com/register/.

Some of the people who helped bring this book to market include the following:

Acquisitions, Editorial, and Media Development

Project Editor: Blair J. Pottenger

Acquisitions Editor: Terri Varveris

Senior Copy Editor: Teresa Artman

Technical Editor: Roy Laudenslager

Editorial Manager: Kevin Kirschner

Media Development Manager:
Laura VanWinkle

Media Development Supervisor:
Richard Graves

Editorial Assistant: Amanda Foxworth

Cartoons: Rich Tennant
(www.the5thwave.com)

Composition Services

Project Coordinator: Adrienne Martinez

Layout and Graphics: Andrea Dahl,
Lauren Goddard, Joyce Haughey,
Stephanie D. Jumper, Barbara Moore

Proofreaders: Leeann Harney, Jessica Kramer,
Carl Pierce, Dwight Ramsey,
Susan Sims, TECHBOOKS Production
Services

Indexer: TECHBOOKS Production Services

Publishing and Editorial for Technology Dummies

    Richard Swadley, Vice President and Executive Group Publisher

    Andy Cummings, Vice President and Publisher

    Mary Bednarek, Executive Acquisitions Director

    Mary C. Corder, Editorial Director

Publishing for Consumer Dummies

    Diane Graves Steele, Vice President and Publisher

    Joyce Pepple, Acquisitions Director

Composition Services

    Gerry Fahey, Vice President of Production Services

    Debbie Stailey, Director of Composition Services

Table of Contents

Introduction

● ●

*A*CT! is the best-selling contact manager that's used by more than 4 million professionals and 11,000 corporations worldwide. For many of these users, ACT! represents their first foray into the area of contact relationship management (CRM). Contact management software is a little more complex to understand than other types of software. With a word processor, each document that you create is totally separate; if you make a mistake, you need only to delete your current document and start fresh. Contact management, however, builds its way into a final product; if you don't give a bit of thought as to what goal you wish to achieve, you could end up with a muddled mess.

I am a *fanACTic,* and I'm not ashamed to admit it. I use ACT! at work. I use ACT! on the road. I use ACT! at home. I've even inspired my friends to use ACT!. I'm excited about the product and know that by the time you learn to unleash the power of ACT!, you'll be excited, too.

So what am I so excited about? I've seen firsthand how ACT! can save you time and help make you more efficient in the bargain. To me, accomplishing more in less time is an exciting thought — it allows more time for the fun things in life. Best of all, ACT! is a program that's very easy to get up and running in a very short time. You'll be amazed not only at how quickly you can set up a database but also at how easily you can put that database to work.

Maybe by the time you finish this book, you, too, will become a fanACTic!

About This Book

ACT! 2006 For Dummies is a reference book. As such, each chapter can be read independently and in the order you want. Each chapter focuses on a specific topic, so you can dive right in, heading straight for the chapter that interests you most. Having said that, however, I must say that I've tried to put the chapters into a logical sequence so that those of you who are new to ACT! can just follow the bouncing ball from chapter to chapter. More experienced users can use the Table of Contents and the index to simply navigate from topic to topic as needed.

Essentially, this book is a nuts-and-bolts how-to guide for accomplishing various tasks. In addition, drawing on many of my own experiences as a full-time ACT! consultant and trainer, I include specific situations that should give you a feeling for the full power of ACT!.

Conventions Used in This Book

Like in most Windows-based software programs, you often have several different ways to accomplish a task in ACT!.

For the most part, I show you ways to perform a function by using the ACT! menus. When an instruction reads Choose File⇨Open, you must access the File menu (located at the top of the ACT! screen) by clicking it with the left mouse button and then choosing the Open option from the subsequent menu that appears. In most cases, you can access these commands from anywhere within ACT! although I generally advise new ACT! users to always start a task from the Contact Detail view, which is the first window you see when ACT! opens. If you must be in a particular area to complete a task otherwise, I tell you where.

I also present you with keyboard shortcuts here and there. Generally, ACT! shortcuts are triggered by simultaneously pressing the Ctrl key and another key on the keyboard. For instance, the shortcut for recording a history is Ctrl+H.

When you need to access one of ACT!'s hidden menus, click an appropriate area of the screen with the right mouse button and then choose from the contextual menu that appears. In these instances, I simply say *right-click* when you need to right-click.

What You Should Read

Of course, I hope that you're going to sit down and read this entire book from cover to cover. But then again, this book isn't The Great American Novel. And, come to think of it, the whole reason why you bought this book in the first place is because you want to get your ACT! together (no groans, please!) as quickly as possible because you're probably finding yourself with too much to do and too little time in which to do it.

For the time being, I'm going to let you get away with reading just the parts that interest you most. I'll let you read the last chapter first and the first chapter last if you like because this book is designed to allow you to read each chapter independently. However, when you find yourself floating in a swimming pool, soaking up the sun, and wondering what to do with all your spare time, you might want to go back and read some of those chapters you skipped. You just might discover something!

What You Don't Have to Read

This book is intended for both new and existing ACT! users. Most of the instructions apply to both groups of readers. Once in a while, I include some information that might be of special interest to more advanced readers. Newbies, feel free to skip these sections! Also, any information tagged with a Technical Stuff icon is there for the truly technically inclined. Everyone else can just skip this info.

Foolish Assumptions

One of my least favorite words in the English language is the word *assume*, but I've got to admit that I've made a few foolish — albeit necessary — assumptions when writing this book. First of all, I assume that you own a Windows-based computer and that ACT! is installed on it. Secondly, I assume that you have a basic knowledge of how to use your computer, keyboard, and mouse, and that ACT! isn't the very first application that you're trying to master.

I also assume that you have a genuine desire to organize your life and/or business and have determined that ACT! is the way to go.

Finally (and I feel quite comfortable with this assumption), I assume that you'll grow to love ACT! as much as I do.

How This Book Is Organized

I organized this book into six parts. Each part contains several chapters covering related topics. The following is a brief description of each part, with chapter references directing you where to go for particular information:

Part I: The Opening ACT!

In Part I, you get an introduction to the concept of a database and why ACT! has become such a popular choice of database users (Chapter 1). In this part, you read about what to expect the first time you fire up ACT! (Chapter 2) and how to set the main preferences in ACT! (Chapter 3).

Part II: Putting the ACT! Database to Work

Part II focuses on putting your contacts into ACT! (Chapter 4) and, more importantly, how to find them again (Chapters 6). I show you how to view all the details about one contact, how to pull up a list of all your contacts, and even how to create an easy list report.

After you master organizing your contact information, Part II helps you organize your day. ACT! makes it easy to take notes (Chapter 7) so that you start relying on ACT! more and your memory less. You find out how to schedule appointments, calls, and to-do's — and other important events in your life. And, you discover how to view those activities in the daily, weekly, and monthly calendars (Chapter 8). Your life can become complicated, but have no fear because ACT! does its best to help you navigate through the maze. The History, Documents, and Secondary Contacts tabs allow you to accumulate lots of information about each and every one of your contacts (Chapter 5).

Part III: Sharing Your Information with Others

Corporate America lives for reports, and ACT! is up to the challenge. Whether you want to print labels or telephone directories on commercially printed forms or prefer to utilize the ACT! built-in reports (Chapter 9), Part III shows you how. I even tell you about building your own reports from scratch (Chapter 10).

One of the best features of ACT! is the ability to communicate easily with the outside world. Part III shows you how to work with templates to automate routine documents as well as how to send out mass mail merges — whether by snail mail, fax, or e-mail (Chapter 11). You also discover the advantages of using ACT! for your e-mail client (Chapter 12).

Part IV: Advanced ACT!ing

We're all different and often like to do things in our own unique way. ACT! understands that concept, and Part IV helps you to customize ACT! to your heart's content. At first glance, ACT! might seem like just an over-the-counter piece of software, but by adding fields (Chapter 13) and placing them on customized layouts (Chapter 14), you can make it perform as well as an expensive piece of proprietary software.

Every database needs an administrator. If you're elected to the job, you need to know how to perform administrative tasks, such as performing routine maintenance, backing up your database, and checking for duplicate data entry (Chapter 15). You'll learn about *ACT8diag,* the higher-level maintenance tool, and how to add multiple users to your database (Chapter 16). For those of you using ACT! 2006 Premium for Workgroups, you can read about enhanced security and automation of common maintenance tasks. If you have remote users who need to access all or parts of your database, you need to know how to synchronize your database (Chapter 17).

Part V: Commonly Overlooked ACT! Features

Part V focuses on four of the most frequently overlooked ACT! features:

- ✔ **Microsoft integration:** Synchronize your ACT! and Outlook address books and calendars; attach a Web site in Internet Explorer directly to an ACT! contact; and explore the various ways that you can use ACT! and Excel together (Chapter 18).

- ✔ **Sales opportunities:** Track your prospective sales, prioritize them, and analyze what you did right — or wrong — in making the sale (Chapter 19).

- ✔ **Groups:** Group your contacts to add a new dimension to your database (Chapter 20).

- ✔ **Companies:** This is an exciting new feature of ACT! 2006. The Company feature enables you to view and edit contacts that all "belong" to the same company (Chapter 21).

In addition, I show you how to install and customize ACT! Premium for Web, the online version of ACT! (Chapter 22).

Part VI: The Part of Tens

With apologies to David Letterman, Part VI gives you two of my favorite ACT! lists. First, I discuss the top ten benefits of using the ACT! Premium for Web product (Chapter 23). Finally, I give you ten of my favorite ways to help you utilize ACT! to its fullest extent (Chapter 24).

Icons Used in This Book

A Tip icon indicates a special timesaving tip or a related thought that might help you use ACT! to its full advantage. Try it; you might like it!

A Warning icon alerts you to the danger of proceeding without caution. *Do not* attempt to try doing anything that you are warned not to do!

Remember icons alert you to important pieces of information that you don't want to forget.

A Technical Stuff icon indicates tidbits of advanced knowledge that might be of interest to IT specialists but might just bore the heck out of the average reader. Skip these at will.

Where to Go from Here

For those of you who are ACT! old-timers, you might want to at least skim the entire contents of this book before hunkering down to read the sections that seem the most relevant to you. My experience is that the average ACT! user probably uses only a portion of the program and might not even be aware of some of the really cool features of ACT!. You might be surprised to discover all that ACT! has to offer!

For the ACT! newbie, I recommend heading straight for Part I, where you can acquaint yourself with ACT! before moving on to other parts of the book and the ACT! program.

Part I
The Opening ACT!

In this part . . .

I know that you're excited about all the possibilities that ACT! has to offer and want to dive into the program as soon as possible. Here's where you find an overview of some of the cool features that you find in ACT!. You also become familiar with the many faces of ACT!; after all, you wouldn't want to get lost along the way. But first, you have to do a bit of homework and whip ACT! into shape by fiddling with a few preference settings to ensure that ACT! produces the type of results that you're looking for.

Chapter 1

An Overview of ACT!

In This Chapter
- ▶ What is ACT!?
- ▶ Who uses ACT!?
- ▶ Basic ACT! concepts
- ▶ A few basic ground rules
- ▶ The "Two ACT! Flavors"

So what is ACT!, anyway? I find that one of the hardest things that I have to do with ACT! is to explain exactly what it is. I like to initially explain ACT! by using very politically correct terminology. For example, ACT! 2006

- ✔ Is a contact management software package
- ✔ Provides users and organizations with powerful tools to manage their business relationships
- ✔ Can be customized based on your company's requirements
- ✔ Is the world's leading contact management software

Feel free to use these points to impress your friends. You might want to mention some of the wonderful features of ACT!, which I do in the first section of this chapter. I also describe the typical ACT! user and give you a brief primer on some pertinent ACT! terminology. I give you a few ground rules that I've established over the years after watching new users wrestle with certain aspects of using ACT!. Finally, I talk about the two versions of ACT! that are available to you.

What Does ACT! Do?

Because I want you to enjoy the benefits of using ACT!, I've put together a little shopping list of features so that you can see all that ACT! can do for you, too. In parentheses after each item, I include a chapter reference where you can find more information about a particular feature (if you're so inclined).

ACT! is a multifaceted personal management tool that

✔ **Stores complete contact information,** including name, company, phone numbers, mailing addresses, and e-mail addresses. (Chapter 4)

✔ **Comes with over 50 predefined fields for each contact** that you add to your database. If you want to add additional fields to meet your specific needs, go right ahead. (Chapter 13)

✔ **Records an unlimited number of dated notes for each of your contacts** so that you can easily keep track of important conversations and activities. This feature is particularly useful for those of us who (unlike our friend, the elephant) do forget things on occasion. (Chapter 7)

✔ **Keeps more than a boring old calendar.** Your scheduled activities are cross-referenced with the appropriate contact so that you have a full record of all interactions that you've had — or will have — with that contact. In addition, you can set an alarm to remind you of the important stuff as well as roll over less-important things until the next day. (Chapter 8)

✔ **Prints out anything** from simple phone lists or address books to detailed reports on activities, notes, leads, and sales opportunities. You can print reports of your reports if you feel so inclined. (Chapters 9 and 10)

✔ **Creates mailing labels and envelopes.** Or, if you prefer, perform broadcast faxes and e-mails with ACT!. (Chapters 11 and 12)

✔ **Manages your sales pipeline** with built-in forecasting tools. You can easily print a few sales reports or create a graph showing your open, won, or lost sales. (Chapter 19)

✔ **Synchronizes data with remote users.** If you have other ACT! users in remote locations, you can send database changes to them and vice versa. (Chapter 17)

✔ **Lets you design and activate a series of activities** to automate your tasks, thus assuring that none of your contacts "fall through the cracks." (Chapter 8)

The Typical ACT! User

So just who is the typical ACT! user? Well, with more than 4 million registered ACT! users and 11,000 businesses currently using ACT!, you're safe to assume that nearly every industry is represented among its user base. Although ACT! started primarily as a tool for salespeople wanting to follow up on their prospects and customers, ACT! has evolved into a tool used by any individual or business trying to organize the chaos of daily life.

I think it's only fair to warn you about one of the possible side effects that you might develop if you use ACT!. If you're anything like me, you'll become addicted to ACT! and eventually use it to manage all facets of your busy existence. You might just become a fanACTic. (Quite simply, a *fanACTic* is an ACT! user who has become addicted to using ACT!.)

So just who is using ACT!? Everyone.

- A CEO uses ACT! because he wants to know what his salespeople are doing and how his customers are being treated.

- An administrative assistant uses ACT! it to automate routine tasks and to keep a schedule of various tasks and activities.

- A salesperson uses ACT! to make sure that she's following up on all her prospects.

- A disorganized person uses ACT! to help him become more organized.

- A smart person uses ACT! because she knows that she'll have more time to play by working more efficiently.

- A lazy person uses ACT! because he knows it's more fun to play than to work.

So what kinds of businesses use ACT!? All kinds.

- Large businesses that want to improve communication among employees

- Small businesses that have to rely on a small staff to complete a multitude of tasks

- Businesses of all sizes looking for software that can automate their businesses and make them more productive in less time

- Businesses looking to grow by marketing to their prospects

- Businesses looking to retain their current customers by providing an excellent level of customer service and developing lasting relationships

So who's *not* using ACT!? Okay, I just said that simply *everyone* is using ACT!, but a few stubborn folks remain out there who aren't looking to organize their lives, such as

- Workaholics who live to spend every waking moment at work

- Hermits who don't need to schedule any appointments or remember to make follow-up phone calls

- Individuals with photographic memories who retain all information and never need to take a note

- Companies that require no paperwork

- Businesses that do no marketing or that have no interest in expanding their customer base

A Few Concepts to Get You Started

Nobody likes technical jargon, but in the course of showing you how to use ACT!, I might end up lapsing into Geek Speak and use a handful of somewhat technical terms; I just can't avoid it. Becoming familiar with them now is less painful in the long run.

First things first. ACT! is a database program. A *database* is a collection of information organized in such a way that the user of the database can quickly find desired pieces of information. Think of a database as an electronic filing system. Although most ACT! users create a database of contacts, some users develop ACT! databases to collect information about things other than contacts. For example, you might create an ACT! database to catalog all the CDs and DVDs in your collection.

Traditional databases are organized by *fields, records,* and *files:*

- ✔ **Field:** A *field* is a single piece of information. In databases, fields are the smallest units of information. A tax form, for example, contains a number of fields: one for your name, one for your Social Security number, one for your income, and so on. In ACT!, you start with 50 separate fields for each individual contact. You find out how to add information into these fields in Chapter 4. And, in Chapter 13, I show you how to change the attributes of existing fields and how to add new ones to your database if you're the database administrator.

- ✔ **Record:** A *record* is one complete set of fields. In ACT!, all the information that you collect that pertains to one individual contact is a *contact record.*

- ✔ **File:** A *file* is the entire collection of data or information. Each database that you create in ACT! is given a unique filename. You can create more than one file or database in ACT! — head to Chapter 3 to find out how.

The Basic ACT! Ground Rules

Sometimes you just need to learn things the hard way. After all, experience is the best teacher. Luckily for you, however, I've compiled a list of rules based on a few mistakes that I see other ACT! users commit. You're not going to find these rules written down anywhere else, and they might not even make a whole lot of sense to you at the moment. However, as you become more and more familiar with ACT!, these rules will make all the sense in the world. You might even want to refer to them from time to time.

Karen's Four Rules of Always:

✔ Always log in to ACT! as yourself.

✔ Always strive for standardization in your database by entering your data in a consistent manner.

✔ Always input as much information into your database as possible.

✔ Always perform routine maintenance of your database at least once a week and create a backup after any session that involved new data input!

The Two ACT! Flavors

ACT! 2006 comes in two separate editions. Everything I cover in this book applies to both versions of ACT!:

✔ ACT! 2006

✔ ACT! 2006 Premium for Workgroups

Every feature found in ACT! 2006 is also found in ACT! 2006 for Workgroups as well. However, from time to time, I point out a feature that is found only in the workgroup version.

All users sharing the same database must be using the *same* edition of ACT!; this means that one user can't be in ACT! 2006 while another is in ACT! 2006 for Workgroups. It also means that users of an older version such as ACT! 6 can't share a database with users of an ACT! 2006 database.

You'll want to be aware of the basic differences between the two versions, so here they are:

ACT! 2006

ACT! 2006 is geared towards the individual or small business user with less than ten users. Most small environments would typically not use the enterprise features found in ACT! 2006 Premium for Workgroups. ACT! 2006:

✔ Utilizes the Desktop Edition (MSDE) version of SQL

✔ Is designed for individuals and small workgroups

✔ Allows a maximum of ten active named users per database

✔ Has a size limitation of 2GB per database

✔ Considers contacts as *Public* (viewable by all database users) or *Private* (viewable only by the Record Manager who created the record)

✔ Has two methods of synchronizing remote data

✔ Can't open a database created using ACT! 2006 Premium for Workgroups

ACT! 2006 Premium for Workgroups

It's important to note that ACT! 2006 Premium for Workgroups contains all of the features found in ACT! 2006. However, the Premium version also includes several extra features that the corporate user just might find appealing.

✔ Includes Microsoft (MS) SQL Server Standard Edition but can also work with MSDE if preferred

✔ Is designed for the corporate enterprise user

✔ Doesn't place a limit on the number of database users

✔ Is more *scalable,* meaning that it's unlikely you'll outgrow your database

✔ Takes the issue of security one step further by adding a third level of contact access — *limited access.*

Database managers and administrators can allow users or teams of users to access these limited access contacts on a contact-by-contact basis.

✔ Has three methods of synchronizing remote data

✔ Can open a database created using ACT! 2006 and can save a database to ACT! 2006 format

✔ Includes Group Invitations and resource scheduling

✔ Provides advanced administrative functionality, including silent installations and automated maintenance procedures (Chapter 16).

✔ Provides advanced opportunity tracking

So what are you waiting for? Boot up your computer, grab the book, and get going. After all, it's time to ACT! (pun intended).

Chapter 2

The Various Faces of ACT!

*A*fter getting the hang of maneuvering in ACT!, you'll find that it's an amazingly easy program to master. The key is to become familiar with the lay of the land *before* you start building your contact database. By doing so, you avoid playing hide-and-seek *later.* To that end, I show you how to log into and open an ACT! database. Although initially getting around in ACT! is pretty easy, you might become lost in the maze of views and tabs that ACT! is divided into. I help you navigate through that maze by taking you on a tour of ACT! so that you can become familiar with the various ACT! screens. Finally, you discover the places that you can turn to if you need additional help.

Locating the Correct Database

When you open ACT!, by default, ACT! opens up the database that was last open on your computer. Easy enough, huh? If, however, you stumble into the incorrect database by mistake, you need to know how to find the correct one. If you're lucky enough to have inherited a database that someone else developed (someone who maybe even placed that database on your computer for you), be sure to ask where that database is located — before that person walks out of your life.

The *default database location* is the place on your computer that ACT! uses to store any new databases that you create and look in to open any existing database. If your database isn't in the default location, you have to move your database to the correct location, change the default location (as I discuss in Chapter 3), or browse to the location of your database.

The first screen that you see when opening an ACT! database each and every time is the Contacts Detail window. If you click around and end up in any of the other ACT! screens by accident, don't panic. One of the nice things about ACT! is that you can execute most commands from any ACT! screen (unless I tell you otherwise). And I promise that pretty soon, the various screens become so familiar to you that you'll be able to navigate through ACT! with the best of them.

To open an existing database, make sure that ACT! is open and then follow these steps:

1. Choose File⇨Open Database from the ACT! Contact Detail window.

The Open dialog box appears (see Figure 2-1).

Figure 2-1: Opening an ACT! database.

2. Click the drop-down arrow to the right of the Look In box.

3. Double-click the folder that contains your database to expand.

4. Click the name of your database and then click Open.

If you prefer, double-click the name of the database that you want to open.

When you open an ACT! database, you actually use a shortcut; these short-cuts all end with the `.pad` file extension. Every ACT! database actually stores three different groups of data:

- ✔ **Main database:** The main database consists of all your contacts' information, activities, notes, histories, and so on. The database files are stored on your local machine by default. You can move the database and all associated files to another location or even over to a network drive if you so desire.

- ✔ **Database supplemental files:** These files and folders are automatically created when you create a new database and include layouts, templates, e-mail messages, and any attachments associated with a contact record. You cannot change the location of these files in the database; they are automatically stored as part of your database.

- ✔ **Personal supplemental files:** These files, which are saved to your local computer, include files such as word processing documents not associated with a contact, newly created layouts, and templates. E-mail messages and attachments associated with contacts are also saved as personal supplemental files.

The ACT! Login Screen

If more than one person shares your ACT! database, ACT! presents you with a login screen each time you attempt to open your database. If you are the only person using a database, the login screen will not appear. Essentially, the login screen (as shown in Figure 2-2) asks you for your user name and your password. Your user name and password are not case sensitive (that is, you can enter your name by typing either lowercase or UPPERCASE letters). You also need to make sure that you enter your user name and password information correctly. For example, if your user name includes your middle initial with a period, you must type that middle initial — including the period — to gain access to your database.

Figure 2-2:
Logging on
to ACT!.

Generally, the Administrator of your database determines your password. The *database Administrator* is the person responsible for making major changes to the database and for performing routine database maintenance (Chapter 16). Although several users may all have access to an ACT! database, ACT! doesn't require that each user have a password. If the database Administrator didn't assign you a password, just leave the password area blank.

If you are assigned a password, notice that asterisks appear while you type it in. That's normal. Just like when you type your ATM card PIN, your ACT! database password is hidden while you type it to prevent any lurking spies who might be watching from learning your password. You're able to change your own password; see Chapter 3 to find out how.

Figure 2-2 shows that ACT! gives you the option of saving your password (an option automatically selected by default). Although this option helps you to log on to your database a little faster in the future, think about making this decision. First of all, what good is a password if it always magically appears anytime that you attempt to access your database? Secondly, by having ACT! remember your password, you may eventually forget it yourself!

The Importance of Being My Record

The first contact that you see when opening an ACT! database is your own — that's your *My Record*. My Record is nothing more than a contact record that is associated with a user of the database. Your My Record stores all your own information, which automatically appears in some of the preset templates that come with ACT!. For example, a fax cover sheet includes *your* telephone and fax numbers; a report has *your* name at the top; and a letter has *your* name at the bottom.

If someone else's information appears as the first contact record that you see when you open your database, explore these three possibilities:

- ✔ Did you log in as yourself? If not, do so. Then, when you open ACT! again — logged in as yourself — your My Record appears.

- ✔ Did you inadvertently change your own contact information? If that's the case, change it back.

- ✔ If you're 100 percent certain that you logged in as yourself and haven't changed your contact information, your database is likely corrupted. I'm not trying to scare you, but I recommend that you turn to Chapter 15, where I show you how to perform a little CPR on your database.

Taking the time to enter all your own contact information is very important. If you don't, you might find that you're missing key information when you start to work with templates and reports. For example, if you never enter your own fax number, your fax number doesn't appear on the Fax Cover Sheet template, which means you have to fill it in every time that you send a fax. Save yourself the trouble and fill in your My Record right off the bat.

Your My Record also allows you to use a few other important ACT! features:

- ✔ Permission to perform various functions is based on the security level of your My Record.

- ✔ Contacts, notes, histories, activities, and opportunities marked as Private can be viewed only by the Record Manager who created them.

- ✔ Every time you enter a new contact, your name appears as the creator of that contact.

- ✔ When you delete a contact, a history of that deletion appears in the History area of your My Record.

- ✔ Every time that you add a note to a contact record, your name appears as the Record Manager of that note.

- ✔ When you schedule an activity, your name automatically attaches to that activity.

Finding Your Way around in ACT!

The purpose of this book is to serve as a reference for both new and existing ACT! users. I certainly don't want to lose anyone along the way. New ACT! users might be somewhat intimidated when they encounter ACT! for the first time. Be assured that this experience is akin to the first time you drive a new car at night in the rain: momentary panic sets in. After you've driven the car for a week or so, the location of the light and windshield wiper controls becomes second nature. I guarantee you'll have the same experience with ACT!.

Navigating through ACT! is fairly easy. However, to make the navigating even easier, I highlight throughout this section a number of pitfalls that you want to avoid.

The title bar

The title bar at the top of the screen provides you with two pieces of key information:

- ✔ The software name
- ✔ The database name

Don't overlook the importance of this wealth of information! If your title bar reads FreeCell, you've stumbled into the wrong piece of software. If the database name indicates ACT8demo, chances are pretty good that you're in the wrong database and may be adding hundreds of new contacts to the wrong place. And if the user name is not yours, you may not be getting the appropriate credit for all your hours of hard work. You can see the title bar, along with other key areas of ACT!, in Figure 2-3.

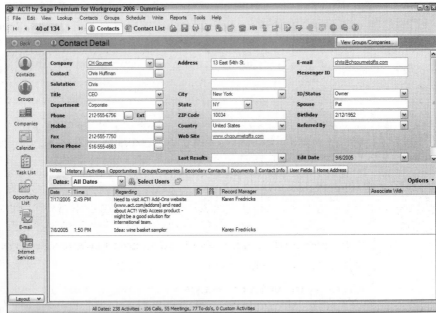

Figure 2-3:
The opening
ACT!
screen.

The record counter

ACT! supplies you with a record counter in the top-left corner of the Contact Detail window (refer to Figure 2-3). The first number indicates the number of your record as it relates alphabetically to the other members of your current lookup. A *lookup* refers to the contacts in your database that you're currently working with. (You can find out everything that you ever want to know about a lookup in Chapter 6.) This number changes when you add or remove contacts. The second number supplies you with the total number of contacts in either your entire database or your current lookup.

To the left and right of the record counter is a set of left- and right-pointing triangles. You can click these triangles to navigate through the contact records. For instance, to go to the previous record, you simply click the left-pointing triangle. Refer to Figure 2-3, which shows how to use these triangles.

I recommend getting into the habit of checking the total number of contacts in your database each time you open ACT!. If the total number of contacts changes radically from one day to the next, you just might be in the wrong database. Worse yet, a dramatic change in the number of contacts may indicate corruption in your database.

The layout

One of the biggest sources of confusion to the new ACT! user is the use of layouts. The *layout* refers to the order in which fields appear on the ACT! screens as well as the colors, fonts, and graphics that you see. You can specify the colors, fonts, and graphics in the layout as well as the position and order of fields. If the database Administrator created new fields for the database, he then needed to add them to a layout. In Chapter 14, I explain how you can create your own customized layouts.

- ✔ **Modify the contact, company, and group layouts or create your own layouts to suit your needs.**

    There's no right or wrong layout — only the layout that you prefer. For example, maybe the Sales Department needs to see one set of fields, but the Customer Service Department needs to see an entirely different group of fields — and want them to appear in a specific order.

- ✔ **Remove fields that you don't use or move fields to other tabs.**

- ✔ **Add fields to your layout**

- ✔ **Change the order of the tabs**

- ✔ **Add your own tabs to the bottom of a layout.**

    Renaming and reordering the tabs to your liking helps you organize your fields. For example, you might want to keep all the personal information about a customer on one tab and the products that he's interested in on another tab.

You can find the name of the layout by clicking the Layout button in the lower-left corner of the ACT! screen, as shown in Figure 2-3. If you inadvertently switch layouts, you might not be able to see all the information in your database, or you might see your information arranged in a different order. At this point, panic often sets in. Don't worry — your data is most probably alive and well and viewable with the help of the correct layout. To switch layouts, click the Layout button to access a list of all layouts; from that list, choose a different layout.

Make sure you take the time to acquaint yourself with the name of the layout that you're using. You might find yourself the victim of one of those random, drive-by clickings you've been hearing so much about and end up in the "wrong" layout. If you know the name of your preferred layout, you can easily find it.

The menu bar

Like most software programs, ACT! comes equipped with a *menu bar* that appears at the top of every ACT! screen. These menus include all the options available for the current view. You can customize all menus to fit your needs; check out Chapter 3 for the details.

A quick way to familiarize yourself with ACT! is to click each and every one of the menu items. You might see something that piques your interest. You might click the Schedule menu and notice the Activity Series option. Hopefully, curiosity overcomes you, and you have an overwhelming desire to find more about that feature. Or you might notice the Sort choice listed in the Edit menu and think hmmm, maybe I can sort my database in a different order than alphabetically by company.

Many times, you'll find that you can accomplish a task in a variety of ways. If you're a keyboard shortcut *aficionado,* you'll find the most frequently used shortcuts in the front cover of this book. Although I know you'll have a copy of this book next to you at all times, you can also glean these shortcuts from the menus. In Figure 2-4, you can see that the shortcut appears to the right of each menu item. In addition, notice that an icon appears to the left of some of the menu items; this means that you'll find that corresponding icon somewhere on the icon bar if you prefer to click rather using the menus or keyboard shortcuts.

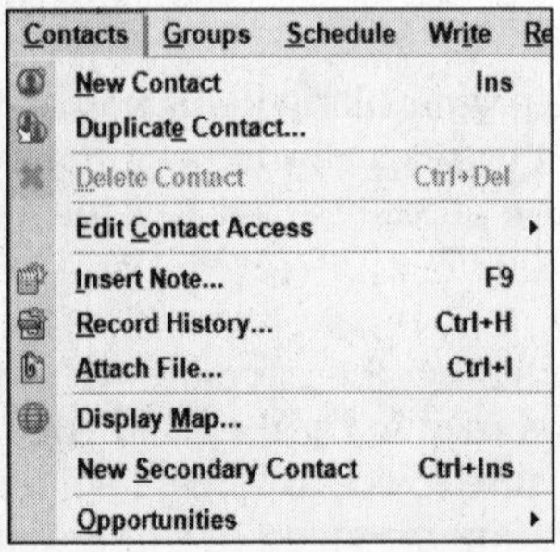

Figure 2-4:
Getting the
most out
of ACT!
menus.

Contacts	Groups	Schedule	Write	Re
New Contact			Ins	
Duplicate Contact...				
Delete Contact			Ctrl+Del	
Edit Contact Access			▶	
Insert Note...			F9	
Record History...			Ctrl+H	
Attach File...			Ctrl+I	
Display Map...				
New Secondary Contact			Ctrl+Ins	
Opportunities			▶	

The toolbar

ACT! also features a *toolbar* at the top of each window. The toolbar includes the most commonly used tasks of the current view. Toolbars work much the same way as the menu bars. You can customize each toolbar to include the tasks that you use most frequently; see how in Chapter 3. And, like the menu bars, toolbars vary depending on the view that you're in. For example, the toolbars that you see in the calendar views include a Show Filter/Hide Filter icon to change the view settings on your calendar, and the toolbar that you see in the Group Detail window include icons for creating groups and subgroups.

The Back and Forward bar

Lurking just below the toolbar is the *Back and Forward bar,* which provides you with a road map of sorts by letting you know the exact area of ACT! you're working in. And, like your Internet browser, the Back and Forward bar has handy-dandy left- and right-pointing arrows that allow you to return to the previous window you were viewing.

The Contact Detail window

When you first open ACT!, you land in the Contact Detail window, which allows you to see all the information about one specific contact. You can use the Contact Detail window to enter, modify, and view information about your contacts. Each contact record displays as a single page that is divided into a top and bottom half:

✔ The top half of the screen contains generic fields such as name, business address and phone that are probably used by just about all ACT! users everywhere. Many of these fields are used extensively in the templates (that is, reports, letters, fax cover sheets, and labels) that ACT! has already set up for you.

✔ The tabs at the bottom provide additional fields for each of your contacts. These are generally the fields that you don't use as much, such as home address and spouse's name.

You can — and should — customize the bottom half of the screen to better serve the needs of your business. You can click through the page tabs in the middle of the screen to get an idea of some of the fields suggested by ACT!. I show you how to add contact information into your database in Chapter 4 and how to modify those tabs in Chapter 14.

The Divider bar

One of the fast food chains used to have a jingle about "having it your way" a number of years back and you might want to hum a few bars of that tune each time you open ACT!. A point in case is the Divider bar that separates the top half of the Contact Detail window containing the fields from the bottom half containing the tabs. Got a lot of fields in the top half of your screen? Grab the Divider bar and drag it down. Want to have more room to view some of the tabs along the bottom? Grab that bar and drag it up a bit.

The Navigation bar

ACT!'s Navigation — or *Nav* — bar is the column of icons located along the left side of the program. The *Nav bar* allows you to move quickly between the various areas in ACT!. For example, to view all the information about one particular contact, click the Contacts icon; to see a list of all your groups, click the Groups icon.

The ACT! tabs

Because ACT! comes with approximately 50 predefined fields — and because your database Administrator might add another 50 or so customized fields — placing those fields where you can see them clearly is important. Plunking 100 fields on one half of your screen gives you a jumbled mess. I suppose that you could lay out those fields by using a smaller font, but the result (although neat) is impossible to read!

ACT! solves this dilemma in a rather unique fashion. The top half of the Contact Detail window displays the most basic fields that are fairly typical to all contacts. In this portion of the screen, the fields include places for the name, address, and phone numbers as well as a few miscellaneous fields. The bottom half of the ACT! screen displays additional information about your contact that's divided into categories, which you access by clicking tabs located across the middle of the Contact Detail window.

The first seven tabs (refer to Figure 2-3) — Notes, History, Activities, Opportunities, Groups/Companies, Secondary Contacts, and Documents — are called *system* tabs. The system tabs are actually *tables;* they don't hold single fields with a single piece of information in each one. Rather, you can add an unlimited number of like items to the same tab. For example, you can add multiple notes about your contact using the Notes tab, or you might have numerous sales opportunities that involve your current contact displayed on the Opportunities tab.

Because the system tabs contain tables rather than fields, you can't customize them in the same way as the other tabs. However, you can remove a system tab or change their order. Chapter 14 shows you how to fix the order.

Depending on the layout you're using, you probably see several additional tabs after the system tabs. These tabs generally display less frequently used information about your contact, such as these:

✔ The User Fields tab displays ten user fields; these fields are just waiting for you to customize them.

✔ The Home Address tab reveals your contact's home address, personal e-mail address, and phone number as well as the spouse's name.

You can find out how to customize the user fields in Chapter 13 and the layouts in Chapter 14.

Do not proceed to add new information in the User Fields without first renaming them. Many new ACT! users make this mistake and end up with an unruly assortment of information in each of these fields. Worse yet, other users of your database might misinterpret this information — or start entering in their own data — further complicating the whole mess.

All the tabs are dependent on the layout that you're currently using. If you switch layouts, your tabs change as well. Some of the ACT! add-on products add new tabs to your ACT! screen. For example, the ACT! QuickBooks link draws information from QuickBooks and plops it into a brand new tab called QuickBooks.

Getting Help When You Need It

In addition to the information that I provide in this book, ACT! 2006 comes with a very good — and quite extensive — online Help system that supplies step-by-step instructions for just about any ACT! feature that you might want to explore.

You can access the ACT! online Help system in one of two ways when ACT! is open:

✔ Press the F1 key on your keyboard.

✔ Choose Help from any ACT! menu bar.

When you access ACT!'s Help menu, you're treated to several options. All these Help options provide a wealth of information, and you shouldn't be afraid to use them.

✔ **Help Topics:** This option supplies you with lots of information based on the window that's open. Use this option when you find yourself scratching your head about something, and you'll probably be rewarded with just the answer you're looking for.

✔ **How to Use Help:** This area of Help provides you with the most information. In fact, you can find so much good information that this section is further subdivided into three tabbed areas:

- *Contents:* Think of the Contents tab as the Table of Contents in a book. The Contents tab presents you with the major topics covered in ACT!. Click the plus sign next to each topic to find a more detailed listing of the subject.

- *Index:* As its name implies, the index is just like the index you find at the back of a book. It provides you with an alphabetical listing of every feature found in ACT!. You can either scroll through the list of features or type in the first few letters of the feature that you're looking for.

- *Search:* The Search tab provides you with the most in-depth information about the various ACT! features. This feature is particularly helpful if you aren't sure of the exact name of the feature that you're trying to find. For example, say you're looking for instructions on how to force a field to display only capital letters. A search of the Index tab doesn't help you (the feature is actually called Initial Capitalization), but you can find the information by typing **capital** in the Search tab. Figure 2-5 gives you an idea of all the help you can find in the Search window.

✔ **Feature Tours:** We all learn in our own way, and the Feature Tours are designed for those of us who want someone to take us by the hand and walk us through a few of the more complex ACT! features. When you open one of the tours, you're treated to ACT! screenshots walking you through a process. All the relevant icons and buttons have been labeled so that you get a real understanding of how the process works. The four Feature Tours are

- *Customizations:* Includes instructions on how to add new fields, drop-down lists, and layouts

- *Groups and Companies:* Instructs you on setting up groups and companies; explains the differences between the two

- *Opportunity Tracking:* Demonstrates how to set up a new sales opportunity and ways that you might want to track it later

- *Handheld Link Installation:* Shows you how to link your PDA to ACT!.

✔ **Online Manuals:** ACT! comes with two nifty PDF files. One is a Quick Reference card that you can print to help you with the most common of ACT! features. The other is a rather large document that you can refer to — or print — when you need extra help.

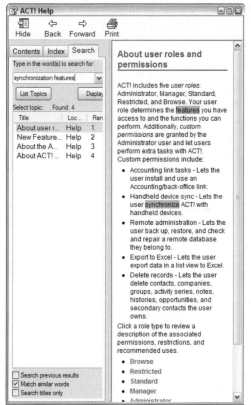

Figure 2-5:
Using the
Search
window in
ACT!'s Help.

✔ **Getting Started Wizard:** In your zealous haste to start working with ACT!, you might have chosen to ignore the wizard that pops up immediately after you first fire up ACT!. The Getting Started Wizard ensures that your word processor and e-mail preferences are set correctly and helps you to either convert an existing database or create a new one.

✔ **ACT! Update:** As much as you might want to think that the software you purchase is perfect in every way, it's not. Very often, users like you discover *bugs,* or little errors in the software. Sometimes, major changes such as the release of a new operating system can cause your software to exhibit some bad behavior. An update patch generally corrects these problems. The ACT! update ensures that you have the latest and greatest release of ACT!; best of all, there is no charge for this service!

✔ **Service and Support:** Ever wonder how to find help when you really need it? Three great options here can provide a bit of extra handholding:

• *Contact information:* Includes a link to the various fee-based support options offered by Best Software.

• *Knowledge Base:* Includes articles written by ACT!'s tech support about commonly asked questions and procedures.

- *ACT! Consulting:* Most of you know a brother, buddy, or colleague who "knows" ACT!. As the old saying goes, a little knowledge is a dangerous thing. In reality, these well-intentioned folks probably know ACT! as it pertains to their business — not yours. Unless they earn a living by consulting in the ACT! program, they're probably not your best source for accurate information.

Your best source of help for ACT! is an ACT! Certified Consultant. These consultants *(ACCs)* earn their livelihood by working with people like you. They are certified ACT! fanACTics who spend a great portion of their day working with any and all things ACT!. They can help you with anything from converting to ACT! from another program and customizing your database to training your employees. Most ACCs even make house calls. Clicking the ACT! Consulting option takes you for a field trip out to an Internet site that contains a listing of all the local ACT! consultants.

Chapter 3

Getting Your ACT! Together

In This Chapter

▶ Creating a new database

▶ Changing the ACT! preferences

▶ Customizing your toolbars and menus

I could easily have titled this chapter "Have It Your Way" because here's where I show you how to set up a new database. You discover some of the preference settings that you can change in ACT!. If you're sharing your database across a network, you'll read about the preferences that are specific to a network. Finally, if you're a real power-user, you'll be excited to know how to change your menus and toolbars.

Creating a New ACT! Database

If your initial meeting with ACT! entailed looking at the Act8Demo database that comes with ACT!, you know that it's a great demo database to use for learning purposes *before* actually starting to work on your own database. After playing with the demo for only a short time, you're probably eager to start working on your very own database. The easiest way to create your first database is by using the Getting Started Wizard. In addition to setting you up with a new database, the wizard helps you to set a few of the most basic preferences needed for ACT! to work correctly.

The Getting Started Wizard opens up automatically when you first installed ACT!. If you you've already gone through it the first time, feel free to skip this section.

Follow these steps to set up your new ACT! database with the Getting Started Wizard:

1. **From any ACT! screen, choose Help⇨Getting Started Wizard.**

   The first of the five Getting Started Wizard screens appears.

   At this point, feel free to put your feet up on the desk, answer a few questions, and let ACT! do the grunt work for you.

2. **On the wizard's introductory screen, click Next to get started.**

   Quick as a flash, the Getting Started Wizard - Word Processor screen appears. Here's where you get to choose your word processor. It's an either/or proposition; you have only two choices (see the next step).

3. **Choose Microsoft Word (if Word is installed on your computer); otherwise, choose the ACT! word processor.**

   Chapter 11 explains how to create a mail merge. If you're using Word, you'll want to use this as your preference because you are already familiar with most of its features.

4. **Click Next.**

   In the next screen, you get to tell ACT! which e-mail client you're using. (For information on determining which e-mail client you need to be using, scurry over to Chapter 12.)

5. **Select the e-mail program of your choice and then click Next.**

   If you prefer, you can even tell ACT! that you prefer to skip the e-mail setup for now. You can read more about setting up your e-mail in Chapter 12.

   By now, I'm sure you realize running a wizard means clicking the Next button a lot. Smart reader! However, the next step in the wizard gets a wee bit more challenging because you have to decide to create a new database, convert an existing database from a prior version of ACT! into ACT! 2006 format, or just skip the database setup. I make the assumption that you are setting up a brand-new ACT! database; that's the direction the steps take.

6. **Select Set Up Database Now and then click Next.**

   In this step of the Getting Started Wizard, you get to make a couple of decisions about the future of your database, as you can see in Figure 3-1.

   • *Database Name:* You might want to give the database a really cool moniker, such as the name of your company, so that you can easily identify it later.

   The name of your database cannot include spaces or punctuation marks. However, you can use an underscore and capital letters. For example, consider naming your database My_Company rather than Mycompany.

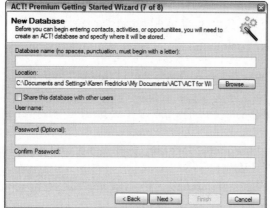

Figure 3-1:
Setting up a
new ACT!
database.

- *Location:* By default, the database is saved to the default database folder. Unless you change that preference, the default location is `C:\My Documents\ACT\ACT for Windows 8\Databases`. You can also indicate whether you want to share this database with other people with whom you might be networked.

- *User Name:* The person setting up the database is also one of the database Administrators. Keeping this in mind, indicate the name of the database Administrator.

- *Password:* The good news is that as you type your password, each character appears onscreen as an asterisk just in case someone is lurking over your shoulder trying to nab your password. The bad news is that because you can't see what you're typing, you might just type something you didn't intend to. ACT! demands that you retype your password to ensure that you didn't misspeak the first time.

An ACT! database does not require a password. It's better to leave the password blank than to add one — and forget what it is!

7. **Fill in the appropriate information and then click Next.**

The final screen of the Getting Started Wizard appears, recapping all the important decisions that you just made about your new database. If you made a mistake or simply change your mind, now's the time to click the Back button and fix things!

8. **Double-check your answers carefully, make the appropriate changes (if any), and then click Finish.**

When you're ready to add contacts to the database, head to Chapter 4.

If you already set your preferences, you don't need to use the wizard to create a new, blank database or to create another database. Just do the following. (To see how to set preferences, see the upcoming section, "Giving ACT! the Preferential Treatment.")

1. **Choose File➪New Database from any of the ACT! views.**

   The New Database dialog box appears. By coincidence, it is identical to the New Database screen of the Getting Started Wizard (refer to Figure 3-1).

2. **Fill in the database name, location, user name, and password (optional), and then click OK.**

   Your currently opened database will close and the newly created database will open.

Copying an Existing Database

Each time you create a new database by using either the Getting Started Wizard or by choosing File➪New Database, you create a new, pristine database based on ACT!'s original out-of-the-box fields. After you use ACT! for a while, you might want to create a new database based on a database that you or someone else has customized.

If you make an exact copy of your database, be careful how you use it. If you merely want to place a database on another computer for reference, making an exact copy by following these steps is fine. However, if your intention is to create a database for a remote user for purposes of synchronization, read Chapter 17 to find out how to create a database for a remote user. If you're creating a copy of a database for backup purposes, check out Chapter 15, where I show you how to create an ACT! backup.

1. **Choose File➪Save Copy As from any of the ACT! views.**

   The Save Copy As dialog box opens (see Figure 3-2), where you decide what type of database you want to create.

2. **Type a name for the copy of the database.**

   Do not make the mistake of assigning the same name to the new database that you use for your existing database. Even though you save the database copy to an entirely new location, there's a good chance that you could accidentally use the wrong database. By default, whenever you open ACT!, it opens the last database that you used; ACT!'s title bar tells you the *name* of the currently opened database but not its *path*. If two databases have the same filename, you could end up working in the incorrect database — without even realizing it.

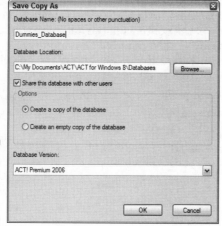

Figure 3-2:
Creating a
copy of a
database.

3. **Specify the location for the new database.**

   By default, the new database is saved to `C:\My Documents\ACT\ACT for Windows 8\Databases`. You can also indicate whether you want to share the database.

4. **Specify the type of database you're creating.**

   Although creating a copy of your existing database is easy, you must understand the consequence of your decision at this point. Consider your choices:

   - *Create a Copy of the Database:* This option creates an *exact replica* of your currently opened database. After you create a new ACT! database and customize it by adding many new fields, you might want to duplicate it for use by other offices or for other businesses that you might own. The new database copies the field structure of your existing database as well as all the actual contact records within the database.

   - *Create an Empty Copy of the Database:* This option creates a blank database that contains all the customized fields that you created in your existing database, but it does *not* contain any of the contact records from your original database.

5. **Click OK.**

   A dialog box appears asking you to insert the name of the primary user of the database, as shown in Figure 3-3.

6. **Fill in the user name and password for the primary user of the database.**

As you see in Figure 3-3, you're also given an option to select a user name from the current database, which is what you want to do if the primary user is already one of the contacts in the database that you're copying. You are now ready to start entering contact records into your new database. Chapter 4 contains the details about adding contact records to a database.

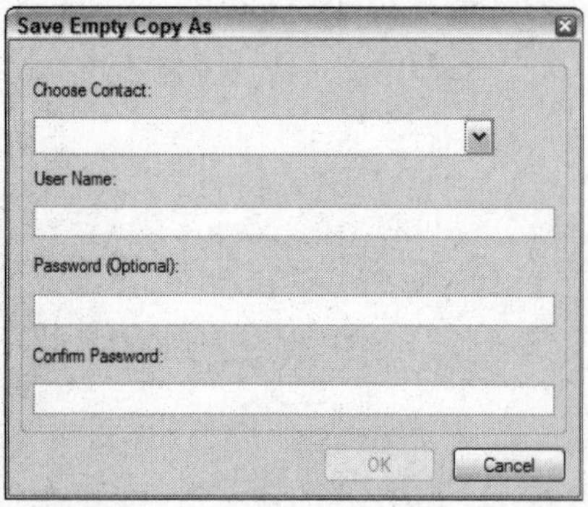

Figure 3-3:
Selecting
the main
user of the
new ACT!
database.

Working with Passwords
=======================

If you're the only user using your ACT! database — or if your clients love you and would chop their arms off at the wrist before turning to one of your competitors — security might not be an important issue for you. When you start ACT! it will not prompt you for a user name and password. But if you're like most people, you probably prefer not to share every tidbit of information in your database with anyone who wanders into your office. Whether you want to prevent certain personnel from changing the basic field structure of your database or adapt a look-but-don't-touch attitude with the unfortunate computer-challenged among your employees, ACT! has a variety of security methods that can help you accomplish your security goals. You can choose one of the following:

✔ Assign a specific security level to each user; I show you how to do that in Chapter 16.

✔ Determine which contacts any one user can access; you can read about ACT!'s Contact Access feature in Chapter 16.

✔ Password-protect your database; I discuss this option throughout the rest of this section.

Unless a contact record is marked as *private,* ACT! 2006 has no way of allowing someone access to only a portion of the contacts in a database. If you want to limit the contacts a particular user sees, you have a couple of options. You can upgrade to ACT! 2006 Premium for Workgroups, which allows access to user records, based on your team preferences. You can also supply the user with his own database and synchronize just those contacts that he has access to from the main database as I show in Chapter 17.

Setting a password

Both the database Administrator and the individual database user can set a password for the user. The theory for this is that the individual can pick a password that has some meaning to him — and so, hopefully, he doesn't forget it. If a user does forget his password, however, the Administrator can reset it; you can see how to do that in Chapter 16.

If you have access to a database and are afraid that some nasty person might use your name to gain access illegally, I recommend assigning a password to yourself, which is ridiculously easy. Here's what you do:

1. **From any of the ACT! screens, choose File⇨Set Password.**

   The Set Password dialog box appears, as shown in Figure 3-4.

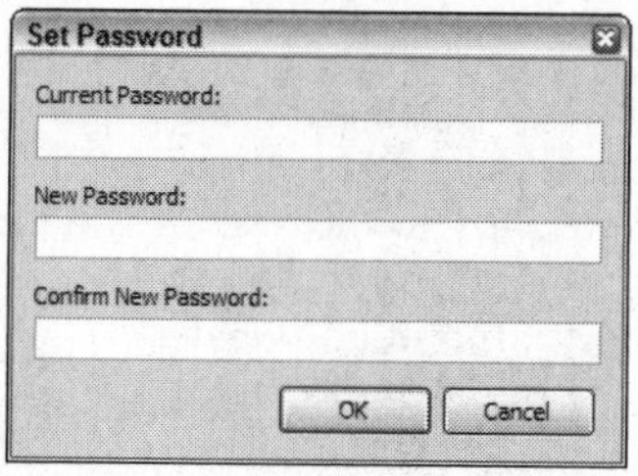

Figure 3-4:
Set a user's
password
here.

2. **Leave the Current Password text box empty.**

3. **Type your new password in the New Password text box. Then, for added excitement, type it once more in the Confirm New Password text box.**

4. **Click OK.**

Changing a password

After you add a password to your database, or if multiple users access your database, you are prompted to supply your user name and password each time you try to open up your ACT! database.

You might not know your password because you don't have one, so before tracking down your Administrator to change a password for you, try leaving the password field blank. (I frequently get phone calls and e-mails from ACT! users who have no idea what password is assigned to them. Guess what? They often don't have one!)

However, if you try every password that you can think of — and even try using no password at all — and still can't gain access to the database, you might have to bribe the database Administrator into resetting your password. I find that chocolate chip cookies work the best, but feel free to pick the bribe of your choice. Then, make sure the Administrator follows these steps:

1. **Choose File⇨Set Password from any ACT! view.**

   If you're going through this chapter section by section, you already know that you can do this from within any of the ACT! screens. I don't mean to sound like a broken record here; I just want you to get used to the idea.

2. **Enter the current password in the Current Password text box.**

3. **Enter the new password in the New Password text box.**

4. **Enter the new password again in the Confirm New Password text box.**

5. **Click OK.**

From time to time, you might want to change your password. Perhaps you feel that a former employee compromised your security, or maybe you've just been watching too many James Bond movies. Whatever the case, remember the new, improved password, or you might be forced to chase the database Administrator around with another batch of cookies!

Giving ACT! the Preferential Treatment

After you install ACT! on your computer, becoming familiar with various preferences is a good practice. If you're the sole user of the database, these settings likely save your sanity. If you share the database with other users, these settings can probably save you all a lot of head scratching.

If you create your original database by using the Getting Started Wizard, some of your preferences are already set. However, reviewing your work never hurts! Your preference settings are the place to turn to if you're the kind of person who likes to have things your own way. You might routinely store all your documents in a specific location and want ACT! to follow that same example. Or you might have a fondness for fuchsia and orange and want to have your ACT! screens coordinate with this color scheme.

Here's how to change several of the most basic preference settings. Feel free to flip through the various preference tabs to get an idea about additional preference settings that you might also want to tweak. You can find the ACT! Preferences dialog box, as shown in Figure 3-5, by choosing Tools⇨Preferences. The Preferences dialog box is arranged into six tabs, each of which I discuss in the following sections.

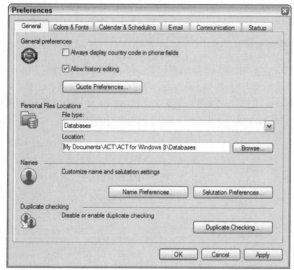

General

As the name implies, you find an assortment of preferences on the General tab. General preferences allow you to specify settings for your database, such as how names and salutations display on your contact records, whether checking for duplicate records is enabled or disabled, and where files associated with your database are stored. ACT! automatically stores your database in the My Documents folder. Your database contains all your basic contact information as well as supplemental files such as layouts, templates, and saved e-mail messages. In addition, you might want to have your own set of personal supplemental files; this area is where you can tell ACT! where you prefer to have them saved.

A few of the preference settings might not be available to you if you're not the database Administrator; for example, you can't change the history or duplicate checking options that appear on the General tab of the ACT! preferences.

Colors & Fonts

You can set the colors and fonts for almost any area of ACT! including all list views, tabs, and calendars. However, there isn't a global color setting; you must set the colors and fonts for each item separately in the Colors & Fonts tab, as shown in Figure 3-6. To set colors and fonts, follow these steps:

1. **On the Colors & Fonts tab, select an item to customize from the Customize list.**

   In the Customize list, you find a list of all the lists, calendars, and system tabs. You'll also notice in Figure 3-6 several items in the list with the words *Detail Composition;* these indicate areas in ACT! in which you can write in extra details when necessary. For example, Chapter 8 talks about scheduling activities; when you schedule the activity you can optionally add extra details or notes about the activity. You can even customize the look of those if you'd like.

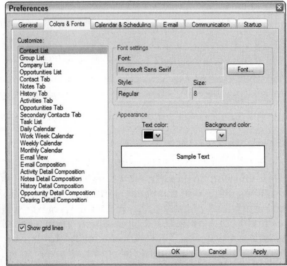

Figure 3-6:
Set color
and font
preferences
here.

2. **Click the Font button.**

   The Font dialog box appears.

3. **Select the font, style, and size of the font.**

4. **Click OK.**

5. **In the Appearance section, select the text and background color for an item you select from the Customize list.**

6. **To change the appearance of another item, select the item from the Customize list and repeat Steps 2–5.**

7. **Click OK to save your color and font preferences.**

You might want to make sure that the colors you pick for the text and background colors result in a legible combination. For example, choosing black text with a black background would not be a great idea, nor would the combination of a yellow font on a white background.

Calendar & Scheduling

The Calendar & Scheduling tab is nothing more than a gateway to the heart of the matter: changing the calendar and scheduling preferences.

When you click the Calendar Preferences button, you can set

✔ The days of the week you want to appear on your work week calendar

✔ The minute intervals for your daily and work week calendars

✔ Various calendar options, such as whether or not you want to see pop-ups when you hold your mouse cursor over a scheduled activity

✔ How you want to banner all-day events so that a border appears on the corresponding day on your monthly calendar

When you click the Scheduling Preferences button, you can get the Activity Type Settings dialog box. From here, you select the activity type for which you want to set options. You can set options for each activity type, but you must set the options one activity type at a time. The options you can include for each activity type are

✔ The priority level you want to display automatically when the activity type is scheduled. For example, you might want phone calls to be marked with a medium priority but meetings automatically set to a high priority.

✔ How long before the activity you want the Ring Alarm to sound for the activity type

✔ The default duration for the activity type

✔ The fields for which you want to display drop-down lists for the activity type

E-mail

Exactly as advertised, the E-mail preference tab is the area where you tell ACT! exactly how you want to handle your e-mail. The preferences you might want to set include

- The e-mail system you want to use with ACT!: Microsoft Outlook, Outlook Express, Lotus Notes, or Internet Mail

- Composing options, including signatures, dealing with forwarded and replied messages, and even how you want the recipient's name to appear when composing a new e-mail message

- How often you want ACT! to notify you about newly received messages

- How you want to handle attachments that you receive

Communication

The Communication tab lets you choose your word processor and fax preferences including

- **The word processing and fax software you want to use with ACT!**

- **How you want ACT! to check your spelling in e-mail messages and word processing documents**

- **The Dialer options if you want ACT! to automatically dial an outgoing number and record the length of the phone call**

Although the Dialer feature can be a great timesaver, you must have the appropriate hardware installed in order to use it. Quite simply, dialing requires that your computer can access a dial tone. This can be accomplished in one of two ways:

- *Your computer has a dialup modem into which you can plug a phone line.*

- *Your telephone system is equipped with Telephone Application Programming Interface (TAPI) hardware and the appropriate telephone driver software is installed on your computer.*

- **The Quick Print header and footer options when printing any of the ACT! lists, including Company, Group, Opportunity, Contact, Notes, History, Activity, and Secondary Contacts**

Startup

The Startup options dictate both the default settings for each new contact added to your database and how ACT! starts up every time you run the program.

✔ The Record Creation setting lets you set the default to Public or Private for each new contact, group, and opportunity you add to the database as well as whether you want to automatically link each new contact to his company record and record a history of the event.

✔ Startup Database lets you specify the database you want ACT! to open automatically as well as how often you want ACT! to check for new software updates.

✔ The Automatic Updates option informs you any time a new update patch is available for ACT!.

Customizing the Navigation Bar

One of the things you might find the most endearing about ACT! is your ability to mold the program how it feels the most comfortable to you. You might decide that for whatever reason, you don't like the look of the Navigation (Nav) bar (those big icons that run down the left side of ACT! as seen in Figure 2-3). No problem — all you have to do to "have it your way" is follow the next few steps:

1. **Right-click the Navigation bar.**

   Note the menu that appears is divided into three sections. You actually get to choose one option from both the top and middle sections.

2. **Chose one of the options from the top section of the menu:**

   • *Large:* That's the size of the Nav bar icons when you first install ACT!.

   • *Small:* If you're working on a small monitor — or just want to have a little more viewing room — you might want the Nav bar icons to be small so the rest of your screen can be larger.

3. **Chose an option for the middle section of the Nav bar menu:**

   • *Standard:* The Nav bar shows you eight of the most common views that will help you navigate to areas in ACT! such as the Task List and calendar.

   • *Expanded:* For those of you who live for detail, the Nav bar shows you 14 icons; you might want to set the size to small so that you don't have to scroll down to see all those options.

- *Classic:* For those of you loyal ACT! fanACTics who want things, well, like you're used to seeing them in versions 6 and earlier, here's your chance to have the Nav bar look "just like it used to."

- *Customize:* If you're still not happy with the look and feel of the Nav bar, feel free to choose the Customize option. A little window opens magically that allows you to drag additional icons to the Nav bar — or get rid of the ones you don't want.

The calendar icon is an example of a Navigation bar icon that you might want to replace. By default, clicking it brings you to the daily calendar. That's fine if that's the calendar you're most comfortable using. However, many of you might prefer to use the weekly — or work week — calendar instead. If that's the case, customize the Nav bar by dragging away the calendar icon and replacing it with the calendar item of your choice.

Modifying the Icon Bar

Customizing the various ACT! menus and toolbars to include functions that you use on a regular basis is a great way to improve your efficiency. Changing your toolbar literally allows you to perform various functions at the click of a button.

Adding items to the toolbar

One thing you might find a little unique in ACT! is the variety of toolbars that you encounter along the way. You see one toolbar while working in the Contact Detail window but a different toolbar when you foray into the Group Detail window. That said, realize that an icon you add to one of your toolbars doesn't appear on another. That's okay because adding icons to any one of the ACT! toolbars is easy.

I encourage you to do a little homework before tackling the toolbar. Don't worry, the assignment is fairly simple; you need to decide in advance which icon you want to add as well as which menu it's located on. Although this step isn't critical, it saves you from floundering around later. After doing your homework, follow these steps to add an icon to any toolbar:

1. From any of the ACT! screens, choose Tools⇨Customize⇨Menus and Toolbars.

For the right-clickers in the audience, you can also give the toolbar a click with the right button of your mouse and choose Customize.

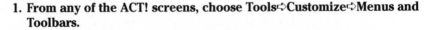

2. **Click the Commands tab in the Customize Menus and Toolbars dialog box (see Figure 3-7).**

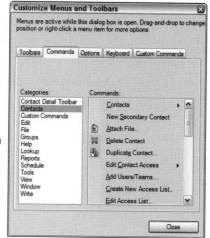

Figure 3-7:
Customize
an ACT!
toolbar
here.

3. **Select the name of the menu that contains the command that you want to add to your toolbar.**

   If you did your homework, pat yourself on the back. If you didn't, have fun flipping through all the choices in the Categories list and scrolling through all the corresponding commands until you stumble upon the item that you want to add to the toolbar. I hate to be an "I told you so," but. . . .

4. **Drag the desired command to the toolbar.**

   As you drag the command to the toolbar, a black line materializes that indicates exactly where the icon is going to appear.

5. **Click the Close button on the Customize Menus and Toolbars dialog box.**

Tweaking the toolbar icons

I'm almost embarrassed to tell you how easily you can further customize the icons on your toolbars. But, because you're such a good person, I am going to tell you. You might store this information away for future reference and use it to impress your friends some time in the near future.

1. **Right-click the toolbar and choose Customize.**

   By the way, Customize is not only the choice you want to choose — it's your *only* choice!

2. **Drag any icon you want to another spot on the toolbar.**

   Now's your chance.

3. **Right-click the icon that you want to modify.**

   Because you're such a nice person, you are treated to the menu shown in Figure 3-8.

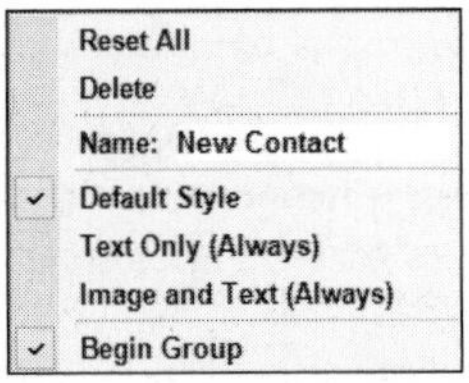

Figure 3-8:
Options for
customizing
the icon bar.

| Reset All |
| Delete |
| Name: New Contact |
| ✓ Default Style |
| Text Only (Always) |
| Image and Text (Always) |
| ✓ Begin Group |

4. **Chose the modification items of your choice.**

   - *Reset All:* Resets all your toolbar and menu customization to the original value

   - *Delete:* Deletes the currently selected icon

   - *Name:* Allows you to rename the icon's ToolTip

   - *Default Style:* Shows just an icon on the toolbar without including any text

   - *Text Only:* Shows only a text command on the toolbar without the icon

   - *Image and Text:* Shows both an icon and text command on the toolbar

5. **Click the Close button on the Customize Menus and Toolbars dialog box.**

Monkeying with the Menus

After you master the icon bar, customizing the menus will seem like a piece of cake. Most of the techniques that I mention here will sound eerily familiar because you modify your menus in pretty much the same way as you do your icon bar.

Ordering additional menu items

For your first feat, add some new goodies to your menus.

1. **Right-click the toolbar and choose Customize.**

   If you feel a slight sense of *déjà vu,* it's because you're treading on very familiar territory.

2. **Click the Commands tab of the Customize Menus and Toolbars dialog box.**

3. **Select the name of the menu that contains the command that you want to add to your toolbar menu.**

4. **Drag the desired command up to the menu that you want to modify.**

   This is where you do things slightly differently than you did with the icon bar (see the preceding section). As you drag the command to the menus, they pop open. Resist the temptation to let go of your mouse button! If you linger your mouse on any of the sub-menu items, they pop open for you as well. When you arrive at your scheduled destination, a black line materializes that indicates exactly where the item is going to appear.

5. **Let go of your mouse button.**

   I'll bet you thought I was never going to say that! If your finger feels numb, that's okay — the reward of having your new items appear on your menus is certainly worth any pain you might have encountered.

6. **Drag any menu item you want to another menu.**

   You'll probably find that ACT!'s menus seem pretty logical, but as they say — different strokes for different folks. If you decide that Preferences should be located on the Edit menu or that the Backup command should really be listed on the Tools menu, go for it. Hover your mouse over the menu with the target item; when the menu pops open, drag it to the correct spot on the new menu.

7. **Click the Close button on the Customize Menus and Toolbars dialog box.**

Adding a separator

Glance at Figure 3-8 to notice a horizontal line separating some of the menu items; this is a *separator.* You can add separators to menus in order to group similar or related commands.

1. **Right-click the toolbar and choose Customize.**

   After the Customize Menus and Toolbars dialog box is open, the menus and toolbars are alive and well and just waiting for you to add a separator.

2. **Right-click the area on a menu where you would like to add a separator.**

   You'll want to click on the menu item just below where you'd like to add the separator. The separator will be added above the selected menu item.

3. **Click Begin Group.**

   Lo and behold, the separator is added right where you aimed.

4. **Click the Close button on the Customize Menus and Toolbars dialog box.**

Adding a custom command

Normally I shudder when someone asks me whether they can perform a task "with the click of a button." As you can see throughout this book, most processes take a couple of clicks. However, you can create custom commands to make ACT! run one of your favorite software programs or some of your customized reports and templates. Want to open Excel from ACT! with the click of a button? Add it to one of your ACT! menus or toolbars. Have you created some templates that you use repeatedly? You might want to think about adding those goodies to the Write menu.

1. **Right-click the toolbar and choose Customize.**

2. **Click the Custom Commands tab (as shown in Figure 3-9) from the Customize Menus and Toolbars dialog box.**

3. **Click the New button.**

4. **Type a name for the command in the Command Name field.**

   The name you choose is simply used to identify your custom command. You don't need to wrack your brain here. If you decide to add Excel to a menu, you might want to name the command *Excel.*

5. **Enter a short description of the command in the Tooltip Text field if you want a pop-up description to be associated with a new icon.**

6. **Click Browse to navigate to either the location of the application's executable file or to one of ACT!'s customized documents.**

7. **Click OK to close the navigation dialog box and then click the Add Command button.**

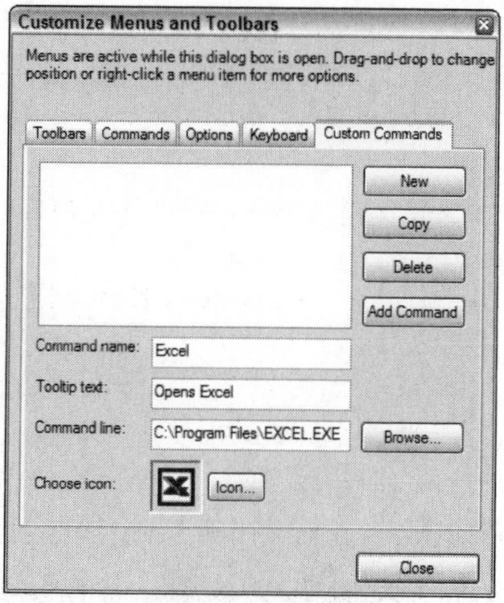

Customize Menus and Toolbars

Menus are active while this dialog box is open. Drag-and-drop to change position or right-click a menu item for more options.

| Toolbars | Commands | Options | Keyboard | Custom Commands |

New

Copy

Delete

Add Command

Command name: Excel

Tooltip text: Opens Excel

Command line: C:\Program Files\EXCEL.EXE   Browse...

Choose icon: [X] Icon...

Close

Figure 3-9:
Make a
custom
command
here.

After you create a custom command, your next task is to get it to magically appear on one of your ACT! menus. I know, by now, you're getting tired of reading all about menu bar customizations. You don't want to follow an entire new set of commands. I don't blame you. But guess what? If you've read through this chapter, you know how to add those new custom command items to your menus. Hop back to the section "Ordering additional menu items" to find that those directions are just about all you need to make it happen.

Refer to Figure 3-7 to see that one of the categories listed is Custom Commands. What a coincidence. You can find all your newly created custom commands just sitting there, waiting to be dragged to the appropriate menu. Time to go put your feet up and rest a bit — you've worked very hard!

Part II
Putting the ACT! Database to Work

The 5th Wave   By Rich Tennant

"I couldn't get this 'job skills' program to work on my PC, so I replaced the motherboard, upgraded the BIOS and wrote a program that links it to my personal database. It told me I wasn't technically inclined and should pursue a career in sales."

In this part . . .

Okay, after you whip ACT! into shape (see the preceding part of this book), it's time to get your life in order. ACT! is a *contact manager,* which (as the name implies) makes it a great place to manage your contacts. First, you add new contacts into your database, and then you need to know how to find them again. After you locate your contacts, you can schedule an activity with any one of them, set a reminder, and maybe add some notes for good measure. (Sure beats the heck out of a yellow sticky note!)

Chapter 4

Making Contact(s)

A database is only as good as the contacts that it contains. In ACT!, adding, duplicating, deleting, and editing the contacts in your database is easy to do. In this chapter, I show you how to do all four of these tasks to maintain an organized, working database. Adding new contacts is only half the fun; being able to find them is why you have the database in the first place. Inputting contacts in a consistent manner ensures that all your contacts are easy to find. And after you add a contact, you can easily duplicate it if you have other contacts that share the same address and phone numbers. If you need to change that contact's information or delete the contact, stay tuned. I demonstrate how to change contact information and even how to "unchange" changes that you might make by mistake!

Adding New Contacts

On the very simplest level, the main purpose of ACT! is to serve as a place to store all your contacts. You can add and edit your contacts from the Contact Detail window because it contains all the information that pertains to one particular record and allows you to see all your contact fields.

Every time that you add a new contact, ACT! automatically fills information in three fields: Record Creator, Record Manager, and Create Date. If you click the Contact Info tab of your layout, you'll notice these three fields. When you add a new contact, ACT! inserts your user name into the Record Creator and Record Manager fields and the current date into the Create Date field. This tab enables you to search for all the new contacts that you created within a given date range. The Record Creator and Create Date fields serve as a permanent record, and you cannot change them. Managers and administrators can override the contents of the Record Manager field if they so desire.

You probably have lots of contacts that you're dying to enter into your database, so what are you waiting for? Jump right in and follow these steps:

1. **If you aren't already in the Contact Detail window, go there by clicking the Contacts icon on ACT!'s Nav bar.**

   Don't know about the Nav bar? Check out Chapter 2, where you find out all you need to know about the Nav bar and then some.

2. **In the Contact Detail window, choose from one of three ways to add a new contact to your database:**

   • Choose Contact⇨New Contact.

   • Click the New Contact icon on the toolbar.

   • Press Insert (on the keyboard).

   Initiating any of the preceding commands results in a blank contact record. You're now ready to enter the new contact's information.

3. **Begin entering information by clicking in the Company field and typing the contact's company name.**

   ACT! doesn't distinguish between actual contacts and blank contacts. Failure to enter information or repeatedly pressing Insert results in numerous blank contact records, which are of no use and serve only to clog the database. So, although you are free to leave any of the ACT! fields blank, you do have to enter something — at the very least, I recommend the key pieces of information such as the contact's name, company name, and phone number — so you might as well begin with the company's name.

   You can always go back to a record and delete, add, or change any information in any field. See the later sections, "Deleting Contact Records" and "The Contacts, They Are A'Changin'."

4. **Click in the next field where you want to enter information and start typing.**

   You can also use the Tab key to advance to the next field. In your initial excitement to start entering all your existing contacts, if you inadvertently press Tab once too often, you might find that you advanced one too many fields and ended up in the wrong field. Don't fret: Press and hold down the Shift key and then press Tab to move your cursor in the reverse direction. If you prefer, you can also get back to any field simply by clicking in it with your mouse.

5. **Continue filling in fields.**

   As I mention in Chapter 2, ACT! comes with approximately 50 preprogrammed fields that reflect the needs of most users. Many of the fields are fairly self-explanatory (and reflect the type of information that you probably expect to find in any address book): contact name, company name, phone, city, state, and ZIP code. These are conveniently located in the top half of the Contact Detail window; see Figure 4-1. A few of the fields are a little less obvious:

- **Address:** If you assume that the three fields ACT! provides for the address is meant to store three *alternative* addresses, you're wrong! The second and third address fields are meant for really long addresses. These fields are good places to include a suite number or building name if it is an integral part of the address.

- **ID/Status:** The ID/Status field is essentially the category field, and it files each of your contacts into categories. By using the ID/Status field, you don't have to manually set up a variety of databases: one for your friends, one for your clients, one for your vendors, and so on. The ID/Status field comes preset with a few dozen of the most commonly used categories in its drop-down list, including employees, customers, vendors, and competitors, which makes searching for each of these categories a snap.

- **Salutation:** This field refers to the name that comes after the word *Dear* in a letter, which is used in your letter templates. By default, ACT! (being the friendly type) uses the first name. Feel free to change the salutation to a more formal one. Read more about changing this in the following section.

If you prefer using the more formal salutation as the default setting, choose Tools⇨Preferences and click the Salutation Preferences button conveniently located on the General tab.

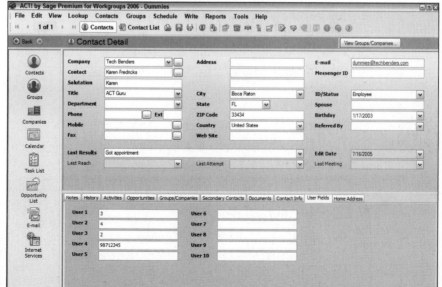

Figure 4-1:
The Contact
Detail
window.

- **Referred By:** This field is one of the most commonly overlooked ones in the database. Information entered into this field is used in the Source of Referrals report; failure to enter Referred By information renders the report useless. So what's the big deal? Suppose you're paying for advertising in two newspapers — wouldn't knowing which one attracted the most prospects be nice? If you're attending trade shows or putting a lot of time and effort into your Web site, wouldn't you like to know whether your efforts result in any new business? And, if an existing customer sends you lots of new leads, wouldn't remembering him with a nice gift at holiday time be nice? Utilizing the Referred By field can help you do all this.

- **User:** Notice the several User fields in the bottom half of the Contact Detail window (refer to Figure 4-1). These fields hold information that's specific to your business. In Chapter 13, I explain how you can change these field names to better reflect their contents. For example, you might rename *User 1* to *Social Security number.*

  I recommend leaving these particular fields blank until you rename them. If you don't, you might end up with various kinds of data entered into one field.

You can always go back and add, change, or delete field data at any time! (See the sections "Deleting Contact Records" and "The Contacts, They Are A'Changin'," later in this chapter.)

6. **Don't be alarmed when ACT! automatically formats some of your field data when you enter information.**

   See the later section, "Letting ACT! do the work for you: Automatic formatting," for the lowdown on what ACT! does and doesn't do for you.

7. **Add your data as uniformly as possible.**

   Check out the later section, "Getting the most out of ACT!: Using the drop-down lists," to find out how to easily keep your data uniform and yourself sane.

8. **If necessary, add multiple entries to a field.**

   Generally, limiting yourself to one item per field is the best practice. From time to time, however, you find a situation in which a contact falls into two categories. For example, a contact might be both a friend and a client. In this situation, you can use a multi-select drop-down list to select more than one item into a field. By default, the ID/Status field is set to be a multi-select field; Chapter 13 shows you how to create as many multi-select fields as you'd like.

To select criteria to be included in a single field, follow these steps:

a. *Place your cursor in the field.*

b. *Select (mark) your desired selections.*

Figure 4-2 gives you an example of a drop-down list.

Figure 4-2:
An ACT!
drop-down
list.

c. *Click the desired entries from the Edit List Values dialog box.*

d. *Click anywhere outside the dialog box to close it.*

The various entries appear in the field, separated by a comma.

9. **When you fill in the information for each new contact, don't forget to click the various tabs at the bottom of your layout.**

You find additional fields lurking on these tabs. The Home Address tab is where you record personal information about a contact. You might have a few other tabs that you can also choose from (see Chapter 14).

Different layouts display different tabs. If you change your current layout, you're probably looking at a different set of tabs. Confused? Check out Chapter 2 for a quick refresher.

If you forget to click those tabs along the bottom of the Contact Detail window, you just might overlook some of the fields that hold important information. Although you can always fill them in later, it's a good idea to input the information while it is still fresh in your memory, so be sure to click those tabs!

10. **Save the new contact information.**

Theoretically, you don't have to save new contact information; it's saved if you do one of the following:

- Execute any other ACT! command, which includes anything from adding a note or sales opportunity to scheduling an appointment.

- Move on to another record in the database.

Although it's not necessary, feel free to do one of the following to save your information:

- Click the Save button (the small floppy disk icon on the toolbar).
- Press Ctrl+S.

Letting ACT! do the work for you: Automatic formatting

Entering a new contact into the ACT! database is so easy that you might overlook some of the magical things that happen when you begin to input contact information. ACT! is here to help by automatically formatting some of the contact information that you input, including

✔ **Automatic phone number formatting:** A great example of ACT!'s magic is found in any of the phone fields. When you type in a phone number, notice how ACT! automatically inserts the necessary parentheses and hyphens. ACT! automatically inserts the dialing format for the United States each time that you enter a new phone number. Have relatives living in Turkmenistan? Have no fear: If you click the ellipsis button (the three little dots) to the right of the Telephone field, ACT! pops open the Enter Phone Number dialog box. By default, the country is listed as the United States, but you can scroll through the list of the countries for just about any country that you can think of, including Turkmenistan (see Figure 4-3). After you click OK, the correct telephone country code and format are applied to the telephone number.

Figure 4-3:
Automatic
telephone
formatting.

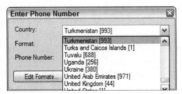

✔ **Automatic name formatting:** Another field that ACT! automatically provides you with is the Salutation field. The Salutation field holds the text that appears after the word *Dear* in a letter. For example, if you enter *Mary Ellen Van der Snob* as the contact name, *Mary Ellen* magically appears as the salutation. Of course, if you prefer to address your contacts in a more formal manner, feel free to change *Mary Ellen* to *Ms. Van der Snob*. When you enter a contact name into the database, ACT! automatically divides it into a first, middle, and last name. Again, if you click the ellipsis button to the right of the Contact field, ACT! shows you how it plans to divide the contact's name. This allows you to sort your database alphabetically by last name or to look up a contact by first name.

This chapter and Chapter 5 both include ways to sort your database. If you attempt to enter a rather large, unique name, ACT! automatically opens the Contact Name dialog box, as shown in Figure 4-4, and asks you how you want to divide the name.

ACT! is an amazingly smart and intuitive program. You might want to input the contact name as Ms. Alyssa Fredricks or Andrea Fredricks, MD. ACT! knows that words like Mr., Miss and Ms. are usually not first names, and PhD, MD, and Esq. are generally not last names, so feel free to add them to the contact name if you'd like.

Figure 4-4:
The Contact
Name
dialog box.

✔ **History fields:** Any changes to a history field are preserved on the History tab. Say you have six steps that you want your staff to perform when dealing with prospects. You might change the drop-down information for your history field to reflect those six steps. When you perform one of the steps and you enter the information into the field, the date and time of the change appear on the History tab so you know exactly when each step took place.

Out of the box, only two fields — ID/Status and Last Results — are history fields. Theoretically, any field can be a history field, and Chapter 13 shows you how to do it.

✔ **Date fields:** The one thing you don't ever want to forget is the birthday of your significant other. However, as you discover in Chapter 6, entering data consistently is important if you have any hope of ever finding it again. What if an important birthday occurs in January, but you aren't sure whether the date was entered as _January, Jan, 01,_ or _1?_ By now, you've probably guessed that ACT! came up with a cure for the birthday blues with the addition of date fields. All date fields have a drop-down arrow, which you can click to bring up a mini-calendar, as shown in Figure 4-5. Click the appropriate date, buy a card, and you're ready to roll. If you prefer, you can also manually enter the date as 01/17/05 or 1/17/05, and ACT! translates it to the calendar mode automatically.

Figure 4-5:
An ACT!
date field.

Getting the most out of ACT!: Using the drop-down lists

One sure-fire way to sabotage your database is to develop new and creative ways to say the same thing. In Florida, users often vacillate between *Fort, Ft,* and *Ft.* Lauderdale, resulting in a bad sunburn and the inability to correctly find all their contacts. You'll notice that several of the ACT! fields contain drop-down lists. In these fields, you can select an item in the list, or you can type the first few letters of an item; the field then automatically fills with the item that matches what you typed or clicked. When you type an entry that isn't in the drop-down list for the Title, Department, City, and Country fields, the item is automatically added to the list so that you can then select it for other contacts.

You have two ways of using the drop-down lists to enter information:

- ✔ Type the first few letters of an entry that already appears in the drop-down list, and ACT! auto-completes the word for you. For example, if you type **Bo** in the City field, *Boise* magically appears, and if you add an S Boston appears.

- ✔ Access the drop-down list by clicking its arrow and then choosing the desired item(s) from the list.

Using these drop-down lists whenever possible helps ensure consistency throughout your database. In Chapter 13, I explain how to add additional drop-down fields to your database and control how you use them.

If you want to change the content of the drop-down lists that come with ACT!, follow these steps:

1. **Click in a field that has a drop-down list.**

2. **Click the drop-down arrow in the field.**

3. **When the drop-down list appears, click the Edit List Values button.**

   The Edit List dialog box appears, as shown in Figure 4-6.

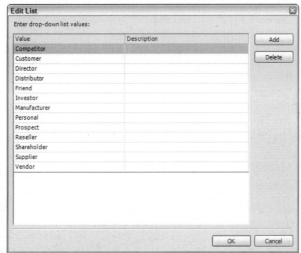

Figure 4-6:
Edit a drop-down list here.

4. **In the Edit List dialog box, do one of the following:**

   - **To add an item to the list:** Click the Add button. A new blank line appears at the bottom of the list. Enter the text that you want to appear in the list.

   - **To remove an item from the list:** Select an item and click the Delete button. Click Yes when ACT! asks you to confirm the deletion.

   - **To modify an existing item:** Double-click it and edit it exactly like you would in a word processor.

5. **Click OK when you finish editing your list.**

That's all there is to it. A pretty easy way to ensure consistency, don't you think?

Duplicating Your Contacts

As you can see from the "Adding New Contacts" section, entering a new contact into ACT! involves quite a few things. Thankfully, ACT! makes duplicating a previously saved record easy.

Suppose that you just entered Jane Jones' contact information, and now you find yourself looking at a pile of business cards from Jane's co-workers. All of them have the same company name and address; the only variables are the contact name and phone number. ACT! gives you two options for duplicating contacts. You can either copy the primary information or all the information. Out of the box, the primary fields are Company, Address 1, Address 2, Address 3, City, State, Zip, Country, and Fax. When you copy all fields, *every* field copies into the new contact record except the Contact and E-Mail Address fields.

To duplicate contact information without extra typing, follow these steps:

1. **Open the record that you want to duplicate.**

2. **Choose Contact➪Duplicate Contact.**

3. **Select either the Duplicate Data from Primary Fields or Duplicate Data from All Fields radio button and then click OK.**

   Chapter 13 shows you how to determine which fields will be used as Primary Fields. Quite simply, these fields represent the data fields that would be the same for each contact. If you choose the Duplicate Date from All Fields options, you might have some strange results; it's pretty hard to imagine that two of your contacts would share the same birthday — and be married to spouses with the same names!

   A new contact record appears, filled in with the copied information from the original contact record.

4. **Continue creating the contact record by filling in the variable information and proceeding as you would with an entirely new contact.**

Your contact information will automatically be saved when you move on to another contact record or switch to another ACT! view.

Deleting Contact Records

What do you do if you find that a contact is duplicated in your database? Or that you're no longer doing business with one of your contacts? For whatever reason you decide that a name no longer needs to be a part of your database, you can just delete that contact record.

ACT! allows you to either delete one contact record or a lookup of contact records. (A *lookup* is the group of contacts that displays after a database search. Peruse Chapter 6 for more information about lookups.) Just realize that you are deleting either the current contact that you're viewing or the current group of contacts that you just created a lookup for. When you're on the contact that you want to delete, do one of the following:

⊾ **Choose Contact⇨Delete.**

⊾ **Press Ctrl+Delete.**

⊾ **Right-click the contact record and choose Delete Contact.**

Clicking the Delete Contact button deletes the current contact you're viewing. If you click the Delete Lookup button, you delete the current contact lookup.

Any one of these choices brings up the warning shown in Figure 4-7.

Figure 4-7:
You get an
ominous
warning
when
deleting a
contact.

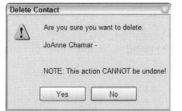

Thinking before deleting a contact

Although the procedure is rather simple, you might want to rethink deleting contacts. When you delete a contact, you also delete all the associated notes and histories tied to that contact. For example, suppose that State College uses ACT! to keep track of all prospective students that it has contacted — or has been contacted by. State College admissions personnel receive thousands of inquiries a month and fear that the database will become too large to manage . . . and subsequently think that deleting all prospects that they haven't had contact with in over a year is the best course of action. However, some of those prospects might be attending different schools that they aren't happy with and might want to enter State College as transfer students. Other prospects might transfer after completing two years at a community college, and still others might consider attending State College as graduate students.

What to do in such a situation? I'd consider moving the contacts that you no longer need into another archival database. That way, should the need ever arise, you can still find all the original information on a contact without having to start again from scratch. How nice to be able to rekindle a relationship by asking, "So tell me, how did you find the accounting department at Podunk University?" Although the setup of an archival database is beyond the scope of this book, an ACT! Certified Consultant can assist you with this matter.

Three warnings before deleting a contact

Losing contacts in your database is a very scary thought. You undoubtedly rely very heavily on your ACT! database; losing that data can be potentially devastating to your business. Worst of all, when you realize that you just accidentally removed several — or even hundreds — of contacts from the database, panic can set in!

Avert this panic by following these tips *before* you attempt to delete any of your contacts:

- ✔ **Know the difference between deleting a contact and deleting a lookup.** That way, you don't delete numerous contacts when you want to delete only a single record.

  - *Contact:* The single record that you view from the Contact Detail window.

  - *Lookup:* The group of contacts that displays after a database search. Chapter 6 gives you a bit more information about creating lookups.

- ✔ **Read the warning and make note of the number of contacts that you're about to delete.** Don't be afraid to click Cancel if a large number of contacts start to disappear.

- ✔ **Remember the three rules of computing: backup, backup, backup!** Chapter 15 provides you with instructions on how to create a backup. A good backup provides the easiest method to restore all your information after you accidentally deleted it.

The Contacts, They Are A'Changin'

Companies relocate and change their names, people move, and your fingers sometimes slip on the keyboard. People change e-mail addresses. You might want to add additional contact information for one of your contacts. All these predicaments require the editing of contact fields. Not to worry; changing the information that you store in ACT! is as easy as entering it in the first place.

ACT! gives you two ways of updating contact information:

✔ Click in the field that you want to change and then press the Delete or Backspace key to remove the existing field information. Then simply type in the new information.

✔ Highlight all the information in a field. By typing in the new information, the old information is automatically replaced.

If you accidentally overwrite information in a single ACT! field, press Ctrl+Z to undo the changes that you just made to that field — *before* you move your cursor to another ACT! record. For those who are keyboard challenged, an alternative is to choose Edit⇨Undo from the main menu. After you move on to another record, neither of these options are available to you.

To undo multiple changes that you make to an ACT! record, choose Edit⇨ Undo Changes to Contact *before* you move on to the next record.

After you execute another ACT! command or move on to another record, ACT! automatically saves the record. At that point, you can't automatically undo any changes you made to a contact record.

Chapter 5

A Few Good Tabs and Lists

*T*hroughout this book, you find all the neat ways in which you can customize ACT!. In this chapter, you discover how to change the appearance of the various ACT! lists and tabs. And, although you encounter numerous lists and tabs in your travels through ACT!, you'll soon discover that you can modify them in exactly the same way.

After you've seen one list or tab, you've seen them all! And, if you're a fanACTic, the lists and tabs work pretty much like they did in previous versions.

Meeting the Lists and Tabs

The bad news is that numerous lists and tabs are sprinkled through ACT!, and new users might find themselves lost in a maze of windows. The good news is that lists and tabs all have pretty much the same look and feel to them — if you master one, you master them all!

You can find all lists by clicking View on the menu bar and then explore one by selecting a list that sounds fun and exciting. Two of the lists — the Task List and the Opportunity List — are so much fun that they are included in the Nav bar running along the left side of ACT!. And, if you feel so inclined, you're welcome to flip back to Chapter 3 to find out how to add all the list items to the Nav bar.

Here's a few of the lists you'll work with most often:

- ✔ **Contact:** Lists all your contacts; the list is filtered based on your current lookup.

- ✔ **Task:** Lists all the tasks and activities you scheduled for all your contacts; you can filter these by date, type, priority, user, public versus private, timeless, cleared status, and Outlook relationship.

- ✔ **Group:** Lists all groups and can optionally include subgroups.

- ✔ **Company:** Lists all companies and can optionally include divisions.

- ✔ **Opportunities:** Lists all the sales opportunities that you enter for all your contacts; you can filter opportunities by date, status, process, stage, probability, amount, and public versus private.

The two types of tabs are

System tabs: These are the same for any and all layouts you use.

User tabs: You can rename and modify these to best fit the way you work (see Chapter 14).

The system tabs are

- ✔ **Notes:** Lists all notes you record for the current contact, company, or group; you can filter the notes by date, private versus public, and user. See Chapter 7 for more on the Notes tab.

- ✔ **History:** Lists all correspondence, activities, and document information that were recorded automatically by ACT! for a contact, group, or company; you can filter the histories by date, private versus public, type of history, and user. Turn to Chapter 7 to find out more about the History tab.

- ✔ **Activities:** Lists all activities for the contact, group, or company; you can filter the activities by date, private versus public, cleared, timeless, type of activity, priority, and user. I go in depth about the Activities tab in Chapter 8.

- ✔ **Opportunities:** Lists the financial lowdown on all the selling opportunities for the current contact, group, or company; you can filter the opportunities by date, status, private versus public, and user. Chapter 19 covers the Opportunities tab.

- ✔ **Documents:** Lists all files attached to the current contact, group, or company; you can't filter this tab. See the section, "Documenting Your Documents," later in this chapter for more about the Documents tab.

- ✔ **Contacts:** Lists all the contacts associated with the current group or company. You only see this tab in the Group Detail window or the Company Detail window.

Minding your filters!

When viewing the various system tabs, you must be aware of the effect that the filters have on what information you see — or don't see. In ACT!, you can choose to filter information or to include it. Different tabs have different filters; however, all tabs include a date filter and a user filter. If the filter is set to show only items in the future and you have an activity scheduled for today, you don't see today's activity. And, if you schedule an activity but you set the filter to include only Alyssa's activities, you don't see your activity either.

When frustrated, check your filters! You might be puzzled at the fact that information you just *know* has been entered into the database has mysteriously disappeared. This becomes increasingly important on the Activities tab, which contains several filter options (including three buried away behind the Option button). The Task and Opportunity lists can be even more confusing; these lists contain a variety of filter options — all of which can be hidden away with one click of the Hide Filters button.

✔ **Secondary Contacts:** Lists the secondary contacts (for example, the butcher, the baker, and the candlestick maker) that are directly associated with the current contact; you can't filter this tab. Flip ahead a few pages to the "Corralling Your Secondary Contacts" section in this chapter where I discuss the Secondary Contacts tab.

✔ **Groups/Companies:** This tab has a dual personality. You'll notice the addition of the Show Membership For drop-down list that lets you indicate whether you want to view the groups or the companies that the contact is associated with. This tab appears only in the Contact Detail window.

You'll notice that the first five tabs appear on the Contacts, Groups, and Companies windows. That's because you can add a note, an activity, and so on to either an individual contact record, or to a company or group record.

Remodeling Lists and Tabs

One of the reasons that you might find the lists and tabs to be so useful is the ease with which you can customize them. You can add or remove columns, change the order of the columns, widen the columns, sort on any one of the columns, and then print out your final product. In this section, I cover a few ways in which you can change the look of your lists and tabs.

Adding or removing columns

Probably the first thing that you want to do to modify your lists and columns is to add or remove a column — or two or three! Follow these steps:

1. **Click the Options button (in the top-right corner) on any list or tab and choose Customize Columns from the menu that appears.**

   The Customize Columns dialog box appears (see Figure 5-1).

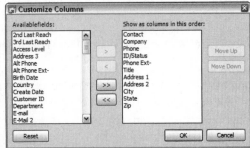

Figure 5-1:
Adding
columns to
the Contact
List.

   Because variety is the spice of life, you right-clickers will also find that you can right-click any of the ACT! lists or tabs to get to the Customize Columns dialog box.

2. **Select the field (column) that you want to add by clicking the appropriate choice in the Available Fields list.**

   Depending on the list or tab you're working with, you see various field choices. Feel free to include as many or as few as your little heart desires.

3. **Click the single right-pointing arrow.**

   If you're really into seeing a lot of information, you can click the double right-pointing arrows; that adds all available fields to your list or tab.

4. **To remove an item, click the appropriate choice from the Show as Columns in This Order list and then click the single left-pointing arrow.**

   If you really want to get rowdy, click the double left-pointing arrows to remove all the current fields. You might do this if you have an overwhelming desire to start from scratch.

5. **Click the Close button when you're done.**

Changing the order and width of columns

You can change the order of the fields from the Customize Columns dialog box that I show you how to access in the preceding section. Click the appropriate choice from the Show as Columns in This Order list and click the Move Up or Move Down buttons.

The order in which items appear in the Customize Columns dialog box is exactly the way they appear in your final product. Knock yourself out, arrange and rearrange all you want, and sleep peacefully knowing that if you don't like the outcome you can always change it again. Now, if I could just do that with my living room!

You can also drag and drop the various column headings to change the order in which columns appear on the lists and tabs. For example, if you want the Date field to appear before the Time field, simply click the Time column heading and drag the heading over to the left of the Date column heading. As you start to drag one of the columns, a black vertical line appears, indicating the intended location of the column.

Changing the width of a column is just as easy. If you move your mouse on the line between any two column headings, your cursor transforms into a double-headed arrow. When that arrow appears, hold down your left mouse button and drag to the left or right to narrow or widen a column. The column to the left of your mouse changes width.

Sorting your lists and tabs

In general, I hate terms like *automatic* and *click of a button* because your vision of *automatic* might be quite different from that of a software engineer. That said, sorting the entries in any of your lists and tabs is, well, automatic and can be done with the click of a button: Just click the column heading that you want to use to sort the list. Want the contacts in your Contact list sorted alphabetically by city? Click the City column heading. Change your mind and want it sorted by ZIP code instead? Click the Zip Code column heading.

ACT! automatically separates the contact's name into a first and a last name. When you click the Contact column heading in any of the lists or tabs, you'll notice that your information is sorted by last name so that Andrea Fredricks appears alphabetically with the Fs rather than with the As.

When you click a column heading, an up arrow appears indicating that the contacts are sorted in ascending order (in alphabetical, A–Z, or 1–10 order). To reverse the sort order, click the column heading again. If the list is sorted in ascending order, contacts that have no information in the selected column appear at the top of the list. In descending order, they appear at the bottom of the list.

Sorting your contacts is so simple that you might decide to get really adventurous and sort based on another criterion. Go ahead — I dare you! Click any column heading to re-sort the list by the field of your choice. Want to have your Contact List sorted by more than one criterion? Sneak a peak at the final section of this chapter for a crash course.

Contacting the Contact List

The Contact List is a good way to view your contacts if you're working with large numbers of contacts at one time. Changing the columns that appear in the Contact List provides you with a way of comparing information between your various contacts. For example, you might want to see how many of your contacts purchased each of your products, and have the name of each product appear in the Contact List, along with their telephone number.

Getting to the Contact List is half the fun

The road to the Contact List is simple to follow — just choose View⇨ Contact List. A list of your contacts appears, displayed in columns as shown in Figure 5-2.

When you come across a contact record in your list that requires a bit of tweaking, you might want to flip to the Contact Detail window to make your changes. You can get to the Contact Detail window in a number of ways:

- ✔ Double-click a contact in the Contact List.
- ✔ Right-click the contact and choose Look Up Selected Contacts.
- ✔ Click the Back button on the Back and Forward bar if you were just in the Contact Detail window.

The Contact Detail window appears with the selected contact's record. To return to the Contact List, choose View⇨Contact List or click the Back button on the Back and Forward bar.

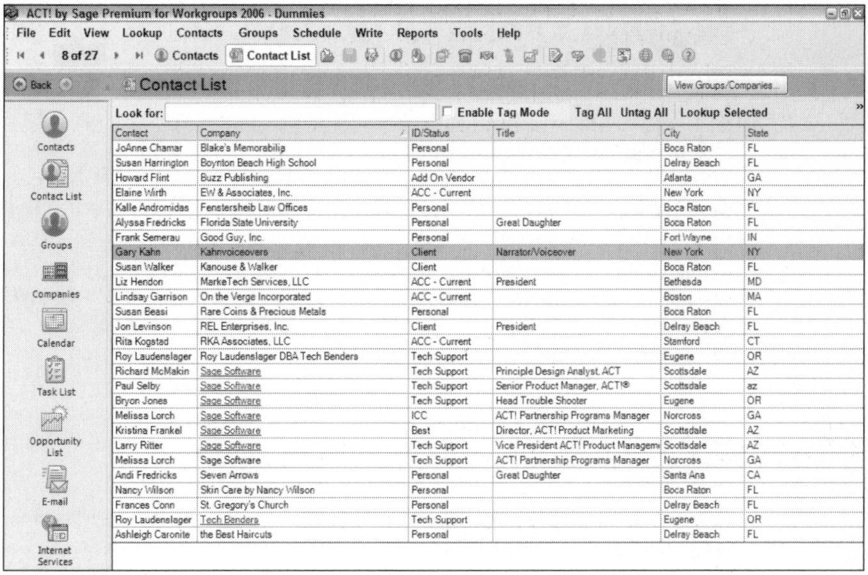

Figure 5-2:
The ACT!
Contact List.

Finding a contact in the Contact List

In Chapter 6, I show you how to create a lookup to find contacts that meet your specific criteria. The Contact List also allows you to go to a specific contact record in the blink of an eye. Here's what you need to do:

1. **Click the column heading to select that column.**

   For example, if you want to find a contact by last name, click the Contact column heading.

2. **Start typing the first few letters of the contact information that you want to find in the Look For text field.**

   If you click the Contact column heading, start typing the first few letters of the contact's last name. If you click the Company Name column heading, type in the first few letters of the company that you're looking for.

   ACT! scrolls down the Contact List to the closest match. For example, if you sorted the list by contact and typed the letter **s**, you might land on the Colonel Sanders contact record. If you typed **sm**, you're probably looking at all your Smiths.

3. **Continue typing until you reach the contact for whom you are looking.**

Tagging contacts in the Contact List

Using the Contact List, you can easily select — or *tag* — contacts to manually create a lookup of your contacts. For example, say that you want to target some of your best clients for a special promotion; a general lookup probably doesn't produce a list of those contacts because you don't have a field that includes special promotions. Instead, you can tag those contacts based on your own instincts.

To switch to Tag mode, just make sure that a check mark is showing next to the Enable Tag Mode option, which is located at the top of the Contact List. You can do the following things in Tag mode:

- ✔ **Tag a contact.** Click anywhere in the contact; a gray bar appears across the contact record indicating that you tagged it. Figure 5-3 shows tagged contacts.

- ✔ **Untag a contact.** Click anywhere in a tagged contact, and the gray bar disappears.

- ✔ **Tag a continuous list of names.** Click the first name in the list that you're selecting, and then press the Shift key while clicking the last name in the list that you're selecting. All the names between the first name and the last name that you're selecting are automatically tagged.

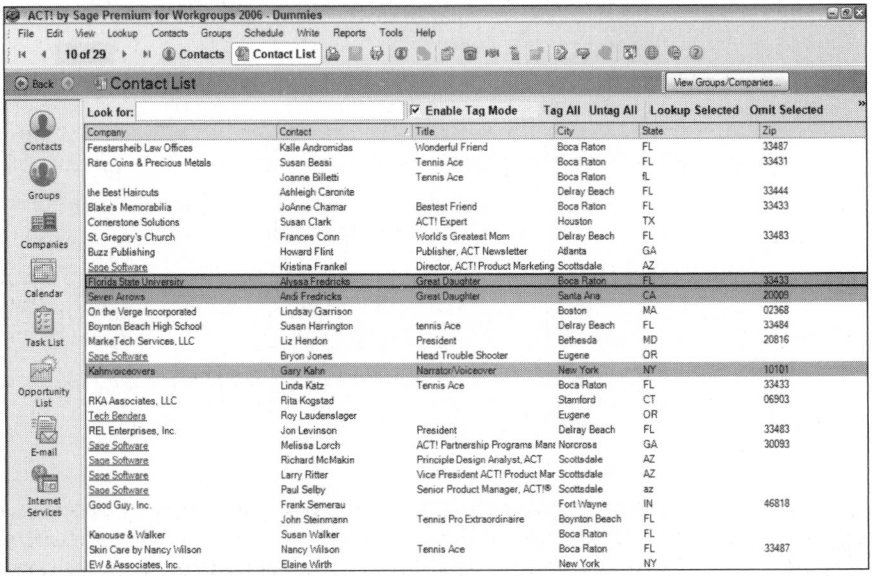

Figure 5-3:
Selected
contacts in
Tag mode.

Notice the four buttons to the right of the Enable Tag Mode option (refer to Figure 5-3). After you tag the contacts that you want to work with or those that you want to omit temporarily, choose one of the following four buttons:

- ✔ **Tag All:** Allows you to select all the contacts currently showing in the Contact List.

- ✔ **Untag All:** Allows you to deselect any contacts that you already selected.

- ✔ **Lookup Selected:** Allows you to create a lookup based on the contacts that you tag.

- ✔ **Omit Selected:** Allows you to remove the contacts that you select from the Contact List. Don't panic — it does not remove the contacts permanently from your database!

If you need to print out any lists or tabs, flip to Chapter 9 for the lowdown on Quick Reports.

Corralling Your Secondary Contacts

Does this scenario sound familiar? You have a main contact, but of course that person, being the big cheese, is rarely available so you often have to work with his assistant. But of course the assistant can't do any true decision making, so you might need to speak to Mr. Big's sales manager on occasion. And, when the sales manager goes on vacation, you need to call the assistant sales manager. Yikes! The Secondary Contacts tab, as shown in Figure 5-4, allows you to store all the pertinent information about Mr. Big and his partners in crime in the same area so you don't have to go on a wild goose chase hunting down names, telephone numbers, and e-mail addresses. And, just like promotions that often happen, you can "promote" a secondary contact into a main contact.

Figure 5-4:
The
Secondary
Contacts
tab.

| Notes | History | Activities | Opportunities | Groups/Companies | Secondary Contacts | Documents | Contact Info | User Fields | Home Address |

| New Secondary Contact | Promote | | | | Options ▾ |

Company	Contact	Title	Phone	City	State
Voice Overs	Ashton Hasher	Voice Over Talent	(212) 555-1212	New York	NY
Rides Alot	Lance Livestrong	Tour de France Wir	(561) 555-1212	Austin	TX
Secrets to Success	Walter Mitty	Analyst	(800) 555-1212	New York	NY
Born in the USA	Bruce Springstein	Vocalist	(917) 492-5555	Asbury Park	NJ

Not sure whether you should add a contact as a primary or a secondary contact? You might want to think of how you are going to use the secondary contact. If you just want to be able to access an assistant's phone number, then the assistant is a good candidate for entry as a secondary contact. However, if you want to be able to e-mail your monthly newsletter to the assistant or include her in some of your mail merges, you need to add the assistant as a primary contact record instead.

Adding a secondary contact

Of course, you can't add a secondary contact until you create a main contact (see Chapter 4 to do so). After you create the head honcho's contact record, here's what you do to create the secondary contact record(s):

1. **From the Contact Detail window, click the Secondary Contacts tab.**

2. **Click the New Secondary Contact button on the top of the Secondary Contacts tab.**

   The New Secondary Contact dialog box appears (see Figure 5-5).

3. **Fill in all the juicy details for the secondary contact.**

   Although you don't fill in quite as much information as you can for a main contact, you do have all the really pertinent fields. Don't forget to click the Business Address tab for even more fields.

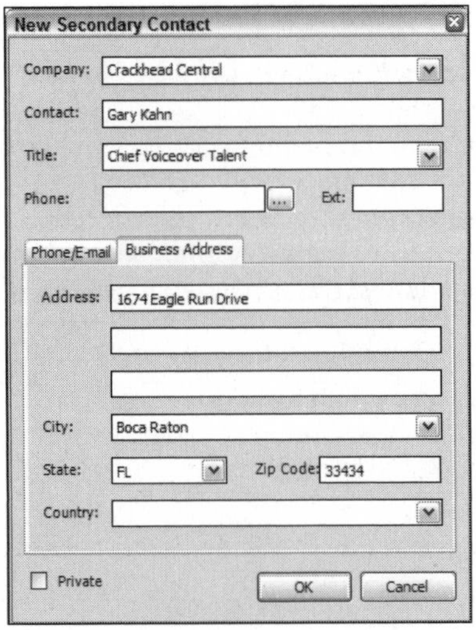

Figure 5-5:
Fill in
secondary
contact
information
here.

4. **Click OK to create the secondary contact.**

Congratulations! Your main contact has now given birth to a secondary contact. All the secondary contacts that you create appear on the Secondary Contacts tab of the primary contact.

If you need to go back and edit or add information for the secondary contact, just double-click the name from the Secondary Contact list and *voilà*, you're back to the Secondary Contact dialog box.

Deleting a secondary contact

Sorry to say, but some of the secondary contacts might drift off into the sunset, leaving you with the need to remove them from your database. Not to worry; you can delete a secondary contact by following the bouncing ball through these steps:

1. **Click the Secondary Contacts tab from the Contact Detail window.**

2. **Right-click the contact you want to delete and then choose Delete.**

   You can never say that ACT! doesn't give you ample warning before deleting a contact. As usual, when you attempt to delete even a secondary contact ACT! shows you a scary warning.

3. **Click Yes to delete the selected secondary contact.**

Promoting a secondary contact

Promoting, promotion — it has a lovely ring to it, don't you think? That lowly assistant might be promoted through the ranks and some day become the "big guy" — or at the very least a more important contact than he/she is today. If you're worried that you have to reenter all that basic information in again, don't be. Just promote the contact by following these steps:

1. **Click the Secondary Contacts tab in the Contact Detail window.**

2. **Select the secondary contact that you want to promote.**

3. **Right-click and choose Promote from the menu.**

   The Promote Secondary Contact dialog box appears, as shown in Figure 5-6.

4. **Select whether to duplicate the main contact's primary fields.**

   With promotions come responsibilities and decisions. If the secondary contact is sliding into the role of the current primary contact, you want to copy all of the primary contact's information to the record of the newly promoted contact. If, however, the secondary contact doesn't have the same basic information as the primary contact, you can choose not to copy the primary fields.

5. **Click OK.**

Promote Secondary Contact
When promoting a secondary contact, you have the option to copy data from the main contact's primary fields to the secondary contact fields. Primary fields are displayed in Define Fields.
Options
Duplicate data from main contact's primary fields
Do not duplicate data from primary fields
OK
Cancel

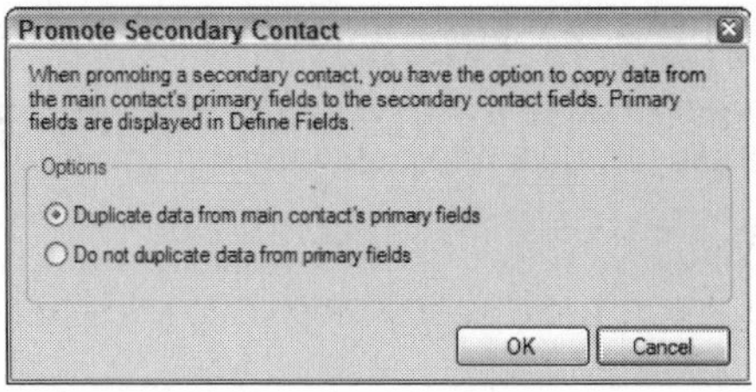

Figure 5-6: Promote a secondary contact here.

Documenting Your Documents

No matter how organized you think your documents might be, you probably occasionally misplace one of them. Of course you can always have Windows search for it, but ACT! offers an easier — and faster solution. The Documents tab, which you can find on the Contacts, Groups, or Companies windows, allows you to attach any and all of your files related to the current contact, group, or company. You can add a proposal created in Excel, a contract created in Word, or even a PDF file that you scanned into your computer. By adding them to the Documents tab, as shown in Figure 5-7, you are actually cloning the original file and placing it in your ACT! database.

Notes
History
Activities
Opportunities
Groups/Companies
Secondary Contacts
Documents
Contact Info
User Fields
Home Address
Add Document
Remove Document
Edit Document
Map To Excel
Name
Size
File Type
Date Modified
Tech Benders Pricing.xls
32 KB
Microsoft Excel Worksheet
7/11/2005
Serial Number.doc
21 KB
Microsoft Word Document
6/25/2005
GapAnalysisAPFWvsAFW1.pdf
31 KB
Adobe Acrobat Document
5/30/2005
3 grads.jpg
1,109 KB
JPEG Image
5/25/2004

Figure 5-7: Locate documents from here.

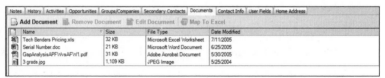

After you add a document to the Documents tab, you can open the file directly from ACT! to view, edit, or print. You can also link the same document to multiple records. Removing a file from the Documents tab does not remove the original document from your computer.

Adding a document

Adding a file to the Documents tab is very easy, and considering the time you save down the road, well worth the effort. Just follow these steps:

1. **Display the contact, group, or company record to which you want to add a document.**
2. **Click the Documents tab.**

3. **Click the Add Document button on the Documents tab icon bar.**

   Alternatively, you can right-click in the file list area and then choose Add Document from the menu.

   The Attach File dialog box opens.

4. **Browse to the document you want to add, select it, and then click Open.**

   ACT! adds the document to your ACT! database and displays the filename, size, type, and last modified date on the Documents tab. Because the document is now part of your database, remote synchronization users can now access the document as well.

You can also drag and drop a file to the Documents tab from Windows Explorer or My Computer by dragging the document's icon to the Documents tab.

Opening a document

The true benefit of adding documents to the Documents tab is the speed in which you can open the documents that pertain to a specific contact, group, or company. Follow these steps:

1. **Click the Documents tab.**

2. **Select the document you want to open.**

3. **Click the Edit Document button on the Documents tab icon bar.**

   Alternatively, you can right-click in the file list area and choose Edit Document from the menu.

   Magically, the program associated with the document opens, revealing the document. You're on you own here — just remember that you can now edit, save, or print the document as you normally do. Any changes you make are reflected the next time you open the document through ACT!.

Removing a document

After you add a file to the Documents tab, you might change your mind and decide to make it go am-scray. Easy come, easy go. Follow these steps to rid yourself of the offending document:

1. **Display the contact, group, or company record that contains the document you want to eliminate.**

2. **Click the Documents tab.**

3. **In the Document List, select the document you want to remove.**

4. **Click the Remove Document button on the Documents tab icon bar.**

   Alternatively, you can right-click in the file list area and then choose Remove Document from the menu.

   ACT! makes sure you want to remove the document by presenting a warning. Software programs very often present you with scary messages before deleting important information. This is a good thing. Heed the warnings!

   ACT! deletes the document permanently from the database. And, because the document doesn't end up in the Recycle Bin, think very carefully *before* deleting the document.

5. **Click Yes to confirm that you really, truly want to remove the document.**

If you originally created the document somewhere in your computer, the document is still there. However, if you are a sync user who received the document as part of the synchronization process, you might want to first open the document and save it to your computer before removing it from the Documents tab — otherwise, it's gone for good!

Changing the Order of Columns

By default, ACT! automatically sorts your data alphabetically by the company name. If you open the Contact List, you see your contacts listed there in company order. Scroll to the first contact in the Contacts view — that contact probably works at a company that starts with the letter A. But, like just about all of ACT!, you can change that order.

As I mention earlier in this chapter, by default, your contacts are sorted alphabetically by the Company column. You can see this two different ways:

- ✔ A small triangle appears in the Company column heading in the Contact List.
- ✔ Companies starting with the letter *A* appear before those starting with the letter *B* as you scroll through your contacts.

Although the Contact List provides you with a quick-as-a-bunny way to sort your contacts, it sorts the contacts based on the contents of a *single* field. If you want to sort your contacts based on multiple criteria, you have another way to do it:

Why don't my contacts sort correctly?

At times, your contacts might appear to not alphabetize correctly. Possible reasons for this include

✔ **A stray mark or a blank space leads the field name.** For example, *'Zinger & Co.* appears alphabetically in front of *Gadgets R Us.*

✔ **Numbers appear alphabetically in front of letters.** For example, *1st Financial Savings* *& Loan* appears alphabetically in front of *AAA Best Bank.*

✔ **ACT! might be a little confused about the first and last name of a contact.** A quick trip to the Contact Detail window is worth your time. Click the ellipsis button next to the Contact's name and then double-check that the correct first and last names appear in the appropriate spots.

1. **Choose Edit⇨Sort from either the Contact List or Contact Detail window.**

   The Sort dialog box appears (see Figure 5-8).

2. **Choose an option from the Sort By drop-down list to specify the first-level sort criterion.**

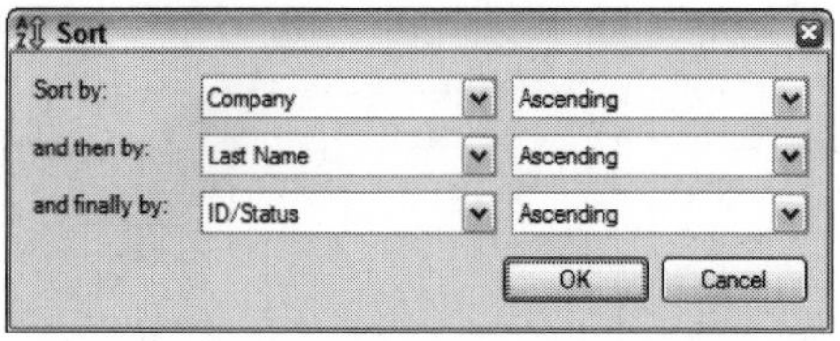

Figure 5-8: Set your sort here.

3. **Select the sorting order (Ascending or Descending).**

   Ascending sort order means from A–Z or from the smallest number to the largest number. Records with no information in the field used for the sort appear first. *Descending* means from Z–A or from the largest number to the smallest number. Records with no information in the field used for the sort appear last.

4. **Choose a second field option from the And Then By drop-down list and specify Ascending or Descending.**

5. **If you want a third level of sorting, choose a field from the And Finally By drop-down list and specify Ascending or Descending.**

6. **Click OK.**

Chapter 6

The ACT! Lookup: Searching for Your Contacts

. . . .

In This Chapter

▶ Understanding the basic ACT! lookup

▶ Querying companies, groups, and opportunities

▶ Special searching

▶ Performing advanced queries

. . . .

*I*f all roads lead to Rome, then surely all processes in ACT! lead to the lookup. A *lookup* is a way of looking at only a portion of the contacts in your database, depending on your specifications. A good practice in ACT! is to perform a lookup first and then perform an action second. For example, you might perform a lookup and then print some labels. Or you might do a lookup and then perform a mail merge. Need a report? Do a lookup first! In this chapter, I show you how to perform lookups based on contact information, notes and history information, and advanced query information.

ACT! Is Looking Up

The theory behind the lookup is that you don't always need to work with all your contacts at one time. Not only is working with only a portion of your database easier; at times, doing so is absolutely necessary. If you're changing your mailing address, you probably want to send a notification to everyone in your database. Comparatively, if you're running a special sales promotion, you probably notify only your prospects and customers. And if you're sending out overpriced holiday gift baskets, you probably want the names of only your very best customers.

Don't create an extra database — Use the ACT! lookup instead

Some ACT! users originally create several databases, not realizing that one database can be used to store information about various types of contacts. Although you might want to create two separate databases — for instance, one for customers and one for vendors — a better alternative is to include both your customers and vendors together in one database. To this one database, you can then add a few miscellaneous contacts, including prospects who aren't yet customers or referral sources that might lead to new customers. Just make sure that each contact is identified in some specific way; I recommend using the ID/Status field. Then when you want to see only vendors or only prospective customers, simply perform a lookup to work with just that particular group of contacts.

Most computer programs use the term "query" to indicate the result of a database search. However, ACT! generally uses the term "lookup." Feel free to use the terms interchangeably.

In ACT!, you can focus on a portion of your contacts by

✔ Creating basic lookups based on the information in one of the nine most-commonly used contact fields in ACT!. (See the later section, "Performing Basic Lookups.")

✔ Conducting a query based on information stored in your groups, companies, and opportunities. (See the later section, "Searching Your Groups, Companies, and Opportunities.")

✔ Creating lookups based on information from other areas in your database including notes, histories, activities, annual events, and contact activity. (See the later section, "Performing Special ACT! Lookups.")

✔ Creating your own, more advanced, queries based on the parameters of your own choosing by using logical operators. (See the later section, "Creating Advanced Queries.")

Performing Basic Lookups

The easiest way to pose a query is to choose one of your main contact fields from a menu and then fill in the search criteria. Although this way is easy because the menus guide you, it's also the least flexible way. The Lookup menu that ACT! provides is probably the best — and simplest — place to start when creating a lookup; just follow these steps:

1. Choose the Lookup menu from the Contact Detail window.

Figure 6-1 shows you the Lookup menu that drops down and the criteria that you can use to perform your lookup.

Figure 6-1:
Define your
lookup here.

2. Choose one of the criteria listed in Figure 6-1 to create a basic lookup.

The ACT! Lookup Contacts dialog box appears, as shown in Figure 6-2.

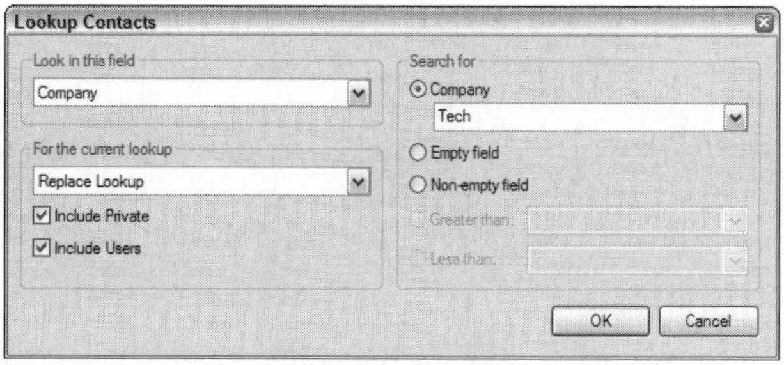

Figure 6-2:
The ACT!
Lookup
Contacts
dialog box.

3. If you're searching based on an Other field, click the Look in This Field drop-down arrow and choose a field from the drop-down list.

If you come from a long line of right-clickers, you might prefer to simply right-click whatever field for which you want to create a lookup and then click Lookup. Sharp as a tack, ACT! opens up the Lookup Contacts dialog box, with your field already selected in the Look in This Field text box.

4. **In the For the Current Lookup area, select an option:**

   • **Replace Lookup:** Creates a brand-new lookup based on your criteria.

   • **Add to Lookup:** Adds the contacts based on your criteria to an existing lookup. For example, if you create a lookup for your contacts based in Chicago, select this option to add your New York clients to the set of Chicago clients.

   • **Narrow Lookup:** Refines a lookup based on a second criterion. For example, if you create a lookup of all your customers, you could select this option to narrow the lookup to only those customers based in Philadelphia.

5. **In the Search For area, select an option:**

   • **Company:** Type the word to search for or select a word from the drop-down list to look for contacts that match a specific criterion.

   • **Empty Field:** If you're looking for contacts who don't have any data in the given field — for example, people who don't have an e-mail address — choose this option.

   • **Non-Empty Field:** If you want to find only those contacts who have data in a given field — for example, everyone who has an e-mail address — choose this option.

When typing in the match criterion, remember that with ACT!, less is more. ACT! automatically searches by the beginning of your string. For example, in the sample database for this book, typing **Tech** returns *Tech Benders* and *Technology Consultants*. However, typing **Technology** returns only *Technology Consultants*.

6. **Click OK.**

   If only one contact record matches your search criteria, that's the record that you see. However, if several contact records match your criteria, the Contact List appears with a list of all your matches. In either case, the record counter now reflects the number of contacts that match your search criteria.

7. **Choose Lookup⇨All Contacts when you're ready to once again view all the contacts in your database.**

Don't panic right after performing a lookup, wondering what happened to the rest of your contacts. You can always reassure yourself by doing a lookup of All Contacts after each and every one of your lookups. Although this won't hurt anything, this step is entirely unnecessary. After you finish working with your current lookup, you can simply wait until you need to create another lookup. Just do a lookup for your next criterion and save yourself a step.

Playing the wild card

Some of you old-timers might remember that an asterisk (*) was the DOS wild card. That same concept exists in Structured Query Language (SQL)-based products like ACT! except that the percent sign (%) replaced the asterisk (for some reason known only to the technical gods).

Say you're trying to find all companies that are carpet cleaners. If you create a lookup using the word **carpet**, you find *Carpet Cleaning by Joanne Chamar* but not *Joanne's Carpet Cleaning*. Enter the wild card and create your lookup using **%carpet**. ACT! finds companies that both begin and end with *carpet*.

Searching Your Groups, Companies, and Opportunities

Probably the most common lookups you create are based on your contact fields. However, you aren't limited to searching by just those fields. You can also query your groups, companies, and opportunities for key information. The best part is that all three queries work in pretty much the same way.

Grappling with your groups

When performing a Group lookup, you might look for the name of one specific group or for a group or groups that all contain the same information. In other words, I might look for all groups whose names start with *Technology*, or I might look for all groups that are located in New York City. To find the groups that match your search criteria, here's all you need to do:

1. **Choose Lookup⇨Groups and then choose from the following options:**

   • **All Groups:** Opens the Group List showing you a list of all the groups in your database.

   • **Name:** Finds all groups that match the name you specify.

   • **Other Fields:** Allows you to search through any and all group fields for the groups that match your desired criterion. The list shows all group fields that you can search in the database.

   • **Save Lookup as Group:** If you just created a lookup (as described in the previous section) and want to save your results into a new group, this is your option. You can also see other ways to create Groups in Chapter 20.

If you choose the All Groups or Save Lookup as Group option, you're finished. If you choose the Name or Other Fields option, the Lookup Groups dialog box opens, as shown in Figure 6-3. You have to continue along your merry way following these remaining steps:

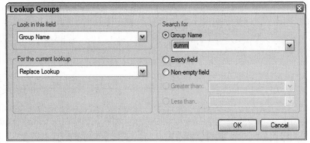

Figure 6-3:
The Lookup
Groups
dialog box.

2. **In the Look in This Field area, select the Group field you want to query from the drop-down list.**

3. **In the Search For area, type the word to search for or select a word from the drop-down list.**

4. **In the For the Current Lookup area, select the Replace Lookup option.**

5. **Click OK.**

   Like magic, the Group List pops open, displaying a list of all the groups that match your specifications.

Calling all companies

Hopefully, creating a lookup of companies seems vaguely familiar because it is so similar to creating a group lookup. To find the companies that match your search criteria, here's all you need to do: Choose Lookup⇨Companies and then choose from one of the following options:

- ✔ **All Companies:** Opens the Company List showing you a list of all the companies in your database.
- ✔ **Name**
- ✔ **Main Phone**
- ✔ **City**
- ✔ **State**
- ✔ **Zip Code**

✔ **ID/Status:** Just like you use the ID/Status field to classify each of your contacts into a separate category, assign your companies an ID/Status. For example, if one of your company ID/Status options is *wholesale,* it's a snap to find all your "wholesale" companies.

✔ **Other Fields:** Provides you with a drop-down list of all your company fields.

✔ **Save Lookup as Company:** Lets you create a company based on the currently displayed contacts. Chapter 21 will show you how to create a company.

The Company Lookup works the same way as the Group Lookup. If you choose the All Companies or Save Lookup as Company option, you're finished. If you choose any of the other options, the Lookup Companies dialog box opens. From there, you can follow the same steps that you did for the Group Lookup.

Ogling your opportunities

Those of you who won't be using ACT! to help keep track of all your past, pending, and future sales can skip this next section. However, if your company has an active sales force, you'll want to run (don't walk) to Chapter 19 to read everything there is to know about ACT!'s cool Opportunity feature. After an opportunity is created, you can search through all your sales opportunities in a variety of ways.

1. **Choose Lookup⇨Opportunities.**

2. **Choose one of the following options:**

   • **All Opportunities:** Opens the Opportunities List, showing you a list of all the opportunities in your database.

   • **Name:** Finds opportunities that match the name you specify. Typically, you want to use the quote number as the name of your quote so that you can lookup based on that criterion. Chapter 20 shows you how to name your quotes.

   • **Stage:** Finds opportunities that match a specific sales stage.

   • **Product:** Finds opportunities that pertain to a specific product.

   • **Total:** Finds opportunities that match the total sale you specify. You can also search for opportunities that are larger or smaller than a specified dollar amount.

   • **Status:** Finds opportunities that match a specific sales status.

- **Record Manager:** Lets you find any of the opportunities that are associated with any one particular user.

- **Other Fields:** Finds all opportunities that match any other opportunity fields, including the eight opportunity fields that you can customize.

If you choose the first option, you're whisked away to the Opportunity List. If you opt for one of the other options, the Lookup Opportunities dialog box appears, as shown in Figure 6-4. If you're getting bored, I apologize — ACT! is just so darned consistent that you're probably finding that querying your sales opportunities is every bit as easy as any of the other lookups I cover throughout this chapter.

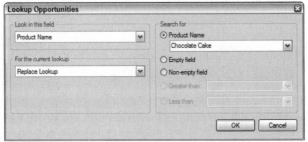

Figure 6-4:
The Lookup
Opportu-
nities dialog
box.

3. **From the Look in This Field drop-down list, select the field on which you wish to search.**

   The list shows all opportunity fields that you can search.

4. **In the Search For area, type the word to search for or select a word from the drop-down list.**

   For example, if you're looking for all opportunities that are in the Negotiation stage, select Stage from the Look in This Field drop-down list and Negotiation from the Search For drop-down list. To find out how well your chocolate cake is selling, choose Product from the Look in This Field drop-down and Chocolate Cake from the Search For box.

5. **Select Replace Lookup from the For the Current Lookup drop-down list.**

6. **Click OK.**

Although you might be as happy as a little clam using the Opportunity lookup, you can achieve the same results by filtering your Opportunity List. Filtering might even make you ecstatic because you'll probably find it a bit easier and much more flexible. Chapter 5 shows you how to filter your Opportunities List. Chapter 19 will further astonish you when it reveals some of the other great Opportunity party tricks!

Performing Special ACT! Lookups

The ability to perform a simple lookup based on a single field criterion is an element common to most databases, but ACT! isn't your average database. All databases contain fields, but only special databases contain things such as notes and activities. And after creating a note to store a useful tidbit of information (which I show you how to do in Chapter 7), you might want to find that information again. Some of you might want to use ACT! to send monthly birthday and anniversary greetings. ACT! provides you with three special query options to find information that was entered into ACT! in a special way.

Searching by keyword

A *keyword search* can be an extremely useful way to find data about your contacts no matter where that information might be lurking. In fact, I've gotten many ACT! users to start calling this search the "Senior Moment" Search. As your database increases, you might find yourself in a situation in which you can only remember one tiny piece of information about a contact. ACT!'s keyword search enables you to dig for that information in the Activities, Opportunities, Histories, Notes, and Fields portions of ACT!. For example, suppose that you're looking for someone to design a new logo for your business but you can't remember where you stored that information. Is *logo* part of the company's name, did you enter it into the ID/Status field, or did you stick it in a note somewhere? A keyword search searches throughout your database, checking all fields, until it finds the word *logo*.

Here's how to perform a keyword search:

1. **From the Contact Detail window, choose Lookup⇨Keyword Search.**

   The Keyword Search dialog box opens (see Figure 6-5).

2. **In the Search For area, enter the key piece of information that you're searching for.**

3. **In the Record Type drop-down list, indicate whether you're looking for a Contact, Group, or Company record.**

4. **In the Search These Records area, choose an option:**

   - **All Records:** ACT! sifts through all records in your database.

   - **Current Record:** ACT! searches only the record that was onscreen when you opened the dialog box. Use this option if you know that somewhere in the deep, dark past, you entered a specific tidbit of information as a note.

   - **Current Lookup:** ACT! searches only the records that you selected in your most recent lookup.

Figure 6-5:
Run a
keyword
search from
here.

5. **In the Look In area, select all options that apply.**

   The keyword search is a powerful searching tool, and it does take a bit longer to run than other searching methods. When you perform a keyword search, ACT! sifts through every last bit of information in your database, hoping to find a match that fits your specifications.

   To speed up the process, limit the amount of elements to search.

   - **Activities:** Searches in your activities

   - **Opportunities:** Searches the information on the Opportunities tab

   - **Histories:** Searches through the histories that ACT! created

   - **Notes:** Searches in the notes you created

   - **Fields:** Searches through all your contact fields

6. **After making all your choices, click the Find Now button.**

   ACT! responds with a list of records, similar to what's shown in Figure 6-6. The lookup results show the contact's name and company, the field in which ACT! finds the matching data, and the data that it finds. For example, if you search for the word *ACT,* your search includes such diverse words as *interactive* and *contractor* because the letters *act* appear in the middle of these words.

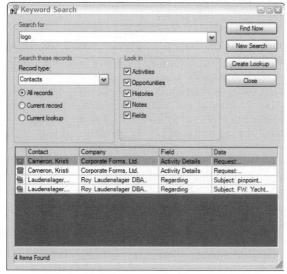

Figure 6-6:
Results of a
keyword
search.

7. **Decide what you want to do with the results.**

   Like the old saying goes, be careful what you search for because you just
   might find it! Okay, the saying doesn't go exactly like that, but after you
   find a number of records using the keyword search, you must decide
   which one(s) to focus on. Here are some of your options:

   - Click the Create Lookup button to see all the records in the
     Contact Detail window.

   - Double-click any part of a single record, and you land on that con-
     tact record. To get back to your search, double-click the Keyword
     Search tab that now appears in the bottom-left corner of the
     Contact Detail window.

   - Select multiple adjacent records by clicking the first record, press-
     ing Shift, and then clicking the last record. Right-click one of your
     selections and choose Lookup Selected Records. You now have a
     lookup that consists of only the contacts that you selected.

   - Select records that aren't adjacent by clicking the first record,
     pressing Ctrl, and then clicking the other records that you want.
     Right-click one of your selections and choose Lookup Selected
     Records. You now have a lookup that consists of only the contacts
     that you selected.

Annual event lookups

In Chapter 13, I show you how to create Annual Event fields. Annual events help automate the processes of tracking important dates, such as birthdays or anniversaries. When you enter a date in an Annual Event field, ACT! automatically tracks the event date from year to year. Because annual events don't appear on your calendar, you must perform an Annual Event lookup to display them. You can use the Annual Event lookup to generate a printed list to display events for the current week, the current month, or a specified date range.

Combining the power of an Annual Event lookup with an ACT! mail merge is a great way to save lots of time. Birthdays and anniversaries are good examples of annual events; like it or not, they happen once per year. The Annual Event lookup tracks them all down regardless of the year. You fellows out there will be happy to know that you need only ask a woman her birthday, regardless of the year. (I show you how to perform a mail merge in Chapter 11.)

Here's all you need to do to create an Annual Event lookup:

1. **From the Contact Detail window, choose Lookup⇨Annual Events.**

   The Annual Events Search dialog box opens, as shown in Figure 6-7.

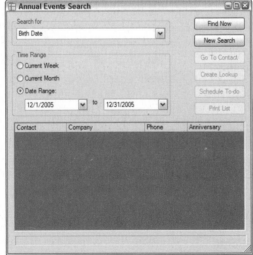

Figure 6-7:
The Annual
Events
Search
dialog box.

2. **Select an annual event from the Search For drop-down list.**

   If you've added more than one annual event field to your database, you can search for more than one of them at a time by selecting each one or by selecting the All option to search through all your annual event fields.

For example, you might want to find everyone who has either a birthday or anniversary in the month of June.

3. Choose a Time Range option in which you want to search.

Your options are the current week or month, or a selected date range.

4. Click the Find Now button.

The results appear in the lower half of the Annual Events Search dialog box. Your results vary, depending on the number of contacts that meet your search criteria. If no contacts meet your search criteria, you receive a message nicely telling you so.

5. Click one of the following option buttons:

- **Go To Contact:** Go to the contact record of the selected contact.

- **Create Lookup:** Create a lookup of all the contacts.

- **Schedule To-Do:** Schedule an activity for the selected contacts. Unfortunately, you can schedule only one activity at a time.

- **Print List:** Print a list of the contacts.

Searching by contact activity

I've often estimated that at least 20 percent of the average database consists of long-lost contact information. You can either ignore these forlorn contacts, or you might realize that there's gold in them thar hills! What if you could find all the contacts that you haven't contacted in, say, the last two years? Chances are that many of those contacts will be glad to hear from you. Maybe they lost your contact information or chose a company other than yours that they weren't happy with. Suddenly those "lost" contacts have become a virtual treasure trove.

You can create a lookup of contacts based on the last time that you made any changes to their record or contacted them through a meeting, call, or to-do. You can look for the contacts that either have or have not been changed within a specified date range. You can also narrow the search according to activity or history type.

To create a lookup by contact activity, follow these steps:

1. Choose Lookup⇨Contact Activity.

The Contact Activity dialog box opens, as shown in Figure 6-8.

Figure 6-8:
The Contact
Activity
dialog box.

2. **Select either Not Changed or Changed in the Look for Contacts That Have area.**

   The neat thing about using the Contact Activity lookup is that you can look for "touched" or "untouched" contacts. In other words, you can search for all the contacts that you contacted in a certain time frame or for all the contacts that you didn't contact in a certain time frame.

3. **Select a date.**

   The date tells ACT! to look for records that have been changed — or not changed — since that date.

4. **Select one or more options in the Search In area to narrow your search.**

   You can search in the following areas of ACT!:

   • Contact fields

   • Notes

   • Opportunities

   • Histories

   • Activities

   If you decide to search through your History and/or Activities tabs, you can even indicate which specific types of histories or activities you want to include in your search.

Many users make the mistake of using only a portion of ACT! — and then find out later that they can't take advantage of some of its coolest features. In order for this search to work, you have to input information in the appropriate spots. For example, you can't look for modified Opportunities if you never created them!

5. Click OK.

ACT! searches for the selected field or activity that was/was not modified within the specified date range. The Contact List appears and displays your selection.

ACT! searches through all your contact fields, notes, histories, and
opportunities, so it might take a moment or two to create your search
results. Relax and practice a few deep-breathing exercises while you
wait.

In Chapter 4, I mention some of the system fields; these are the fields that
ACT! fills in for you automatically. These fields are easily identifiable because
they are grayed out. Although you can't change the information in these
fields, you are free to create lookups on them. For example, every time you
change any of the information for a contact, ACT! automatically updates the
Edit Date field. Feel free to give any of the system fields a right-click and
search on them. For example, if you're looking for all the contacts that have
been created since before or after a given date, give the Create Date field a
right-click!

Creating Advanced Queries

You might want to consider the final two lookup options to be "powerful" and
not "advanced"; many of you might associate *advanced* with *difficult,* and that
is certainly not the case here.

If you need to base your lookup on multiple criteria, you can perform a basic
lookup and then use the Narrow or Add To Lookup options (refer to Figure
6-2) in the Lookup Contacts dialog box to create a more specific search. This
option works fine if you're willing to create several lookups until you reach
the desired results. A better alternative is to use a query to create a lookup. A
query searches all the contacts in your database based on the multiple criteria that you specify and then creates a lookup of contacts that match those
criteria.

Looking up by example

The Lookup by Example function allows you to create an exact profile for the
contacts you're hoping to find. For example, you might look for all customers
in the state of Arizona who expressed interest in a specific product. When
you create a Lookup by Example, ACT! responds by presenting you with a
blank contact record and lets you specify the fields and values that define the
query.

This is what you do:

1. **Choose Lookup⇨By Example.**

    The Lookup By Example window opens. The Lookup By Example window, as shown in Figure 6-9, looks just like any other contact record with one major difference — all the fields are blank.

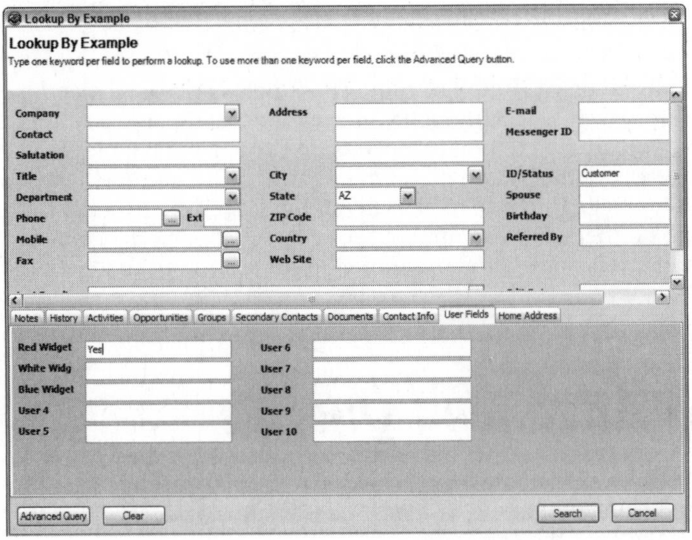

Figure 6-9:
The Lookup
By Example
window is
similar to a
contact
record, but
it's blank.

2. **Click in the field that you want to query.**

    You can create a query on virtually any field in your database. Don't forget to check out some of those neat fields that might be located on your various layout tabs. For example, the Contact Info tab contains the Record Manager and Create Date fields, which are common things to query.

3. **Fill in any criteria on which you want to search.**

    Fill in as many criteria as you need. The whole purpose of doing a Lookup by Example is that you're looking for contacts that fit more than one criterion. If you're looking for all customers who are located in Arizona, type **customer** in the ID/Status field and **AZ** in the State field.

4. **Click the Search button when you are ready to put ACT! to work digging through all your contact records.**

The Advanced Query

After you use your database for a while and it slowly but surely fills up with more and more contacts, you might feel the need to add a little more power to your lookups. You also might find yourself constantly creating the same lookup and wish to save it to save yourself a little time later on. In fact, you might even start using the term *query*, which is computer-speak for *fancy lookup*. Fortunately for you, although an Advanced Query packs a lot of power, it's still a piece of cake to run. Just follow these steps:

1. **Choose Lookup⇨Advanced⇨Advanced Query.**

   The Advanced Query window opens up, as shown in Figure 6-10.

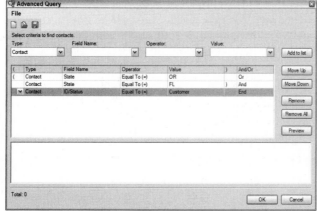

Figure 6-10:
The
Advanced
Query
window.

2. **Select Contact or Opportunity from the Type drop-down list.**

3. **Select one of the available contact or opportunity fields from the Field Name drop-down list.**

   To make life easy for you, you find all your fields listed in the Field Name drop-down list.

4. **Select one of the operators in the Operator field.**

   Knock yourself out! Indicate whether you're looking for a specific word, a field that contains a part of a word, or even a range of figures or dates.

5. **In the Value field, select one of the available items that corresponds to the selected Field Name item.**

   If the Field has a drop-down list, you'll be happy to discover that it is also available in the Advanced Query window.

6. **Click the Add to List button.**

   The query criteria appear in the columns in the middle part of the Advanced Query window.

7. **To select more than one criterion, repeat Steps 2–6.**

8. **Optionally, click in the And/Or column for the item and select an option if necessary.**

   As you build the query, you might want to make use of the And/Or column to help you group your criteria to indicate the relationship between each set of criteria. In Figure 6-10, notice that the two state criteria are bracketed together and joined by the word *or,* indicating that you're looking for contacts from either Florida or Oregon.

9. **Optionally, use the parenthesis column if necessary.**

   The example in Figure 6-10 groups the two state criteria together with parentheses so that these queries are carried out together. This is a particularly important step if your query contains both "and" and "or" criteria.

10. **Click Preview.**

    For those of you in need of instant gratification, you can see a list of all the contacts that match your specification. And, if you goofed and no contacts show up, you can quickly remove a few of your criteria by clicking the Remove button, and try again before anyone notices.

11. **Choose File⇨Save As if you'd like to use your query later.**

    The next time you want to run the same Advanced Query, you'll be able to return to the File menu, choose Open, and open your saved query.

12. **When you finish selecting criteria, click OK.**

13. **At the Run Query Options message, select the Replace Lookup option and click OK.**

    The results of the query display in the Contact List or Opportunities List.

Although the process of saving and reusing an Advanced Query is relatively easy, you can combine this process with the Menu Customization techniques outlined in Chapter 3 to really save yourself oodles of time. Yes, Virginia, you can most definitely add saved Queries to the Lookup menu so that you can find all those Customers in Oregon and Florida who love red widgets!

Chapter 7

Stamping Out the Sticky Note

. . . .

. . . .

ook around your desk. If you have more than one sticky note attached to it, you need to use ACT!. Look at your computer monitor; if it's decorated with sticky notes, you need to use ACT!. Does a wall of sticky notes obscure your file folders? Do you panic when you can't find your pad of sticky notes? Do you have small sticky notes clinging to larger sticky notes? You need to use ACT!!

In this chapter, I show you how to make a note in ACT!. I also tell you all about the notes or *histories* that ACT! creates for you automatically, and then I give you a short course in reviewing your notes.

Getting to Know ACT! Notes

What if one of your best clients calls requesting a price quote? You jot down some information on a piece of paper, only to have the paper disappear in the mountain of clutter that you call your desk.

Or imagine that one of your more high-maintenance customers calls you on March 1 in immediate need of an imported Italian widget. You check with your distributors and guarantee him one by March 15. On March 10, he calls you, totally irate that he hasn't yet received his widget.

Sound familiar? The ACT! note is one of the easiest features to master but one that too many users overlook. A simple note in ACT! provides you with several benefits:

  ✔ Your entire office can operate on the same page by having access to the same client data.

  ✔ You have a record, down to the date and time, of all communications that you have with each of your contacts.

  ✔ You won't forget what you said to your customer.

  ✔ You won't forget what your customer said to you.

  ✔ You'll be able to have pertinent information at your fingertips without having to strip search your office looking for a lost sticky note.

Adding a note

Considering the importance of notes to the overall scheme of your business, they are amazingly easy to add. Here's all you have to do to add a note to a contact record:

1. **Make sure that you're viewing the contact for which you're creating a note.**

   If you need help here, see Chapter 6 to help you look up the contact and land in the Contact view.

2. **On the Notes tab (middle of the screen), click the Insert Note icon.**

   The Insert Note window appears, date- and time-stamped with the current date and time. Take a look at Figure 7-1.

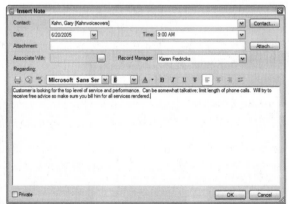

Figure 7-1:
Create a
note in ACT!
here.

3. **Start typing your note in the Regarding area.**

   Your note can be as long or short as you want. You can use the formatting options exactly as you do in any word processor to **_emphasize_** any portion of your note.

4. Click OK to record your note.

That was almost too easy for you; now you can move on to a few tricks that I have up my sleeve.

Working with notes

After you create a note (see the preceding section), you might need to change it. To edit a note, just double-click it to get back to the Insert Note window. After you open it, here are a few things you can change:

- ✔ **Change the note information.** Start typing in the Regarding area exactly as you do with any word processor.

- ✔ **Change the date on a note.** No matter how much you depend on your computer, sometimes you still rely on good old-fashioned paper. Maybe you jotted down a note after you turned off your computer for the day or made notes — both mental and on paper — at a trade show. When you start to input those notes into ACT!, they all have the current date rather than the date when you actually created them. To change the date on a note, simply click the date and choose a new date from the drop-down menu that appears.

   Not all notes are created equal; some of your notes might be more important than others. As your list of notes becomes longer, various key notes can get lost in the shuffle. A real low-tech solution is to postdate the note by giving it a date several years into the future so that your note always appears at the top of the Notes tab.

- ✔ **Attach files to a contact record.** In Chapter 5, I talk about adding files to the Documents tab so that you can view and edit them right from the Contact Detail window. In addition, you can attach a file to a note in a contact record. To attach a file to a note, follow these steps:

   a. Click the Insert Note icon on the Notes tab.

   b. Click the Attach button in the Insert Note window.

   c. Navigate to the file that you want to attach and then click Open.

   d. Click OK to record the note.

   To view the attached file, simply open the note and click the attached file.

- ✔ **Spell-check a note.** If you're like me, you type notes while doing a hundred other things and end up with a lot of typos. Don't fret; just run a spell check by clicking the Spell Check icon in the Insert Note window. ACT! opens the spell checker and locates any misspellings. Unfortunately, you can check the spelling for only one note at a time.

> ✔ **Add Associate With info.** If the note you're adding is specific to a group or company, a click of this button allows you to attach your note to that group or company. Later, when viewing the group or company, you can filter your notes to include just the ones that are associated with that group or company. You might want to head over to Chapter 20 to glean insight into Groups and Chapter 21 to comprehend Companies.

Discovering ACT! Histories

If you insist on doing things the hard way, feel free to skip this section. If you love the thought of having someone else doing your work for you, read on!

Maybe you've noticed that the History tab is called, well, the History tab. In the earlier sections of this chapter, I show you how to add and modify notes. ACT!'s history entries are items that magically appear on the History tab after you

> ✔ Delete a contact (Chapter 4).
>
> ✔ Complete a scheduled meeting, call, or to-do item (Chapter 8).
>
> ✔ Write a letter, fax, or mail merge (Chapter 11).
>
> ✔ Change information in a field designated to create history (Chapter 13).

When you clear an activity, a history of the activity is recorded in the contact record of the person with whom you scheduled the activity. You can also edit or add activity details to the history, such as adding information about the decisions made during the meeting. View these histories again later or create reports based on activities with your contacts.

Creating field histories

ACT! provides you with a very powerful tool when you combine the use of drop-down lists with the ability to create a history based on the changed information in the field. By default, ACT! automatically creates a history when you change the information in either the ID/Status or Last Results field. When you enter information into either of these fields, it's automatically saved on the contact's History tab.

Suppose that you create a ten-step sales process to coincide with the average progression of one of your prospects into a customer. You can change the Last Results field's drop-down list to reflect those ten stages. As you progress through the sales cycle and change the content of the Last Results field, ACT! automatically creates a history indicating when the change took place. Figure 7-2 shows both the content of the Last Results field and the automatic histories that are created as the contact progresses through the sales stages.

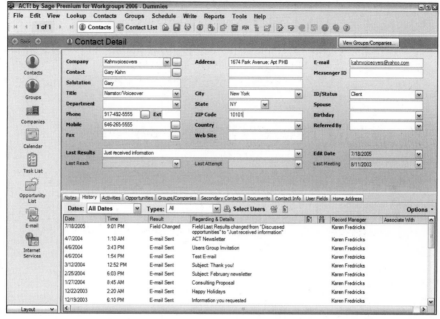

Figure 7-2:
Change the
sales step in
the Last
Results
field.

By relying on the field's drop-down list to create new content information, you ensure that your information remains consistent. You can then create reports on the various sales stages by creating a lookup based on the notes and histories.

In Chapter 6, I show you everything you need to know about creating lookups — and then some! Chapter 9 explains the various ACT! reports and shows you how to filter them by date range.

Clearing activity histories

In Chapter 8, I explain how to use ACT! to plan your busy schedule. After you hold or attend a meeting, place a call, or complete something on your to-do list, clearing the activity is important. Figure 7-3 shows you the Clear Activity dialog box that opens each time you clear an activity.

Select the Add Details to History check box, and ACT! automatically inserts your notes as well as the history of the event on the History tab. ACT! provides you with the same option when you get in touch with a contact through a letter, an e-mail, or a fax. Figure 7-4 shows the Create History dialog box that appears after you create a letter in ACT!. Of course, you can always choose not to include a history, but you'll probably find recording one more useful. You can even add more details in the Regarding area.

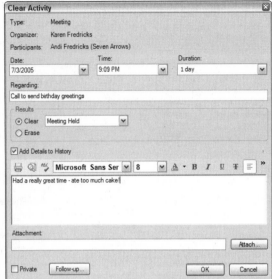

Figure 7-3:
Clear an
activity
here.

Figure 7-4:
Attach a
history to a
letter.

Manually recording a history

Situations arise when recording a history of an event just isn't practical. You can create a history record for a contact without scheduling and clearing an activity for that person. You can even add a history for someone who isn't yet in your database. For example, you might have called a potential new client from your car and found juggling the steering wheel, your phone, and your lunch while typing on your laptop a bit too daunting. However, when you return to the office, you still need to record the calls that you made and the tasks that you completed.

You can also record one history for an entire group of people. For example, you might have attended a meeting at your local Chamber of Commerce and want to record a few details about the meeting for each of the attendees. Regardless of why you need to do it, here's how you create a history after the fact:

1. **Find the contact for whom you want to record a history.**

   If you're creating a history for an entire group of people, create a lookup of the contacts for whom you want to add a note.

2. **Choose Contacts⇨Record History.**

   The Record History window opens, as shown in Figure 7-5.

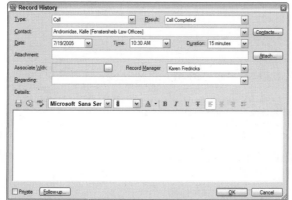

Figure 7-5:
Record a
history here.

3. **Select an activity type from the Type list.**

   If you need more activity types, don't worry. Chapter 16 shows you how to increase your selection of activity types.

4. **Select a Result option.**

5. **Click the Contacts button if you're creating a history for your current lookup.**

   The Select Contacts window, as shown in Figure 7-6, opens.

   This step isn't necessary if you're creating a history for just one contact because that contact's name would already appear in the Contact text box of the Record History window. However, if you're trying to record a history for the multiple contacts that are included in the lookup that you created in Step 1, you have to do a little extra footwork.

   a. *Choose Current Lookup from the Select From drop-down list.*

   b. *Click the double right-pointing arrows to move all the contacts in your current lookup to the Selected Contacts area.*

   c. *Click OK to return to the Record History window.*

Figure 7-6:
Select the
contacts for
a manual
history.

6. **Enter date, time, and duration information.**

7. **Enter activity information in the Regarding field or select a description from the drop-down list.**

8. **Add additional information in the Details area.**

   The information that you enter here is added to the Regarding field on the History tab.

9. **Click OK to record the history.**

   Your note is recorded in the contact's record. If you created a history for an entire group of contacts, the note appears in the contact record of each individual in the group.

If you click the Follow-up button instead of OK, you can schedule a new, follow-up activity in the same way that you scheduled your original activity. Talk about one-stop shopping! The result of a call might be that you scheduled a follow-up meeting for the next week. By scheduling a follow-up activity, you have the results of your original meeting as well as a reminder of the meeting scheduled in the future. You can also schedule follow-up activities for the next step in your sales process.

Working with Your Notes and Histories

The Notes and History tabs are very similar; consequently, you can use them in similar ways. They are so similar, in fact, that in previous versions of ACT!, they were actually combined into one single tab. Here are a few things that you can do to edit your notes and histories:

✔ **Delete a note or history.** To delete a note or history, you must first select it and then press Delete. You can also right-click the selected note and choose Delete Selected from the contextual menu. Either way, ACT! presents you with a warning before you remove the note permanently.

✔ **Delete several notes and/or histories.** Eventually, you want to delete certain notes or even histories. To delete several notes in one fell swoop, just select the notes that you want to delete and then press Delete:

- If you're selecting several contiguous notes, click the first note and then press Shift while clicking the last note that you want to delete.

- If the entries aren't contiguous, press Ctrl while clicking each note individually.

Now that you know how easy deleting a history is, you might want to prevent other users of your database from deleting them. If you're the database administrator, choose Tools⇨Preferences. Then, on the General tab, remove the check mark next to the Allow History Editing option.

✔ **Copy a note.** When you find duplicate contacts in your database, you probably want to delete them — but not any notes attached to them. Or, maybe you want a note from one contact record also attached to another record. Luckily, ACT! gives you the ability to copy notes from one contact to another contact with a simple copy-and-paste procedure:

a. *Highlight the notes or histories that you want to copy and then press Ctrl+C.*

b. *Find the contact where you want to insert the copied notes, then on the Notes or History tab, press Ctrl+V.*

If you're feeling somewhat artistic, in need of a change, or just plain having trouble with your forty-something eyesight, you might want to either add gridlines around your notes or change the color and/or font style. Or, you might just decide to walk on the wild side and change the whole ball of wax. Take a stroll down preference lane to accomplish this:

1. **Choose Tools⇨Preferences from any ACT! screen.**

   The Preferences dialog box opens.

2. **Click the Colors and Fonts tab.**

3. **Click the Notes tab.**

4. **Click the Font button to select a different font, style, or size.**

5. **Click OK to close the Font window.**

6. **Choose a text color and background color from the Appearance area.**

7. **To have gridlines appear on the Notes tab, select the Show Grid Lines check box.**

The ACT! gridlines are just like the gridlines you see in Excel. If you change your preference to show gridlines, horizontal lines appear between each of your notes and vertical lines between columns.

8. **Repeat Steps 3–7 for the History tab.**

9. **Click OK.**

Your Notes and History tabs are now modified according to the preference settings that you selected.

Chapter 8

Playing the Dating Game

● ●

● ●

*I*n this chapter, I show you how to schedule activities with your contacts, how to view those activities and modify them if necessary, and even how to find out whether you completed a scheduled activity. You also discover the intricacies of navigating through the various ACT! calendars, how to use your Task List to keep you on top of your activities, and the joy of sharing a list of your scheduled activities with others.

Scheduling Your Activities

One of the most useful of ACT!'s features is its ability to tie an activity to a contact. Most basic calendaring programs allow you to view your appointments and tasks on your calendar, but they don't offer a way of cross-referencing an appointment to a contact. For example, if you schedule an appointment with me and forget when that appointment is, you have to flip through your calendar until you see my name. Plus, you can't easily see a list of all appointments that you've ever scheduled with me. However, ACT! offers these helpful features.

In ACT!, every activity is scheduled with a specific contact. If the contact doesn't exist in your database, you must add the person to your database — or schedule the appointment with yourself.

Here's what you do to add an activity to your busy schedule:

1. **Go to the contact with whom you're scheduling an activity.**

   Here's the drill. You create a lookup (I show you how in Chapter 6) to find a prospect's phone number. You call the guy, and afterward, you want to schedule a meeting. At this point, you're already on the contact record of the person with whom you're scheduling an activity.

2. **Schedule a call, meeting, or to-do in one of three ways:**

   • Click the Call, Meeting, or To-Do icon on the toolbar in the Contact Detail window or the Contact List.

   • Choose Call, Meeting, or To-Do from the Schedule menu in just about any of the ACT! views.

   • Double-click the appropriate time slot on any of the ACT! calendars.

Using different methods to schedule different activities is a smart plan of action. For example, I recommend scheduling meetings through the calendars to make sure that you don't have a conflict for a specific time slot. When you're scheduling calls and to-dos, however, which are generally "timeless" activities that don't have to be set for a specific time, you can simply click the corresponding icon on the toolbar.

In any case, all roads lead to the Schedule Activity dialog box, as shown in Figure 8-1.

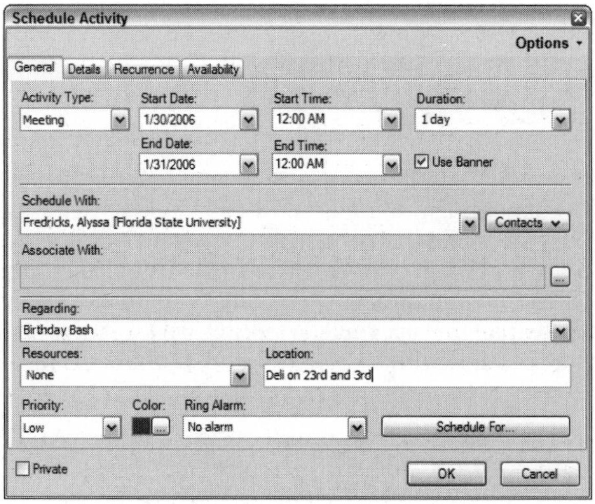

Figure 8-1: Schedule an activity in ACT! here.

3. **On the General tab, fill in the various options.**

If *options* is your name, ACT! is your game! The Schedule Activity dialog box offers a myriad of scheduling options from which to pick, and ACT! has thoughtfully filled in many of these options based on your default scheduling preferences. (Chapter 3 walks you through changing some of these preferences.) You can leave the information in the following fields as is or override the default preferences:

- *Activity Type:* Choose Call, Meeting, To-Do, Personal Activity, or Vacation from the drop-down list.

- *Start Date:* Click the arrow to the right of the field to display the calendar and select the date of the big event.

- *Start Time:* Enter a start time for the event. Choose Timeless for the Start Time if you're scheduling a call or to-do that doesn't need to occur at a specific time.

- *Duration:* Click the arrow to the right of the field to choose the duration for the activity. You can also manually specify a time range; an hour-and-a-half-long meeting can be entered as either **90 m** or **1.5 h**.

The End Date and End Time are automatically set based on the starting date and time you specify. If you change the duration, ACT! automatically adjusts the end date and time.

- *Use Banner:* This option lets you display a banner on the monthly calendar if an activity involves one or more full days.

- *Schedule With:* The name of the current contact automatically appears here. Select a different contact by typing the first few letters of a contact's last name to locate the contact in the list.

If you click the Schedule With drop-down list, you'll notice that the names appear alphabetically by last name. If you're having trouble remembering someone's last name, simply click the Company column heading to arrange those contacts alphabetically by company. You can then type the first few letters of a company name in the Schedule With box.

- *Contacts:* Click the Contacts button and then choose Select Contacts to select more than one contact, New Contact to add a new contact, or My Record to schedule a personal appointment.

- *Regarding:* You'll want to give a brief description of the activity because it is later reflected on the contact's History tab. Type it here or choose an item from the drop-down list.

The Regarding drop-down list reflects the Activity Type that you choose, so scheduling a Call gives you different options from scheduling a Meeting. Don't like the items in the drop-down? As usual, you'll find the Edit List Values options button. Click it to create your very own customized drop-down list for each one of the activity types.

- *Resources:* If you're using ACT! 2006 Premium for Workgroups, you can place first dibs on shared commodities such as the conference room, LCD projector, or the office stash of candy bars.

- *Location:* It never hurts to let everyone know, including yourself, where the big event is going to take place.

- *Priority:* Choose High, Medium-High, Medium, Medium-Low, or Low.

Don't see the Medium-High and Medium-Low options? Chapter 16 shows you how to customize your Priorities list.

- *Color:* Click the arrow to the right of the field to display a color palette, and then choose the color that you want to assign to the activity. Feel free to design your own system of color-coding your calendar.

- *Ring Alarm:* Enabling this sets an alarm to remind you of a scheduled activity at a specified interval before the event.

- *Schedule For/By:* Click this button to assign a task to one of your co-workers (as if ACT! hasn't made life easy enough for you already!).

4. **(Optional) Click the Options button.**

   If you wish, click the Options button select one of these options:

   - **Confirm the activity** with the contact(s) involved by sending an e-mail to the participant(s). ACT! automatically opens up an email message filled in with the critical detail in the body of the e-mail like the one shown in Figure 8-2 and includes an attachment in ACT! format. When the e-mail recipient receives the e-mail, he can double-click the attachment (the instructions for this are also included in the body of the e-mail) and have the activity automatically placed in his ACT! calendar.

   - **Create a separate activity for each participant** if you're scheduling your activity with more than one contact.

5. **On the Details tab, add additional details and print the details (if you want).**

   These are two relatively important tasks:

   - *Details:* Add additional information regarding an activity. For example, you might want to add special instructions about the items that you need to bring to a meeting.

   - *Print:* This is where you can print the activity details.

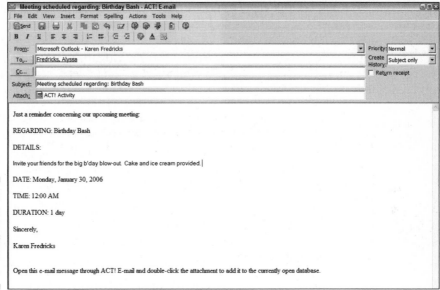

Figure 8-2:
Send an
e-mail
reminder of
a scheduled
activity.

6. **On the Recurrence tab, designate the activity as recurring if that's the case; otherwise, go to Step 7.**

   If the activity that you're scheduling repeats on a regular basis, you can designate it as a *recurring* activity rather than setting up several separate activities. For example, if you're taking a class that meets once a week for the next 12 weeks, you can designate the class as a meeting with a weekly recurrence. Be sure to specify the date on which the activity stops recurring.

   Here are the recurring option settings:

   • *Daily:* Select to schedule an activity that occurs daily and the date on which the activity stops.

   • *Weekly:* Select to schedule an activity that occurs weekly, on which day or days of the week the activity is scheduled, and the date on which the activity stops.

   • *Monthly:* Select to schedule an activity that occurs monthly by indicating the week in the month, the day of the week, or the specific day of the month on which the activity will be occurring and the date on which the activity stops.

   • *Yearly:* Select to schedule an activity that occurs every year, and the date on which the activity stops.

   The Annual Event field can eliminate the need to set reminders for activities, such as birthdays, anniversaries, and renewal dates. Find out how to set up an Annual Event field in Chapter 13.

7. **Click OK.**

   You now have a real, live scheduled activity!

After you create activities, ACT! is a worse nag than your mother! You can see your activities — and ACT! reminds you to complete them — in a number of ways:

- ✔ **Alarm:** If you asked ACT! to ring the alarm when scheduling an activity, the ACT! Alarms window appears at the specified time before the activity is due. It also appears each time that you open ACT!.

- ✔ **Per contact:** The Activities tab for a selected contact enables you to see what specific activities you scheduled with that particular contact.

- ✔ **All contacts:** The Task List shows a listing of everything you scheduled for all your contacts during a specified time period.

- ✔ **Calendar:** All ACT! calendars including the monthly, weekly, and daily views show a listing of the current day's activities.

Later in this chapter, in the section "Exploring Activities," I show you how to view, edit, clear, and share your scheduled activities.

Regardless of your method of viewing your activities, remember this tip: *When frustrated, check your filters.* If you're just not seeing everything that you know is supposed to be showing in your calendar, check your filters! Not seeing anything scheduled for the future? Maybe your date range is set to show the activities for today only. Seeing too much? Perhaps your filters are set to show *everyone's* Task List or calendar. Not seeing *any* of your activities at all? Perhaps your filters are set to include everything *except* your own activities! Flip back to Chapter 5 if you want a refresher course in those frustrating filters!

Working with the ACT! Calendar

The various ACT! calendars are great for viewing scheduled tasks. Here are a couple of ways to get to your calendars:

- ✔ Choose View and specify the type of calendar that you want to view.
- ✔ Click the calendar icon on the Nav bar.

You can view your calendar in any one of four different ways, depending on which way you feel the most comfortable:

✓ **Daily calendar:** Shows you the time-specific activities of the selected day as well as a listing of the day's tasks (see Figure 8-3). The day is divided into half-hour intervals.

Not happy with half-hour intervals? No problem; you can change that default setting in ACT!'s preference settings. Not sure how to do that? Take a peek at Chapter 3 to tweak your preferences.

✓ **Work Week calendar:** Shows you the time-specific activities of the selected week as well as a listing of the day's tasks. Each day is represented by a single column and divided into half-hour intervals.

✓ **Weekly calendar:** Shows the entire week including Saturday and Sunday. (See Figure 8-4.)

✓ **Monthly calendar:** Shows you the time-specific activities of the selected month as well as a listing of the day's tasks (see Figure 8-5).

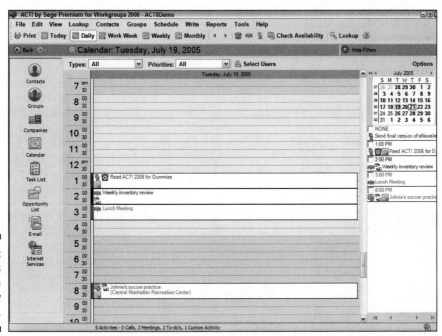

Figure 8-3:
Tame tasks with the daily calendar.

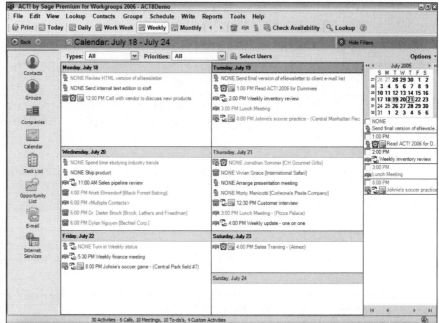

Figure 8-4:
Organize with a weekly calendar.

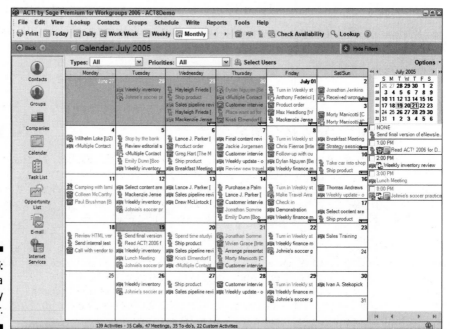

Figure 8-5:
Plan with a monthly calendar.

The mini-calendar

A mini-calendar appears to the right of any of the ACT! calendars. The mini-calendars work a little differently from the daily, weekly, and monthly calendars in that they are used to change a date and not to just schedule an appointment. If you'd like, you can access a three months' supply of mini-calendars by pressing F4 from any of the ACT! views (see Figure 8-6). Right-click the day that you want to check, and a small window appears, displaying all activities scheduled for that day.

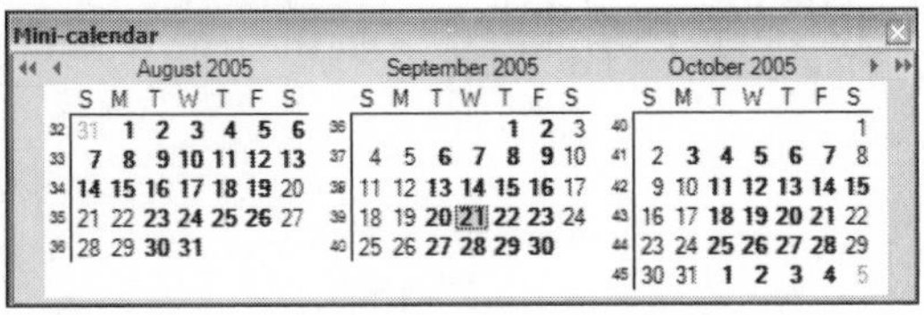

Figure 8-6:
The mini-
calendar.

After you access any of the ACT! calendars, you can navigate to a different date in one of the following ways:

- ✔ View today's activities by pressing Ctrl+Home.
- ✔ Switch to a different day by clicking any day on the mini-calendar.
- ✔ Get a daily synopsis by right-clicking any day on the mini-calendar.
- ✔ Go to a different year by clicking the double arrows.
- ✔ Go to a different month by clicking the single arrows.

The Recap List

If you take a peek at any of the calendars, you notice a mini-calendar up at the top-right corner. As I mention earlier, this calendar provides you with a quick way to view a different calendar date by clicking it. A miniature to-do list — the *Recap List* — appears right below the calendar. The Recap List lists all your scheduled activities on a specific day.

You can view the Recap List of only one user at a time, but you can have access to multiple users' Recap Lists. When you select multiple users, buttons with each user's name appear in the Recap List. Click the user's name to open or close his Recap List. If a selected user has no scheduled activities for the selected date, her name doesn't display in the Recap List. To view another user's Recap List, follow these steps:

1. **Click the Calendars icon on the Nav bar.**
2. **Click the Select Users button.**

The Select Users dialog box appears.

3. Select the users whose Recap Lists you want to view and then click OK.

When you select multiple users, their tasks all appear on both the calendar and the Recap List. This can get confusing — not to mention make you feel that you have too much to do if you forget you're viewing everyone else's activities. This is where a bit of color-coding can come into play. Gary's activities might all be in blue, and Alyssa's might be in magenta. That way, you'll be sure to know which activities belong to whom.

4. From the calendar, select the date for the Recap List you want to view.

The user's tasks display in the Recap List (see Figure 8-7). If you selected multiple users, you can click the button with the user's name to view that user's tasks.

Figure 8-7:
The Recap
List.

Using the Task List

Like the Honey-Do list hanging from your husband's workbench, the ACT! Task List gives you a listing of all the activities for all your contacts.

The Task List is readily accessible by clicking the Task List icon on ACT!'s Nav bar. Figure 8-8 shows a sample Task List.

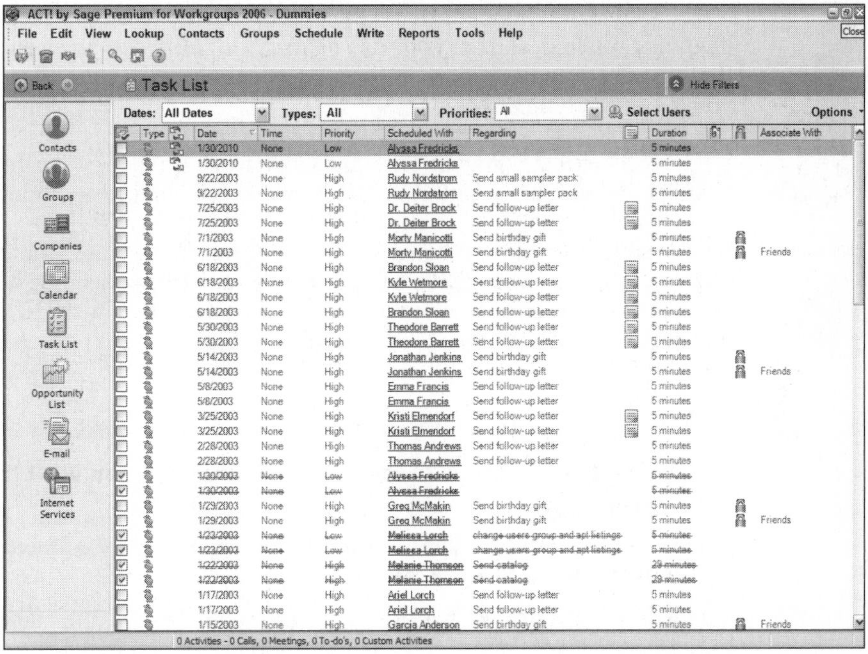

Figure 8-8:
The ACT!
Task List.

You can filter the Task List by using different criteria (as shown in Figure 8-8):

✔ The date range of the activities

✔ The type of activity

✔ The priority of the activity

✔ The users whose activities you want to view

You can also include a few more advanced activity options by clicking the Options button:

✔ Private

✔ Timeless

✔ Cleared

✔ Outlook

Creating a lookup from the Task List

Here's the scenario. You wake up bright-eyed and bushy-tailed, ready to face another new day. You get to the office, view your Task List, and stop dead in your tracks: The length of your Task List is so long that you don't even know where to begin. Consider creating a lookup directly from the Task List. By spending the first hour of your day sending out all those faxes and brochures that you promised — and then the next hour returning your phone calls — you get everything done.

When you break down your tasks into manageable pieces — instead of having a breakdown yourself — the Task List becomes less intimidating.

Having said all that, I feel compelled to add that Rome wasn't built in a day, and you might not be able to complete *all* your tasks in a single day, either. ACT! has a preference that enables you to roll over your tasks to the next day if necessary. Check out Chapter 3 for a quick refresher on changing ACT! preferences.

1. **To open your Task List, click the Task List icon on ACT!'s Nav bar.**

2. **Select the date range of the activities for which you want to create a lookup.**

3. **Select the activity types in the Types area to indicate the activities that you want to work with.**

   As you select these options, hopefully, your Task List became a bit shorter. If you feel so inclined, you can filter your Task List even further by selecting the priority types you'd like to include and making sure that your tasks are the only ones visible in the Task List.

4. **Right-click the Task List and select Create Lookup.**

   ACT! creates a lookup of the selected activities. You can now scroll through your contacts and work on all similar tasks at the same time.

Printing the Task List

As great as ACT! is, it can be totally useless if you don't have access to a computer or hand-held device. Or maybe you work with a technically challenged co-worker (your boss?) who prefers to have a copy of his or her Task List printed on a daily basis. No need to fret; ACT! can easily perform this task for you:

1. **Click the Task List icon on the Nav bar.**

2. **Choose File⇨Quick Print Current Window.**

   The Quick Report dialog box opens.

3. **Click OK to print the Task List.**

Exploring Activities

In the first section of this chapter, "Scheduling Your Activities," I show you how to do exactly that. After scheduling an activity, you'll probably want to take a look at it. Or edit it. Or clear it. Or maybe even share it with others. So in this section, I show you how to do all these things.

Viewing the Activities tab

If you click the Activities tab at the bottom of the Contact Detail window, ACT! displays all the activities scheduled with the current contact. This is a great way to have a list of all the activities that you've scheduled with a contact.

You can see the Activities tab in Figure 8-9. You can filter your activities so that only certain activities show on the Activities tab. Your choices include

- ✔ Dates to show
- ✔ Types to show
- ✔ Priorities to show
- ✔ Users
- ✔ Private activities
- ✔ Timeless activities
- ✔ Cleared activities
- ✔ Outlook activities

Can't find the filter options for Private, Timeless, Cleared, and Outlook activities? Click the Options button, and you'll find them.

Figure 8-9:
The
Activities
tab.

	Type	Date	Time	Priority	Scheduled With	Regarding				Associate With	
☐	☎	8/13/2005	None	High	Chris Huffman	Product order				CH Gourmet Gifts	
☐		8/10/2005	None	Low	Chris Huffman	Remember press kits for trade show				CH Gourmet Gifts	
☐		8/9/2005	3:00 PM	Low	<Multiple>	Team Lunch	📧			CH Gourmet Gifts	
☐		8/8/2005	None	High	Chris Huffman	Product order				CH Gourmet Gifts	
☐		8/7/2005	None	Low	Chris Huffman	Vacation				CH Gourmet Gifts	
☐		8/7/2005	3:00 PM	Low	<Multiple>	Lunch Meeting				CH Gourmet...	
☐		8/1/2005	None	High	Chris Huffman	Product order				CH Gourmet Gifts	
☐		7/27/2005	None	High	Chris Huffman	Ship product				CH Gourmet Gifts	
☐		7/23/2005	4:00 PM	High	<Multiple>	Sales Training	📧			CH Gourmet Gifts	
☐		7/21/2005	3:00 PM	Low	<Multiple>	Lunch Meeting				CH Gourmet Gifts	
☐		7/21/2005	None	Medium	Chris Huffman	Arrange presentation meeting				CH Gourmet Gifts	

Notes | History | Activities | Opportunities | Groups/Companies | Secondary Contacts | Documents | Contact Info | User Fields | Home Address

Dates: All Dates | Types: All | Priorities: All | Select Users | Options

All Dates: 64 Activities - 11 Calls, 22 Meetings, 22 To-do's, 9 Custom Activities

After you set your filters, you can also determine the columns that you want to appear on the Activities tab. These are the possibilities:

✔ The type, date, time, and duration of the activity

✔ The priority that you set for the activity

✔ The regarding information and any details that you entered for the activity

✔ The company and contact name

✔ The name of the group or company that the activity might be associated with

✔ The contact's phone number, extension, and e-mail address

✔ Additional activity details

✔ What ACT! user the activity was scheduled for and the ACT! user who scheduled the activity

✔ Any attachments associated with the big event

After you determine the columns that you want to view onscreen, you can easily print a down-and-dirty report. In Chapter 5, I give you all the juicy details for rearranging the columns on the Activities tab — or on any other ACT! list for that matter — and turning it into a Quick Print report.

Editing your activities

Like all the best-laid plans of mice and men, your activities will change, and you need a way to make note of these changes in ACT!. Changing an activity is all in the click — or in this case, the *double-click* — of the mouse. If you can see an activity, you can edit it. That means you can edit your activities from the Activities tab, the Task List, or from any of the ACT! calendars. The only activities that you can't change are those that you've already cleared.

Resist the urge to simply change the date for rescheduled activities. Although this is easy enough to do, you might end up losing some key information. Say, for instance, that a particularly high-maintenance customer stands you up four times — and then complains to your boss about your lack of service. If you had simply edited the original activity, you wouldn't be able to document the dates of all four activities. You might like to think of this as CYA (um, *cover your ACT!*) technology!

Clearing activities

After you complete a task, clearing the task is very important because then ACT!

✔ Stops reminding you about the activity

✔ Allows you to add some additional details about the activity

✔ Lets you schedule a follow-up activity if necessary

✔ Automatically updates the Last Reach, Last Meeting, or Last Attempt fields with the current date

✔ Creates an entry on the History tab of the contact with whom you had scheduled the activity

Clearing an alarm is not the same as clearing an activity. You might clear an alarm when you first open ACT! or when the activity is scheduled to occur, and not actually clear the activity. Eventually, your Task List will grow dangerously long, in which case, you're probably going to start ignoring it all together. Worse, you won't have a history of the activity because theoretically *it never occurred!*

To clear an activity, follow these steps:

1. **Select the activity that you want to clear by doing one of the following:**

   • In any Calendar view, select the check box next to the activity in the Recap List.

   • In the Task List or on the Activities tab, click the check mark column.

   • Right-click the activity and choose Clear Activity.

   Using any method, the Clear Activity dialog box appears (see Figure 8-10). The current date and time appear automatically. The Regarding information that you had originally entered for the activity appears as well. This information later appears in the Regarding column of the history that is automatically created when you clear an activity.

   The Clear Activity dialog box enables you to clear just one activity at a time. You can clear multiple activities from the Activities tab or the Task List:

   a. *Hold down the Ctrl key while selecting additional activities to clear.*

   b. *Right-click the selected activities and then choose Clear Multiple Activities from the shortcut menu.*

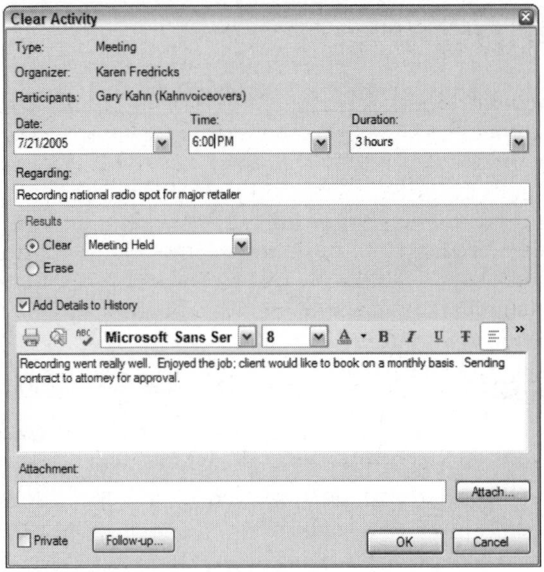

Figure 8-10:
Clearing an
activity.

2. **Select a Result option.**

    The result determines the type of note that's added to the History tab as well as the system field that is affected. For example, if you indicate that a call was completed, two things happen:

    • A history is added to the History tab with Call Completed showing in the Type column.

    • The Last Reach field is changed to include today's date.

    The results vary according to the type of activity that you scheduled. If you schedule a meeting, the results are either Meeting Held or Meeting Not Held. If you schedule a call, you see different result options including Call Attempted, Call Completed, and Call Left Message.

3. **Select the Add Details to History check box if you want to edit or add activity details.**

    Changes that you make to the Add Details area appear in the Regarding field on the History tab for the contact.

4. **Click the Follow Up Activity button to schedule a follow-up activity (if you want).**

    This is a very cool concept. When you clear an activity, ACT! gives you the option of scheduling a follow-up activity. Schedule a follow-up exactly like you schedule an original activity.

5. **Schedule the follow-up activity in the Schedule Activity dialog box and then click OK to return to the Clear Activity dialog box.**

6. **Click OK again, and you're done.**

Creating an Activity Series

Quite simply, an *activity series* is a series of steps that you might want to follow to achieve a specific goal. For example, you might have a six-step plan of action for every prospect that heads your way, or seven things you need to do during each of your customer-related projects. Every time you meet a new prospect, you might want to lure him into using your services with a specific plan of action: send a brochure, follow it up with a phone call, send out a letter explaining some of the things you discussed in the phone call, and then finally send an e-mail further explaining your business. After the prospect becomes a customer, you might want to routinely send a welcoming letter, send out a proposal, wait for approval, and then wait for the deposit check to slide into your mailbox.

ACT! allows you to group these steps into one list in order for you to auto-mate your process. By using an activity series, you can stick to your game plan. And, hopefully, some of those hot prospects turn into customers because you don't allow any of them to fall through the cracks.

Using the Activity Series Template Creation Wizard

Before you can schedule an activity series, you must create one using the Activity Series Template Creation Wizard. Here's where you develop the series by naming it, setting it as public or private, and adding activities. The wizard also allows you to edit or delete an existing activity series template. Follow these steps to start the wizard:

1. **Choose Schedule⇨Manage⇨Activity Series Templates from any ACT! screen.**

2. **In the Activity Series Template Creation Wizard, select the Create a New Activity Series radio button and then click Next.**

   The wizard walks you through the next three steps.

3. **Fill in the name of your new activity series, indicate whether it's public or private, give it a description (if necessary), and then click Next.**

   The Activity Series Template Creation Wizard opens, as shown in Figure 8-11.

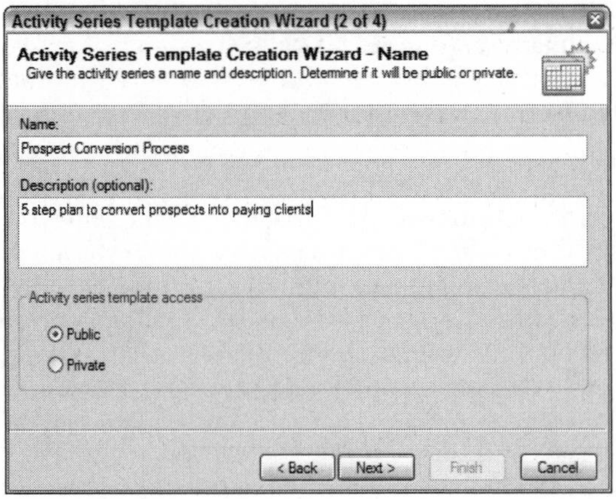

Figure 8-11:
Creating an
activity
series.

4. **Click the Add button to add all the steps you want to include in your activity series.**

   The Add Activity dialog box opens; you can take a peek at it in Figure 8-12.

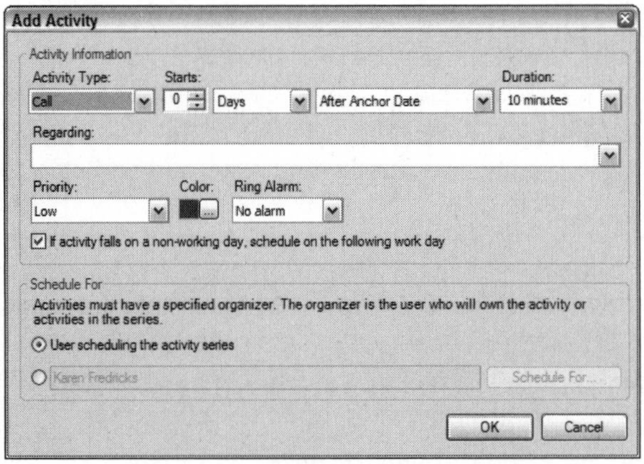

Figure 8-12:
Add a new
activity to
an activity
series.

5. **Fill in the Add Activity dialog box and click OK.**

   Here's where you indicate all the pertinent details for each and every step of your activity series. You have to enter several key pieces of information; don't worry if you make a mistake because you can always go back and edit these steps if you don't get them right the first time.

   • *Activity Type:* Indicate whether you're scheduling a call, meeting, to-do, or a custom activity (skip ahead to Chapter 16 for more info about custom activities).

- *Starts:* Activity series are based on an *anchor date.* You can either schedule an activity that occurs after the anchor date (which is generally the day you begin the series) or activities that must be completed before the anchor date.

- *Regarding, Priority, Color, and Ring Alarm:* These fields are the exact same ones you encounter when scheduling a regular, run-of-the-mill activity.

- *If Activity Falls on a Non-Working Day, Schedule on the Following Work Day:* Select this check box to prevent an activity from being scheduled on a Saturday or Sunday.

- *Schedule For:* If you're like me, you like nothing better than delegating work to another person. Here's where you can assign each Activity Series step to a poor, unsuspecting co-worker!

6. **Repeat Step 5 as often as you need and then click Next.**

7. **Indicate Yes if you want to schedule the series now or No if you want to start it later and click Finish.**

Scheduling an activity series

After you create the template, you can schedule the series with one of your contacts and set the anchor date. All the activities link together so that if one activity changes to another date, you have the option to change only that activity to another date or to reschedule all the remaining activities.

1. **Create a lookup to find the contact or contacts with whom you want to schedule the activity series.**

   I warn you repeatedly that ACT! saves you lots and lots of time. If scheduling an activity series with one person saves you time, just think of what scheduling one with a *bunch* of people does for you!

2. **Choose Schedule⇨Activity Series.**

   The Schedule Activity Series dialog box appears, as shown in Figure 8-13.

3. **Select the activity series template that you want to use, indicate the anchor date, and click OK.**

   If you forgot to create a lookup or if you want to include a few more contacts, you can do it. Select one contact from the With drop-down menu, or select multiple contacts from the Contacts dialog box by clicking the Contacts button and selecting Select Contacts.

   The activities are scheduled and appear on the appropriate spots on the contact's Activities tab, the Task List, and on the calendars. No time is yet associated with any of the activities because activities scheduled as an activity series are automatically timeless.

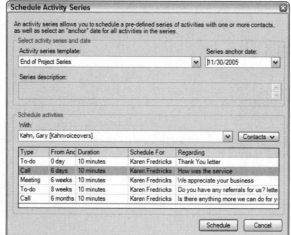

Figure 8-13:
Schedule an
activity
series.

No conflict checking is performed when the activities are scheduled using an activity series. Your tasks are scheduled regardless of whether you are already scheduled to be on vacation or off attending a conference in Kalamazoo.

Before scheduling the series with a large number of contacts, test the series by scheduling it with just one contact. Then, take a gander at that contact's Activities tab to make sure that the activities appear in a logical sequence. If something appears amiss, delete all the scheduled activities from the contact's Activities tab and read on.

Modifying an activity series

Mistakes happen — and you might make one when initially setting up your activity series. Or you might wish to assign another employee to one of the steps in the series. Not to worry; here's all you need to do to modify the series:

1. **Choose Schedule⇨Manage⇨Activity Series Templates.**

2. **Select the Edit an Existing Activity Series radio button in the first screen of the Activity Series Template Creation Wizard and then click Next.**

3. **Select the activity step that you wish to edit and click the Edit button.**

4. **Make the appropriate changes in the Add Activity dialog box and click OK.**

5. **Click OK in the Schedule Activity Series window when you finish modifying all the activities.**

Part III
Sharing Your Information with Others

The 5th Wave   By Rich Tennant

FIRED

YOU

"NIFTY CHART, FRANK, BUT NOT ENTIRELY NECESSARY."

In this part . . .

Entering contacts into ACT! is only half the fun. The other half consists of communicating with the outside world. In this part, you find out how to run and create reports for your internal purposes and also how to reach an audience of one or thousands through the use of snail mail or e-mail. You'll even find a large collection of commercial forms for printing (buried deep inside ACT!).

Chapter 9

Using the Basic ACT! Reports

*A*fter you build your database, the fun part is sitting back and using it. If paper is your game, then ACT! is surely the name — at least of the software that you should be using for any type of reporting. Here in this chapter, I discuss the various ACT! reports that are available. In Chapter 10, I demonstrate how to design your very own reports.

In this chapter, I show you everything you always wanted to know about ACT! reports but were afraid to ask. After reading this chapter, you'll be familiar with the various reports, know how to run them, and also know techniques for sharing those reports with colleagues. You also find out about some of the "non-reports" such as labels, address books and list views that are buried away in some unexpected places.

Knowing the Basic ACT! Reports

ACT! comes with a menu of 40 basic reports right out of the box. In Chapter 10, I show you how to customize existing reports or create new ones. Here I list the basic reports, briefly describing each. Chances are good that at least one of the basic ACT! reports gives you exactly the information that you're looking for.

If you really want to see firsthand what each ACT! report looks like, open the Act8Demo database and print out the first page of each report. Then, stick all the reports in a notebook. (If you want to get really fancy, stick them in sheet protectors first.) That way, if you ever need to run a report, you can go back to your sample printouts for a quick reference before you start running a lot of unnecessary reports.

The first three reports in the ACT! Reports menu are probably among the most useful because they supply you with information for each of your contacts. You can determine which one best suits your needs by deciding whether you want to view a page, a paragraph, or simply one line of information about your contact.

- ✔ **Contact Report:** A one-page report showing all the contact information for each contact, including the notes, history, and activities.

- ✔ **Contact Directory:** Prints the primary address and home address for each contact in paragraph form.

- ✔ **Phone List:** Prints the company name, company phone number, phone extension, and mobile phone number for each contact; the report displays one line of content for each contact.

The next several reports display information that's pertinent to you and your notes and activities:

- ✔ **Activities:** Shows you the scheduled and completed calls, meetings, and to-do's scheduled with each contact during a specified date range. The Task List is sorted by contact so that you can see a listing of all the time that you've spent — or are scheduled to spend — with any given contact.

- ✔ **Notes/History:** Lists the notes and history items for each contact during a specified date range.

- ✔ **History Summary:** Produces a tally of the number of attempted calls, completed calls, meetings held, letters sent, and fields changed for each contact during a specified date range sorted by contact. Figure 9-1 shows you the top part of a History Summary report.

- ✔ **History Summary Classic:** Shows the numerical total of attempted calls, completed calls, meetings held, and letters sent for each contact during a specified date range sorted by contact.

The History Summary report displays only those contacts that you've contacted during a specific date range. Comparatively, the History Summary Classic report displays a list of all your contacts, including contacts that you've contacted as well as those that you have not. If you end up producing a 50-page report, I suggest creating a Contact Activity lookup before running the report. If you need help creating a lookup, turn to Chapter 6.

- ✔ **History Time Spent:** Shows the date, time, duration, and information regarding activities scheduled with each contact during a specified date range. You get a subtotal of the time that you spend with each contact as well as of the time that you're still scheduled to spend with them — if you assign a time duration to your meetings, calls, and to-do's.

History Summary

Chris Huffman, CH Gourmet
13 East 54th St.

New York, NY 10008

Date Range: 6/1/2005 - 6/30/2005
Number of Contacts: 77

Contact			
Ashley Allen, Tiny Town Productions			
	Call Completed	Total:	1
Ernst Anderson, CH Gourmet Gifts			
	Meeting Held	Total:	1
Garcia Anderson, Searchlight Casting			
	Call Attempted	Total:	1
	Meeting Held	Total:	1
Bruce Baker, SimAero			
	Call Completed	Total:	2
	To-do Done	Total:	1
	Call Left Message	Total:	1
Theodore Barrett, Verge Records			
	Call Received	Total:	1
	Field Changed	Total:	1
Albert Barry, Mercury Production Management			
	Call Completed	Total:	1
	To-do Done	Total:	2
Paul Brushman, Brushy's Golfing World			
	Call Completed	Total:	3
	To-do Done	Total:	2
Ethan Campbell, MegaGadgets Catalog Co.			
	Meeting Held	Total:	1
Silvia Carlini, Hospital de la Gente			
	Call Completed	Total:	1
Cecil Carter, CH Gourmet Gifts			
	Meeting Held	Total:	1
Jane Chen, CH Gourmet Gifts			
	Meeting Held	Total:	1
Bill Craig, KKQS Radio			
	Call Completed	Total:	2

Figure 9-1:
The ACT!
History
Summary
report.

The next two reports are based on information in two of the key ACT! fields:

- **Contact Status:** Shows you the ID/Status, last reach, last meeting, and last results for each contact during a specified date range. You'll likely want to create a Contact Activity lookup before running this report to avoid having a lot of empty contact information in your final report.

- **Source of Referrals:** The Source of Referrals report relies on the information in the Referred By field. Figure 9-2 shows you an example of the Source of Referrals report and plainly shows what happens if you don't enter data consistently. *Dave* Davis and *David* Davis are probably the same person, yet they show up in two different spots in the report.

You can find the Group reports together in a subsection of the main Reports menu. These reports give you different ways to view the information in your groups. If you aren't using groups (which I explain fully in Chapter 20), these reports might not be of any benefit to you.

- **Group Membership:** Lists all groups and their members

- **Group Summary:** Lists the notes, histories, and activities for all groups or for specific groups

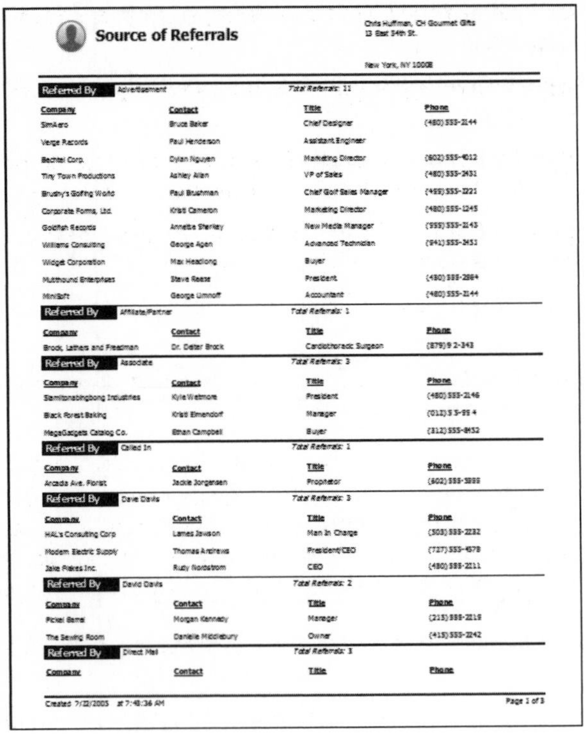

Figure 9-2:
ACT!'s
Source of
Referrals
report.

✔ **Group Comprehensive:** Lists all information (including notes, histories, and activities) for each group, subgroup, and their respective members

✔ **Group List:** Lists all groups and their description from the Group Description field

You find the Company reports together in a subsection of the main Reports menu. These reports give you different ways to view the information in your companies. If I sound like a broken record, it's because the five Group reports that I mention earlier all come in a "company version."

ACT! provides you with a variety of Opportunity reports, funnels, and graphs. The Opportunity reports use information entered onto the Opportunities tab. If you aren't using the Opportunities feature (head to Chapter 19 for the low-down), you can't use these reports. The Opportunity reports are all housed in a separate Opportunity section in the Reports menu.

✔ **Sales Analysis by Record Manager:** Shows the total sales by Record Manager, including everything from the average dollar amount of his sales to the average number of days it takes to close a sale

✔ **Totals by Status:** Garners totals of all sales opportunities and sorts them by Closed/Won Sales and Lost Sales

- ✔ **Adjusted for Probability:** Lists all sales opportunities showing a weighted sales total

- ✔ **Pipeline Report:** Gives information about sales opportunities at each stage in the sales process

- ✔ **Opportunities by Record Manager:** Lists sales opportunities, Closed/Won Sales, and Lost Sales sorted by Record Manager

- ✔ **Opportunities by Contact:** Provides complete sales information for each contact with a sales opportunity or a closed sale

- ✔ **Opportunities Graph:** Gives forecasted or closed sales, in a bar or line graph

- ✔ **Opportunities Pipeline:** Gives the number of sales opportunities at each stage of the sales process, in a graphical form

More than a dozen more ACT! reports are, unfortunately, buried. The Report menus include several "other report" options, which would lead you to believe that they would lead you to, well, some of the "other" reports. Not so. If you click any of the "other reports" menu options, you land in a folder that contains **all** the ACT! reports. If you look carefully, you'll find the following reports:

- ✔ **Birthday List:** Shows contact name, company name, and birth date for each contact

- ✔ **E-mail List:** Lists contact names and their primary e-mail addresses

- ✔ **Task List:** Gives the 411 about the activities scheduled with each contact and the status of each activity

- ✔ **Fax List:** Lists contact names and their fax numbers

- ✔ **Lost Opportunities by Competitor:** Shows subtotals of lost opportunities by competitor

- ✔ **Lost Opportunities by Reason:** Shows subtotals of lost opportunities by reason

- ✔ **Lost Opportunities by Record Manager:** Shows subtotals of lost opportunities by Record Manager

- ✔ **Opportunities by Company:** Show information for each company and any open opportunities

- ✔ **Opportunities by Group Summary:** Shows information for each group and any open opportunities

- ✔ **Opportunities Referred By:** Shows opportunities subtotaled by who referred the opportunity

- ✔ **Gross Margin by Contact:** Shows the gross margin by contact

- ✔ **Gross Margin by Product:** Lists each product and gross margin for each product

> ✔ **Gross Margin by Record Manager:** Shows the total sales, total cost, average discount, and gross margin as a percentage of sales by Record Manager
>
> ✔ **Sales Analysis by Record Manager:** Lists Record Manager and total sales
>
> ✔ **Sales by Reason:** Closed/Won opportunities listed by reason

Running an ACT! Report

The following steps apply to all ACT! reports. The dialog box is the same for all reports. Depending on the report that you're running, however, some of the options might be unavailable — and thus, appear grayed out.

To run an ACT! report, just follow these steps:

1. **Perform a lookup or display the contact record or records that you want to include in the report.**

   All roads in ACT! lead — or at least pass by — the lookup. Before running a report, decide which contact's or group's data you want to include in your report. For example, you might run a History Summary report for a single contact or a Contact report for all contacts in a state or region. You can include data from the current contact or group record, the current contact or group lookup, or from all contacts or groups.

2. **Choose the Reports menu and then select the name of the report that you want to run. To run a report that doesn't appear in the menu, choose Reports⇨Other Contact Reports and select the appropriate report.**

   The Define Filters dialog box opens, as shown in Figure 9-3. The General tab is identical for any and all ACT! reports that you create.

   All reports come equipped with a General tab. However, all reports are not created equally when it comes to the other tabs. Depending on the report you run, you'll notice different tabs available to you.

3. **In the Send the Report Output To drop-down list, select an output for the report:**

   - *Preview:* Choose the Preview option if you're at all hesitant about your reporting capabilities. A preview of the report appears onscreen. After previewing the report, print it or run it again if it doesn't look exactly how you want.

   - *Rich-Text File:* Saves the report as an RTF file, which you can open in Word.

   - *HTML File:* Saves the report as an HTML (HyperText Markup Language) file. Choose this option if you want to use the report on your Web site.

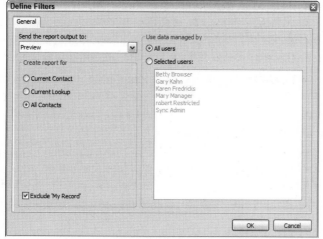

Figure 9-3:
The Define
Filters
dialog box.

- *PDF File:* Saves the report as a PDF file that can be read in Adobe Reader.

- *Text File:* Saves the report as a TXT file, which you can read with a wide variety of software, including Excel.

- *Printer:* Sends the report directly to your default printer. If you're fully confident that your report will print correctly the first time, go for it!

- *E-mail:* Sends the saved report as an attachment to an e-mail message. The attachment has an `.rpt` extension and can be read only by recipients who have ACT! installed on their computers.

4. **In the Create Report For area, specify the contacts to include in the report.**

   The choices are self explanatory. You run a report for the current contact, the current lookup, or all contacts.

5. **Select the Exclude 'My Record' check box if you don't want to include information from your My Record in the report.**

   This option is not available for all reports.

6. **In the Use Data Managed By area, select the Record Manager of the contacts that you're including in your report.**

   - *All Users:* Includes contact records managed by all users of the database.

   - *Selected Users:* Includes contact records managed by selected users of the database. If you're the only user of the database, only your name appears in the list.

7. **Click the Activities, Note, and/or History tabs, if you're running any of those reports, and make the appropriate selections.**

   • *On the Activities tab,* select the type of activities and the corresponding date range of the activities to include in your report.

   • *On the History tab,* select the type of histories and the corresponding date range that you're including in your report.

   • *In the Use Data Managed By area,* select the users who imputed the data that you want to include in the report.

By default, any of the activity, notes, or history reports show you data for the current month. If you don't change those date ranges, your report might not give you the information that you're expecting to see.

8. **Click the Opportunity tab, if you see one, when running a Sales report.**

   Seems a bit hokey, but sometimes the Opportunity options appear on the General tab, and sometimes they appear on their very own tab as illustrated in Figure 9-4.

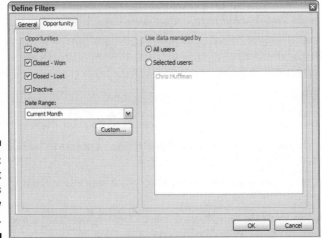

Figure 9-4:
The report filter's Opportunity tab.

Regardless of where you find the Opportunity options, you still have the same choices:

   • *In the Opportunities area,* select whether you want to include Open, Closed - Won, Closed – Lost, and/or Inactive sales in your report.

   • *In the Date Range drop-down menu,* specify the date range of the Sales Opportunities to include in the report.

   • *In the Use Data Managed By area,* choose to include the opportunity information from All Users or Selected Users of your database.

9. **Click OK.**

   ACT! runs the report. If you aren't happy with the results, run the same report a second time by using different criteria or try running a different report. Better yet, read Chapter 10 to discover how to create your very own ACT! reports.

Printing Address Books

Printing an address book is probably one of the more common tasks used by ACT! users, and ACT! makes the chore an extremely simple one to perform. Creating a hard copy of your ACT! address book is basically a three-step process:

1. Add all your contact information into your ACT! database, making sure that your information is as complete as possible.

2. Create a lookup of the contacts that you want to include in your address book.

   Of course, you might want to include all your contacts in the print copy of your address book. You might even want to print separate address books for each of the different types of contacts in your database.

3. Choose the format for your address book. ACT! comes equipped with some neat choices including Day-Timer and Franklin address books.

Those are the basic steps. The following steps include all the down-and-dirty details for creating your own printed address book:

1. **Create a lookup if you intend to print only a portion of your address book that I show you how to create at the beginning of this section.**

   Refer to Chapter 6 if you need a refresher course in creating an ACT! lookup.

2. **From any of the ACT! windows, choose File⇨Print.**

   Okay, I know you're probably scratching your head wondering why I'm asking you to print when you haven't created anything yet. That's the concept with these non-reports: They aren't actually reports by definition, so ACT! just threw them into the Print menu. Go figure!

   The Print dialog box opens, as shown in Figure 9-5.

3. **Choose Address Book from the Printout Type area.**

4. **Select the paper type for printing the address book.**

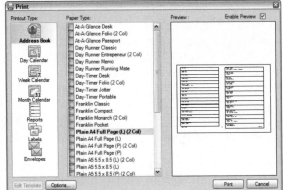

Figure 9-5:
Choose the
form you
want to
print.

ACT! enables you to print contact addresses and phone numbers in a variety of commonly used paper formats, including

- At-A-Glance

- Day Runner

- Day-Timer

- Franklin

You can print all your ACT! information onto preformatted addressing systems. ACT! provides you with the most popular, commercially available addressing systems. The preprinted forms are available at any of the large office supply warehouse stores. If you use an address system from one of these manufacturers, choose it from the Paper Type list.

Figure 9-5 shows you some of your choices. The Edit Template button is grayed out because you can't make changes to the Address Book templates.

Of course, if you don't want to spend the money on preprinted forms or you just want a printout of your address book on a plain sheet of paper, you can always use my particular favorite form for printing an address book: plain paper.

A preview of the selected printout appears in the Preview pane on the right if you have the Enable Preview option checked.

5. **Click the Options button to specify the information to include in the address book.**

The Options dialog box opens, as shown in Figure 9-6.

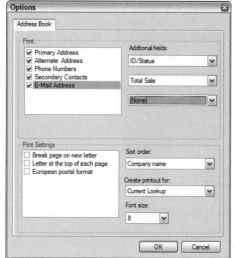

Figure 9-6:
The Options
dialog box.

6. **In the Print area, select the fields to include in your address book:**

   - *Primary Address:* Prints the contact's main address

   - *Alternate Address:* Prints the contact's alternate address

   - *Phone Numbers:* Prints the contact's phone numbers, including Work, Alternate, Fax, Mobile Phone, Home Phone, and Pager

   - *Secondary Contacts:* Prints the secondary contacts' names and phone numbers

   - *E-mail Address:* Prints the contact's e-mail addresses

7. **In the Additional Fields drop-down menus, you can add up to three additional fields.**

   The choices in Step 6 are based on the default fields that come with ACT!. If you've added several new phone number fields, they don't appear in the printout of your address book, but ACT! allows you to add up to three additional fields.

8. **In the Print Settings area, select your printing options.**

   Here's where you get to determine how your address book is going to print:

   - *Break Page on New Letter:* Starts a new page for each letter of the alphabet

   - *Letter at the Top of Each Page:* Prints the current alphabetic letter at the top of each page

   - *European Postal Format:* Prints the postal code before the city

9. **In the Sort Order drop-down menu, select the order in which you want entries to appear in your address book — alphabetically either by company name or contact last name.**

10. **In the Create Printout For drop-down men, specify whether to include the Current Contact, the Current Lookup, or All Contacts.**

11. **If desired, change the Font Size option.**

12. **Click OK.**

Creating Mailing Labels and Envelopes

All right. You've created a brochure that's guaranteed to knock the socks right off of your customers — and potential customers. Now all you have to do is send out those puppies in the mail. There is no easier method to do this than by creating mailing labels or envelopes using ACT!.

Some of you might be snickering about now because you're much too sophisticated to be using snail mail. You've probably already raced over to Chapter 12 to find out how to create e-mail blasts. But you might still want to use the ACT! labels to create everything from file tabs to name badges.

You print out labels and envelopes in ACT! in exactly the same way. At first glance, printing envelopes in ACT! to match a customized letter template seems like a great idea. After all, they look a lot more personalized than an ordinary mailing label. However, if your mailing entails sending personalized letters to a large number of people, consider rethinking your decision. Unless you have a specially designed envelope tray, you're probably going to have to print your envelopes in batches. And remember that 30 envelopes are much bulkier and harder to store than a page of 30 labels. While you print each batch of envelopes, you have to make sure that they remain in the exact same order as your letters, or matching them to the corresponding letter could become a nightmare.

If you're printing envelopes, I suggest limiting the number of envelopes that you print at any one time. If you're just printing a single envelope for one person to go with a letter that you just created using a document template, using your word processor to create the envelope is probably easier than using ACT!. ACT! automatically asks whether you want to print an envelope after you create a letter when using a document template. (See Chapter 11 for the details.)

To create labels or envelopes using ACT!, just follow these steps:

1. **Create a lookup of the contacts for whom you want to create labels or envelopes.**

If you're creating a personalized mailing, I'd guess that you've already created a lookup of the contacts that get the mailing. By creating the corresponding labels using the existing lookup, you're guaranteed to have the same number of contacts and to have your labels print in the same sort order.

2. **Choose File➪Print from any ACT! window.**

3. **Choose either Labels or Envelopes from the Printout Type list.**

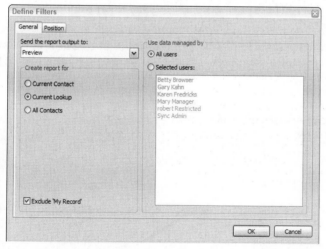

   From this point forward, I focus on creating labels, but these directions also work for envelopes. Just substitute the word *envelope* for the word *label* in any of the directions.

4. **Select a template from the list and click the Print button.**

   The available label templates are listed on the Paper Type area of the dialog box.

   Notice that all the labels are Avery labels. Chances are that even if you're using a generic label, you find the magic words *Same as Avery Label #XX* printed on the side of the box.

   The Define Filters dialog box appears, as shown in Figure 9-7.

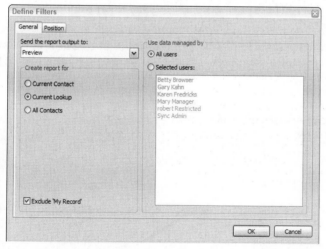

Figure 9-7:
The Define
Filters
dialog box.

5. **In the Send the Report Output To drop-down menu, choose your print option.**

   You'll find all the same printing options that you have when you print reports. Theoretically, you could save your labels in HTML format or e-mail them to someone. Previewing the labels before printing them is always a good idea. You can then print them directly from the Preview screen if everything looks hunky-dory.

6. **In the Create Report For area, specify whether you want to create labels for the Current Contact, the Current Lookup, or All Contacts.**

   If you've sorted your database, choose the Current Lookup option to retain the sorting, even if you're printing your entire database.

7. **Select All Users or Selected Users from the Use Data Managed By area.**

   This option refers to the Record Manager of each contact. You might want to print labels for just your own contacts.

8. **Click the Position tab.**

   This is how you're going to make your first million dollars. According to the rules of probability — or just your dumb luck — chances are that if you use labels that come 30 to a page, you end up needing 32 labels. This leaves you with a sheet of 28 unusable labels — unless you use ACT!, that is. The Position tab allows you to start printing your labels on the appropriate spot on your page.

9. **Click OK.**

   You're now the proud owner of a beautiful set of labels.

Modifying Labels and Envelopes

You might decide that your labels or envelopes need a little extra pizzazz. Maybe you want to add another field or make a field longer. Maybe you think a font change is in order. Most modifications that you have in mind can be accomplished from either the label or envelope template editor:

1. **Choose File⇨Print from any ACT! screen.**

2. **Choose either Labels or Envelopes from the Printout Type list and select the label or envelope type that you'd like to modify. For our purposes we're going to choose Labels; however, you'd follow the same steps if you were modifying an Envelope template.**

3. **Click the Edit Template button to make changes to an existing label template.**

   The Label Designer dialog box opens, as shown in Figure 9-8. The Label Designer toolbox also opens; you recognize this toolbox if you design layouts (Chapter 14) or reports (Chapter 10) in ACT!.

4. **Before making adjustments to the existing label formats, save the template using another name by choosing File⇨Save As, typing the name of the template in the File Name field, and then clicking OK.**

   The next time that you run a set of labels, the template that you create appears as one of the label template choices.

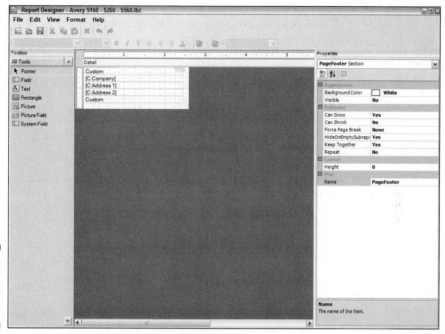

Figure 9-8:
The Label
Designer
dialog box.

5. Modify the label formats to your heart's content:

- *To delete a field:* Click the Pointer tool in the top left corner of the toolbox, click a field, and then press Delete.

- *To move a field:* Click the Pointer tool in the toolbox and drag a field to a new position.

- *To change the font for a field:* Double-click a field and then choose the Font menu to specify a different font, size, or attribute.

- *To add a field:* Click the Field tool and draw a rectangle to indicate where you want to place the field. You're then prompted to select the name of the field you wish to add.

- *To close the template:* Choose File⇨Close and then click Yes to save.

6. Click OK.

If the label that you ordinarily use isn't listed, changing your labels to correspond to one of the labels listed in ACT! is probably your easiest choice. But if you rely on a special label, you can create a document template that corresponds with the dimensions of your labels. Check out Chapter 11 to find out how to create custom templates.

As you poke around in the various templates, notice a few fields labeled Custom. Avoid the tendency to delete these custom fields — they're there for a reason. The custom field at the top of the label provides the contact name using the Prefix, First Name, Last Name, and Suffix. The custom field at the bottom provides the City, State, and Zip code. The custom fields can be moved, resized, and the font changed, but they should not be deleted.

Working with Quick Report

I like to think of the ability to print the various ACT! lists and tabs as somewhat of a secret weapon. By being able to print these lists, you can report quickly on just about anything that you can view throughout your database. This ability enables you to quickly create a report based on the specifications and criteria that you need immediately.

You're able to create a Quick Report for the following ACT! lists:

✔ Contact List

✔ Task List

✔ Group List

✔ Company List

You can also create a Quick Report for the following system tabs in the Contact, Group, or Company Detail windows:

✔ Notes

✔ History

✔ Activities

✔ Opportunities

✔ Groups/Companies

✔ Secondary Contacts

✔ Documents

Basically, if you're viewing a *list,* such as the Task List, ACT! can print the list. If you're viewing a *tab* that contains a list of items, such as the Notes, History, or Opportunities tab, ACT! can print those items as well.

Creating a Quick Report

Follow these steps to create a report:

1. **Display the list view or tab that you want to print.**

   - *To display a list,* such as the Task List or Contact List, choose View and then the appropriate list.

   - *To display a tab,* click the tab from the Contact, Group, or Company Detail window.

2. **Arrange the columns exactly as you want them to appear on your printout.**

   If you need help adding/removing columns or changing the order or size of existing columns, check out Chapter 5.

   All the lists and tabs that you see in ACT! are customized in exactly the same way.

3. **Choose File⇨Quick Print Current Window.**

   The Windows Print dialog box opens.

4. **Click OK.**

   Some of you might be thinking that you can print a Quick Report pretty quickly. You're right! Guess that's why they're called *Quick Reports!*

Setting the Quick Report preferences

You can read in the preceding section that when you run a Quick Report, it moves along quickly. You're not asked for any customization options other than your initial determination of the columns and column order that you wish to print. Quick Print preferences allow you to modify the content of the headers and footers that appear on all your Quick Reports.

1. **Choose Tools⇨Preferences from any ACT! screen.**

2. **Click the Communication tab and then click the Quick Print Preferences button.**

   The Quick Print Preferences dialog box opens, as shown in Figure 9-9.

3. **Select a view from the When Printing This section.**

   You might want a Quick Report of your companies to look differently than the Quick Reports of your opportunities. Here's where you get to assign the various attributes for each view you plan to print.

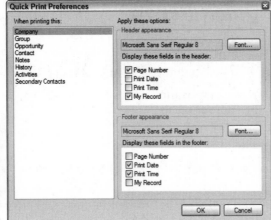

Figure 9-9:
The Quick
Print
Preferences
dialog box.

4. **Choose from the following options for both the header and footer for each view that you choose.**

   • Font

   • Page Number

   • Print Date

   • Print Time

   • My Record

   You can see that the settings in Figure 9-9 tell ACT! to place the My Record and page number information in the header and to place the print date and print time information in the footer.

5. **Click OK.**

Chapter 10

Designing Your Own Reports

In This Chapter

▶ Using the ACT! Report Designer

▶ Modifying an existing ACT! report

▶ Filtering report content

▶ Creating report sections

*A*CT! comes with 40 reports right out of the box. Chances are that one of these reports can give you exactly the information that you need, and Chapter 9 shows you how to run any of the existing ACT! reports. But, just in case you can't find exactly the report you want, this chapter shows you how to create brand new reports or modify an existing one. If you want to add it to the Reports menu after designing a report, head to Chapter 3, where I show you how.

Understanding the Report Designer

Designing a database report can be a bit intimidating if you've never done it before. I like to think that you can tackle the chore of creating a report in one of two ways: the hard way or the easy way. The hard way consists of creating a brand new report entirely from scratch, which entails placing each and every element of your report onto a blank report template. The easy way consists of taking an existing report that's kinda what you're looking for and modifying it.

You might want to open the Act8demo database and print out a page of each of the existing ACT! reports for reference. Doing so helps you decide which report works as the best starting point for your modifications.

Being familiar with the structure of your existing database can prove helpful when you attempt to create a report. Thus, you need to know the field names that you're working with as well as their location in ACT!. For example, if you want to include the name of a company, you must know that the field is called Company and that you find the field in the Contact Detail window. If you want to include notes that you've added, you must know to include the Regarding field from the Notes tab.

Before starting to create or modify a report, create a lookup of the contacts that you're including in your report. This step is optional but can be timesaving. As you design your report, you'll notice that sometimes certain fields aren't large enough to contain their data or that columns don't line up correctly. By creating a lookup, you can check the progress of your report-designing efforts by running a preview of your report each time that you add a new element to it.

Mastering ACT! Report Basics

After you pick the report you want to modify — or decide that you're a glutton for punishment and start from scratch — you're ready to begin.

1. **Choose the Reports menu from any ACT! screen.**

   You have two choices here:

   • *New Template:* Even if you choose this option, ACT! shows you a list of all the report templates. The top choice, Empty Report, is the one you want to choose if you're adventurous enough to want to start working without a net.

   Yikes! The problem with designing an ACT! report from scratch is, well, that you have to create the report from scratch. As shown in Figure 10-1, a blank template with Header, Detail, and Footer section titles appears on the left.

   • *Edit Template:* For me and most ACT! users, this choice is safer. You can now open the report that most closely matches your desired results. To make things even less confusing, you'll discover that the filenames of the reports match the names of the reports. Compare Figures 10-1 and 10-2 to see the difference between a blank report and an existing one.

   Notice what appear to be duplicate fields. The first field that you see is the Field label. You can edit any of these labels by double-clicking the label, and then typing in any desired changes. You can distinguish the field itself by the colon that appears in each field. The actual data from your ACT! database appears in this area when you run the report. The letter in front of the colon indicates the Field type. For example, if you add your name in the Header section, the field appears as My:Contact. If you add a contact's company, it appears on the report template as C:Company.

2. **From the Report Designer, choose File⇨Save As.**

   I highly recommend giving your report a brand new name even if you're just tweaking an existing report. That way, you still have the original report to go back to, just in case.

3. **Fill in a name for your new report and then click Save.**

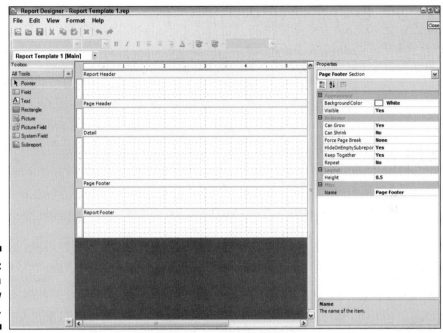

Figure 10-1:
Creating a
brand new
ACT! report.

Figure 10-2:
Modifying
an existing
ACT! report.

Saving early and often

Creating a report requires a great deal of patience. Even the most expert of report designers run into problems at times or (gasp) make a mistake. Imagine how you'd feel if after spending several hours working on a report, you made a huge mistake without realizing it until you ran your report for the first time. You'd head back to the drawing board (none too happily, I might add). For that reason, I suggest that you keep repeating the following procedure each and every time you make a change to the structure of your report.

From the Report Designer, choose File➪Print Preview and give your report a good examination:

✔ If you like what you see, close Print Preview and choose File➪Save. Your changes are now safe and sound.

✔ If something is wrong in Houston, or at least somewhere in the body of your report, close Print Preview and then close the Report Designer without saving your changes. Cutting your losses is easier now rather than trying to untangle the mess you might inadvertently create later on.

Most of you have discovered the wonderful Undo feature that allows you to take back what you just did. You can "undo" an incorrect change to your report template by choosing Edit➪Undo (or holding down the Ctrl key and tapping the Z key on your keyboard). Unfortunately, you'll find that very often the Undo won't work in the report designer. All the more reason to save *early and often*. Talk about working without a net!

Using the toolbox and properties

An ACT! report template consists of a number of elements. For example, you might have your company logo at the top of your report and a series of column headings that appear at the top of each page in your report. ACT!'s Report Designer lets you modify those various elements using the toolbox and Properties features.

Tooling around in the toolbox

Refer to Figure 10-2 to see the toolbox running along the left-hand side of the Report Designer. It consists of the following eight tools:

✔ **Pointer:** You must click the Pointer tool in order to select any element in the Report Designer that you wish to modify.

✔ **Field:** Click this tool if you want to add a new field to the body of your report.

✔ **Text:** This tool allows you to create a descriptive text box.

- ✔ **Rectangle:** As its name implies, this tool allows you to draw a box or rectangle in your report. Use this option to highlight a section of your report. The rectangle is also used to create lines by making the border and background solid and the same color.

- ✔ **Picture:** This tool allows you to add a graphic, such as your company logo, to your report.

- ✔ **Picture Field:** This tool allows you to add a contact's picture to your report.

- ✔ **System Field:** This tool allows you to add fields including date, time, and number of pages in your report.

- ✔ **Subreport:** Using this tool shows multiple objects for each contact in a report. For example, you might want to show activity information for each contact listed on a contact report.

Using the properties properly

In addition to the toolbox, the Report Designer comes equipped with a Properties window guaranteed to give you more options than your local ice cream store. The Properties window runs along the right side of the Report Designer (refer to Figure 10-2). You can see what I mean by the options available to you. The purpose of the Properties window is to show you all the applied formatting of the currently selected element.

Feel like the Properties window is infringing on your territory? You can send it packing. A simple press of the F4 key closes the Properties window. Want to bring it back? Simply press F4 again.

If you want to move the toolbox or Properties window out of the way, just double-click the window title bar. Each of these windows now detach themselves from the side of your screen. At this point, you can drag them to whatever area of the Report Designer you're not using. Want to put them back? Double-click the title bar and whoosh!, there it is!

The Properties window reflects the properties of the field or element that's currently selected. The left side of the Properties window lists all the aspects available for the field or element that you select. The right side shows you the currently selected choice. If you want to change any particular aspect, simply click the option on the right side and choose a different formatting option from the drop-down list that appears. For example, if I want to change a font color from black to red, I click the word *black* that appears to the right of the font color and then choose *red* from the drop-down list.

You can also use the Properties window to change the attributes of several elements at the same time. You can click several elements at the same time by holding down either the Shift or the Control key while clicking the elements you want to change. After you make your selection, you can change as many attributes as you want all in one fell swoop.

Changing the Report Content

I mention earlier that chances are that you began with a basic report and decided to modify it somewhat — or even give it a complete makeover. Probably the first thing you want to do is decide which fields will — or won't — appear in your report. After you make that momentous decision, you might decide to tweak the order of the fields. Of course, then you're going to have to realign some of the fields that you moved so that they line up in an orderly fashion. You also have to decide how long a field should be — for example, the State field needs to house only 2 letters, but the City field might need to hold 30. Whew! You have a lot of work to do, so read on!

Working with existing fields

Start by tweaking some of the fields already on your report template. You could start by removing some of the fields from the Contact Report, or you might want to make the font a wee bit larger to accommodate your 40-something eyes. The more ornery members of the crowd might not be happy with the order in which the fields appear in one of the opportunity reports. Like anything else, it's simple if you know the trick.

1. **From the Report Designer, click the Pointer tool in the toolbox.**

2. **Select the fields you want to modify.**

   To select multiple fields, hold down the Shift or Control key while clicking any additional fields. If you're a mouse lover, you can also drag your rodent around several adjoining fields to select them.

   You can identify selected fields by the little boxes that now appear along their edges and centers.

After you select the fields you want to work with, you can change your selection in a number of ways:

✔ **To change field properties:** Select an item from the Report Designer Properties window and edit the properties. You can also select font attributes such as bolding, centering, and size from the Report Designer toolbar.

✔ **To delete a field or a field label:** Press the Delete key on your keyboard.

   Many of the ACT! reports include *custom fields,* which contain special scripts to make the reports do special things. Refrain from deleting those custom fields unless you can completely determine their function.

✔ **To resize a field:** Grab one of the selection handles on either side of the field and drag to either the left or right, depending on whether you want the field larger or smaller.

✔ **To move a field:** Place your cursor in the middle of a field or group of fields and drag them to the desired location.

✔ **To align fields:** First select all the secondary fields and then select the anchor field. The *anchor field* is the one that is correctly placed on the report template and the one you should click last; all the other fields are the ones that you want to align horizontally or vertically with the anchor field. Choose Format⇨Align from the Report Designer menu and indicate how to line up the fields.

As you modify and move fields, you'll probably start to notice that the fields no longer line up as neatly as they once did. Although you can physical drag a field or fields around in an attempt to line them back up again, you'll probably end up wasting a lot of your valuable time. Using the Align Fields options is much more accurate — and better on your blood pressure!

You can distinguish between the anchor field and the other fields that you select by carefully examining the selection handles. If you look at Figure 10-3, the anchor field has light gray handles, whereas the secondary fields all have black ones.

Figure 10-3:
The anchor and secondary selection handles.

Adding a field

After you modify, move, and delete fields from your template, you might want to start adding in a few additional fields. If so, follow these additional steps.

A dozen of the basic ACT! reports are invisible to the naked eye — or at least not seen on the Report menus. Save yourself a bunch of time and check whether one of those reports fits the bill. It's always easier to delete and move existing reports rather than having to add new ones. You can see a list of those reports in Chapter 9.

1. **In the Report Designer, click the Field tool in the toolbox.**

2. **Place your cursor on the template where you want to insert a field and then drag down and to the right to define the field's length and position.**

Most probably, you want to add the new field to the Detail section of your report. However, you can also add fields to any of the other sections, including the header and footer as well.

You can read more about the other sections later in this chapter. When you work with a report, you might find it helpful to enlarge the sections to give you a bit more elbowroom. You can do this by grabbing the gray horizontal line that appears at the bottom of each section and dragging it down an inch or two. Just remember to drag the section line back up again when you're finished adding new fields to avoid seeing huge gaps between the lines of your report.

When you release the mouse button, the Select Field dialog box appears, as shown in Figure 10-4. You can now choose any of your existing ACT! fields to add to the report templates.

Figure 10-4:
The Select
Field dialog
box.

3. **Select the record type that you want to add from the Select a Record Type drop-down list.**

   Typically, you want to add a new Contact field to the body of your report. However, you might decide to add My Record fields to the header so that your name and other pertinent information appears at the top of the report. You might also want to include Secondary Contact information. You can even choose to add Activity, History, Note, and Opportunity fields to your report.

   As you make a record type selection, notice that the list of fields changes. If you decide to add a Note field, the choices include Date and Time, whereas a selection of Contact Opportunity allows you to include any of your Opportunity fields.

4. **Indicate whether you want to include a field label.**

   A label appears on the report regardless of whether any information appears in the field. If you don't want to include a field label for a field in the template, deselect (clear) the Include a Label check box.

5. **Click the Add button.**

   The Report Designer now contains the fields and field labels that you added. Refer to Figure 10-2 for an example of a report template that contains several sections, subsections, and fields.

6. **Continue adding additional fields if desired. Click the Close button when you finish adding new fields.**

ACT!'s Report Designer is deceptively powerful. Although it is beyond the scope of this book, an advanced user can add custom fields to any of the ACT! reports. These custom fields contain Visual Basic scripting, which can let the ACT! reports return information in just about any form.

Adding a summary field

After you add a field to a report template, you might want to add a summary field. Summary fields can be used to give you a count of all the contacts that appear in a report or a total for a column containing numeric data.

1. **Add the field in the Report Designer that you want to convert into a summary field.**

   Although this sounds fairly straight-forward, you've got several things to think about here:

   - Summary fields usually appear above or below the rest of your data, so you'll probably want to put these fields in your headers or footers.

   - The summary fields usually match the data type and field. In other words, if you want a count of all your contacts, your summary field will be the Contact contact field. If you want a total of all your sales, the summary field will be the Total opportunity field.

   - The data doesn't actually have to appear in the report in order to be summarized. For example, you might want to have a list of contacts with a total representing the number of purchases they've made.

2. **Right-click in the field and choose Properties from the Field Properties displayed.**

3. **Click the Data tab and select the Summary option from the Field Type area.**

   You can check out the Data tab of the Field Properties dialog box in Figure 10-5.

Figure 10-5:
Creating a
summary
field.

Your summary options include

- *Count (count):* This field counts the number of records for the selected field.

- *Total (sum):* This field calculates the total of all values in the selected field.

- *Average (avg):* This field calculates the average of all values in the selected field.

- *Minimum (min):* This field finds the lowest number or earliest date in the selected field.

- *Maximum (max):* This field finds the highest number or latest date in the selected field.

If some of the options are grayed out, those options don't apply to the field that you selected. For example, I could count a list of contacts, but I can't add them together because you can't add character fields.

4. **Click OK to add the field to your report.**

   After you create a summary field, you'll recognize it because ACT! inserts several letters in front of the field name to indicate the type of summary field that you just created. To make life easy for you, I included clues for you in the parentheses above.

Filtering Data in a Report Template

Just like you can filter heaven knows what out of your water, you can filter data out of a report. You can change the filters each time that you run a report, or you can include filters in your report template to save you from having to do it later. Any filters that you set become defaults that you can change later when you actually run the report. Here's all you need to do to add that timesaving feature to your report templates.

1. **Choose Edit⇨Define Filters from the Report Designer.**

   The Define Filters dialog box appears. You can sneak a peak at it in Figure 10-6.

   The Define Filters dialog box is divided into five tabs. Depending on the type of report you're creating, some of the tabs might not be available:

   - *General:* Selects the default output for the report, the contacts to include, and the Record Manager of the contacts

   - *Activity:* Lets you select whether you want to include calls, meetings, to-do's, and cleared activities within a given date range

   - *Note:* Lets you specify the date range and creator of the notes to appear in a report

   - *History:* Lets you determine whether you want to include histories, e-mails, and attachments within a given date range

   - *Opportunity:* Lets you filter for Sales Opportunities as well as Closed and Lost Sales within a given date range

2. **Select the data to include in the report from the Activity, Note, History, and Opportunity tabs, and then click OK.**

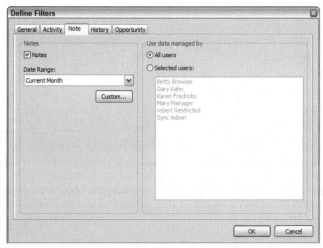

Figure 10-6:
The Report
Designer
Define
Filters
dialog box.

Chapter 9 warns you that you need to change the report filters each and every time you run a report if you don't like the default values. By default, the notes, history, and activity reports all display information from last month. If you run these reports on a weekly basis, here's your chance to change those defaults.

Sectioning Your ACT! Report

You create sections in a report template to help you organize the information that you want to include in your report. In general, the main information that you're reporting on appears in the body of the report. However, you might want your own contact information to appear on the first page of your reports, the page number to appear at the top of every page, the date and time to show up on the bottom of each page, and your totals to magically materialize on the very last page. In this section I'll show you how to do just that.

Defining report sections

A report template is divided into *sections* of information. Each section has a section title that appears in the report template but doesn't appear in the report itself. You can determine which fields you want to appear in each given section. A report template consists of five main sections; you can't delete or change the order of the sections, but you can hide a section if you don't want it to appear in your report (see "Hiding a report section" later in this chapter. The five main sections are

- ✔ **Report Header:** Information that appears at the top of the first page of the report, such as the report's title and creator.
- ✔ **Page Header:** Information that appears at the top of each page, such as column headings.
- ✔ **Detail:** The area that contains one or more of your Contact or Group fields. The Detail section is the meat and potatoes of the report where you find pertinent information, such as the contact's name, address, and phone number.
- ✔ **Page Footer:** Information that appears at the bottom of each page in your report, such as the date and page number.
- ✔ **Footer:** Information that appears at the bottom of the last page of your report, such as a recap or a grand total.

You can resize a section to make room for additional fields by dragging the horizontal gray line that appears at the bottom of the section lower on the template.

After you fiddle with your report template and have it exactly the way you want it, don't forget to resize each section back to the original size — or close it up as much as possible. Any blank areas in a section appear as blank areas in your report!

Modifying report sections

Most of you will be quite happy to rely on the five default report sections. However, from time to time, you might want to get a bit fancier. Maybe you want to list each of your contacts alphabetically by last name grouped by city. You need to create subsections within your report to accomplish this. Not a problem; here's all you need to do:

1. **In the Report Designer, double-click any section header.**

   The Define Sections dialog box opens, as shown in Figure 10-7. Notice that in addition to adding subsections, you can choose a few other options as well:

   - *Page Break:* Indicates whether you want to have each section appear on a new sheet of paper or start a new sheet at the end of a section.

   - *Collapse if Blank:* Closes up a section if no information is contained in it.

   - *Allow Section to Break Across Multiple Pages:* Allows a long section to continue on to multiple pages.

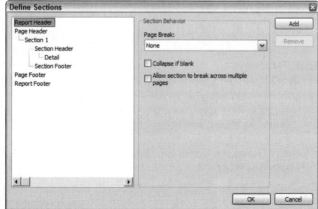

Figure 10-7:
The Report
Designer
Define
Sections
dialog box.

2. **Click the Add button to add a new section to the report.**

   The Select a Field to Group By dialog box opens, as shown in Figure 10-8.

Figure 10-8:
Determine
how
information
is grouped
in a report.

3. **Select the field you want to use to group your report and then click OK.**

   In Figure 10-8, you can see how I decided to group my reports by city.

4. **Select an ascending order from the Define Sections dialog box.**

   Once you select the field you wish to group on in Step 3 above, you'll be returned to the Define Sections dialog box. The new section will be highlighted, and you'll be able to indicate whether the new section appears in ascending or descending alphabetical order.

After you create a new subsection, you can place as many fields on it as you want using the techniques in the "Adding a field" section earlier in this chapter.

Hiding a report section

There might be times when you'll want to hide a section. For example, let's say you want a report that counts the number of contacts in each of your ID/Status fields. Theoretically ACT! needs to list all those contacts so that they can be counted, yet you really don't want to see all those contacts because you are only interested in seeing a total. Although you can't remove any of the default report template sections, you can hide them, which gives you the same result. To hide a section

1. **In the Report Designer, open the Properties window by choosing View⇨Properties Window.**

2. **Select the name of the section that you wish to hide.**

3. **Click the Visible property in the Properties window and change it to No.**

Although you can still see the section in the Report Designer, it doesn't appear in your finished reports.

Chapter 11

Merging Your Information into a Document

• •

• •

A particularly useful ACT! feature enables you to create customized document templates: forms in which ACT! fills in your selected data fields. You can send these forms to a thousand people as easily as you can send them to just one person. You can send out routine documents one at a time on a continual basis, or you can send out the document one time to all or part of your database. After you create a form, you can send it out via snail mail, e-mail, fax, or Pony Express.

Mail Merge Isn't Just about Mailing

Poor mail merge! Folks often have two common misconceptions about mail merge. Some people think that *mail merge* is synonymous with *junk mail*. Also, the word *mail* makes some folks think postage stamps are involved. However, neither of these common misconceptions are true. A mail merge simply takes the content of one or more fields and puts that content into a template or form.

A good way to understand the concept of mail merge is to visualize this simple equation:

template + data field(s) = personalized document

Note the *(s)* at the end of *data field,* suggesting that you can use either one name or many names. Some of you might think that you will never perform a mail merge because you have no desire to send out a mass mailing. Others of you might have already perfected the art of mass mailing but never realized that a mail merge can be directed to one person or to thousands of people. I hate to be the one to break your bubble, but if you have any kind of routine documents that you're generating repetitively, you should be using ACT!'s mail merge to do it.

The three things necessary to create a mail merge are

- ✔ **A name or a list of names:** If you've followed this book to this point, you're the happy owner of a database and know how to create a lookup. (Don't know how to create a lookup? Better check out Chapter 6.) You can merge a document with your current contact, your current lookup, or the entire database.

- ✔ **A program that can combine the names into the template:** After you have a list of names and a document template, you need something to combine them. You could try to use your food processor, but I prefer to use the mail merge feature in ACT!.

- ✔ **A document template:** A *document template* is a letter or form that substitutes field names in place of names and addresses or whatever other information comes directly from your database. ACT! comes with a number of document templates that you can either use as is or modify. You can also create your own document templates by using a word processor.

Picking Your Word Processor

ACT! can use either its own word processor or Microsoft Word to create document templates. By default, ACT! is set to use its own word processor. Most ACT! users prefer using Word as their word processor, and I assume that you're no different. Although the ACT! word processor gets the job done, chances are that you're already using Word — and using an application that you're already familiar with is preferable. You'll also find that the ACT! word processor offers a far smaller array of features than Word.

If your word processing preferences inside ACT! aren't set to use Microsoft Word as your default word processor, you can't use existing Word templates or any templates that you created by using Word. To change your word processor settings, follow these handy-dandy directions:

1. **Choose Tools⇨Preferences from the Contact Detail window.**

2. **On the Communication tab, select a word processor from the Word Processor list.**

    In this case, you're choosing Microsoft Word.

3. **Click OK.**

Using the out-of-the-box templates

For those of you all set to write The Great American Novel, you might want to create all your own original documents. That's great, and I recommend that you skip to the section "Creating a Document Template." The rest of you might be interested in perusing some of the great templates that come prepackaged in ACT!. Even if you decide that these templates aren't exactly what you're looking for, you can use them as a starting point for developing your own unique document templates.

The following figure shows you the Open dialog box that appears when you choose Write⇨Other Document from any of the ACT! windows.

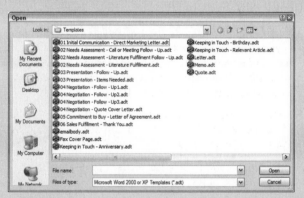

You might want to run each of the templates one time to determine which ones you think will be most useful to you. Later in the section entitled "Creating a Document template," you find out how to modify them to your heart's content. Right now, I want to point out three of my favorites that you might want to focus on. These three document templates are listed for you right up there on ACT!'s Write menu because you'll probably use these three templates the most often.

✔ **E-mail Message:** The E-mail Message template is based on a template with the crazy-sounding file name of `emailbody.adt`. Because you'll probably be sending a lot of e-mail using ACT!, you'll want to polish up this template. The `emailbody.adt` template pops up when you choose Write⇨ E-Mail Message from any of the ACT! windows or when you click a contact's e-mail address.

✔ **Letter:** The Letter (`Letter.adt`) template is a great template to use when you need to create a letter on the fly to one of your contacts. It automatically dates a letter and addresses it to your current contact. It even includes your name, company, and title on the bottom (the closing). All you need to do is fill in the body of the letter and stick on the stamp! You can also use this template as boilerplate for creating the rest of your form letters.

✔ **Fax Cover Page:** If you feel that you have no need for ACT!'s fax cover page because you already created something rather spiffy using Word, you can convert that Word document into an ACT! template to have ACT! automatically fill in all the necessary fields for you. Use the `Fax Cover Page.adt` template for this.

(continued)

(continued)

> You'll notice the Other Document (from template) choice on the Write menu. Click it and you'll find all the ACT! templates. Two templates contain graphics and are ready to send via e-mail; unfortunately, they work only when you set your word processor template to the ACT! word processor.
>
> ✔ ENewsletter
>
> ✔ Special Offer
>
> You might want to hold off using the Quote template — it's designed for use with the opportunities you create. Flip to Chapter 19 for more details.

Creating a Document Template

Before you can win friends and influence prospects with your dazzling display of personalized documents, you need two basic elements: the data and the document template.

You're creating a template, not a document, to perform your mail merge. A *document* is a plain old file that you create and use in Word. You use it once, save it, and store it away for posterity or delete it as soon as you're done with it. Comparatively, a *template* is a form that merges with your contact information. The convenience of templates is that you use them over and over again.

With your data tucked away nicely in your database, all you have left to do is to create the document template, which involves creating a form document. Your document template contains placeholders that are then filled in with information from your database after you perform a merge. Create a document template by following these steps:

1. **Choose Write⇨New Letter/E-Mail Template.**

   If you chose Word to be your word processor of choice, try not to look too surprised when Word opens. (To review how to set this preference, see the preceding section.)

2. **Resist the urge to close the Add Mail Merge Fields dialog box that's obscuring a portion of Word.**

   The Add Mail Merge Fields dialog box, as shown in Figure 11-1, is the main event of this little procedure. If you scroll through the Add Mail Merge Fields list, the various field names should ring a bell. After all — they're all your database fields.

   You can drag those pesky fields out of your way by placing your mouse pointer on the Add Mail Merge Fields title bar and dragging this dialog box out of the way.

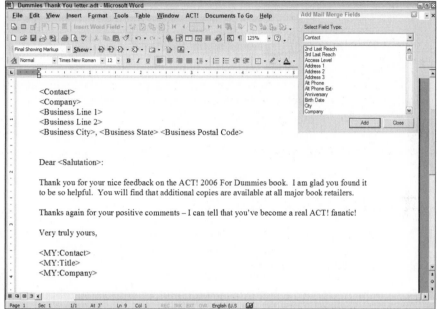

3. Change all your document settings.

Go ahead and change your font, margins, and other formatting items exactly as if you're working in a regular ol' Word document.

4. Create the body of your letter or form.

Nothing new under the sun here. You can backspace, delete, and type just like you do in any Word document.

5. Click the spot in your document where you want to insert a field.

6. Determine what type of field you want to insert into your template.

The Add Mail Merge Fields dialog box allows you to insert three different types of field information.

- *Contact:* If you want your contacts' information to appear when you perform a mail merge, you need to insert a Contact field into your template. In a letter, the name at the top that you're sending the letter to is the Contact field.

  Whatever information you've entered into a field appears in the merged document. If any of the fields in the contact record are empty, ACT! skips that field; you don't see a blank line. In Figure 11-1, I inserted the Company field; however, if your contact isn't associated with a company, that line is skipped.

- *Field Label:* Selecting the Field Label option inserts the name of the field, not the information contained in that field. You might wonder why you want to go through the effort of scrolling through the list of field names to insert a label when you could just as easily type in the field label. I wonder the same thing!

- *My Record:* If you want your own contact information to appear, select the My Record field option. If you're creating a letter document template, the name that appears at the bottom (in the closing) is your name and is represented by the My Record field option.

Your My Record information resides on the first contact record that appears when you open an ACT! database.

7. **Insert fields where you want contact information to appear.**

Here's where the fun begins. Every time you get to a part that could be populated with ACT! information, you must scroll down that long list of fields, select the one to insert into your template, and the click Add.

The field name appears in your document set off by a set of lovely angle brackets. Treat these field names exactly as you do any other words in your template. For example, if you want to see them set in bold, bold the field name. You'll also want to place the appropriate punctuation next to an inserted field if necessary; you'll note that in Figure 11-2 that the <Salutation> field in the greeting line is followed by a colon.

8. **Check your document for accuracy and edit as necessary.**

9. **Choose File➪Save As.**

Okay, I know that you probably already know how to save a document in Word, but I want to draw your attention to an interesting phenomenon that occurs when saving an ACT! document template in Word. Your document is automatically saved with the `.adt` extension. And, unless you specify otherwise, your template is saved to your default template folder. In Chapter 3, I show you how to determine the location in which to save your templates and also how to add a document template to the Write menu.

Document templates created with the ACT! word processor end in the extension `.tpl`.

After you create a template, you can change it whenever the need arises. For example, you might discover a spelling mistake. Or the contact fields that you're using might not work correctly, or they lack proper punctuation. You might even want to make changes to the wording in some of the templates, including the out-of-the-box templates. The procedure for editing your document template varies only slightly from that of creating the document:

1. **Choose Write➪Edit Template.**

2. **When the Open dialog box appears, select the document template that you want to open and then click Open.**

The template opens in Word, and the Add Mail Merge Fields dialog box automatically appears (refer to Figure 11-1).

When you edit an existing template, you see your field names in angle brackets within the document rather than your data. If you see actual data, you aren't editing the template, and the changes that you make affect only the current document that you're in; your document template remains unchanged.

3. **Make the appropriate changes to the template.**

4. **Click Save when you finish editing.**

In general, using an existing template is easier than creating a new template from scratch. Basically, to create a new template, you simply open a similar template and follow the same procedure as if you're editing an existing template — but save the file with a different name. Or, if the document already exists in Word, you might want to first open the existing document in Word, highlight the information that you want to appear in your template, copy it to the Clipboard, and then paste it into the new template.

Grappling with Graphics

You might want to think of e-mail merging as a good news, bad news kind of situation. The good news is you can read here how to create a template and e-mail it out to the entire world. The bad news is that you probably need to understand a little more about the technology that is involved in placing graphics into e-mail.

Basically, the two kinds of e-mail templates that you can create are

- ✔ **Plain text:** These templates consist of plain old, black-and-white verbiage.
- ✔ **HTML:** These templates are colorful and very often contain graphics.

Any of the templates that you create following the techniques in the previous section can be transmitted via either mail or e-mail. These templates can all contain merge fields so that your written letters and your e-mail can be personalized to contain any of the information found on a contact's record. They can be created using any of your font attributes including font type, size, color, bolding, italics, and underlining. You can even add a graphic — but not if you plan on e-mailing the template.

So, what's the hang-up? In a word — graphics. Those company logos that you want to include in your templates can prove to be quite annoying, troublesome, and just downright exasperating. Graphics need to be properly embedded into the body of your template or linked to graphics that are hosted on your Web site in order to avoid being sent as an attachment.

Think about it — have you ever received an e-mail from someone with a graphic attached to it? You open that e-mail and see a big white box with a tiny red X somewhere in it. Puzzled, you open the attachment and see a logo. This is a perfect example of someone who forayed into the exciting world of graphics and lost the battle. Here are a few tips to consider before sticking a graphic into one of your templates:

- ✔ **Word:** If you choose Word as your word processor preference, you need to insert the proper HyperText Markup Language (HTML) code into your template. The best way to accomplish this is to create the contents of your e-mail in a program that can save it as HTML code, such as Microsoft FrontPage. You can then insert the HTML-coded file into your Word template.

Still feeling dazed and confused when it comes to sending HTML e-mail? Consider using an add-on product to help you create those templates. You can read about one of my favorites, Swift Page E-mail, in Chapter 24.

- ✔ **ACT! word processor:** Consider using the ACT! word processor if you're intent on sending HTML e-mail and don't want to rely on any other product. The ACT! word processor lets you insert a graphic into your template and automatically embed it as long as your graphic is stored in the same folder as your template.

Don't lull yourself into thinking that your e-mail is going to properly transmit just because it looks perfect when you edit or preview your template. Consider creating a free Yahoo! or Hotmail e-mail account and send a trial e-mail there to make sure the graphics display properly before sending them off to the outside world!

Reaching an Audience of One

Don't assume that creating a mail merge implies sending out a single message to thousands of people at one time. A mail merge can also be used to automate the most mundane and routine of tasks. You can use ACT!'s document templates to write a thank-you letter every time that you land a new client or to write an inquiry letter each time that you receive a new lead. After you discover this timesaver, I guarantee that you'll never go back to your old way of creating documents again!

To send a document to a single member of your database, follow these steps:

1. **Create a lookup to find the contact to whom you want to send a letter.**

   Feel free to turn to Chapter 6 if you need help creating a lookup.

   The current contact record that you have displayed is the one whose information fills in your template.

2. **Choose Write and then choose Letter, Memo, Fax Cover Page, or Other Document.**

You can modify any of the ACT! menus. You might want to modify the Write menu to include some of your own templates. Flip over to Chapter 3 if you need a little refresher course in adding new items to an ACT! menu. As you start creating new templates, you can add corresponding menu items to the Write menu.

3. **Complete the body of the document.**

Depending on the type of document that you choose to create and the modifications that you made to the document template, you're looking at the start of a document. For example, by choosing to create a letter, the name, address, salutation, and closing are already provided. You just need to add the body of the letter to complete it. If you choose Other Document, you can choose either one of the other ACT!'s templates or one of your own. These, of course, already include the body as well.

If you chose to create a fax cover sheet, you need merely to add the number of pages in the transmittal and an optional comment to proceed.

4. **(Optional) Save your document.**

After you complete your document, you can save it to the location of your choice. If you don't think that it's necessary to save the document that you create from a template (because you can so easily re-create them), you aren't required to.

5. **Print, fax, or e-mail your document.**

If you use Word as the default word processor to create your ACT! documents, you can now print, fax, and e-mail exactly like you're already used to doing in Word.

If you choose to print, the Create History dialog box appears after printing is complete (see Figure 11-2). Now this is cool. I like to refer to this as the "Would you like fries with that?" step. After you create a document using a document template, ACT! will create a record of the document on the History tab. You now have a history of the date on which you sent a document. Better yet, other people in your organization are also aware of your interactions with the contact. If you don't want to record a history, select the No, Do Not Record History radio button.

- *To attach the document to a note on the History tab:* Select the Attach Document to History check box. When you enable this option, a shortcut to the document is automatically added to the History tab; you can access the document by double-clicking the attachment.

- *To have additional information appear in the note that's added to the History tab:* Enter a description of the document in the Regarding field. This description appears on the History tab regardless of whether you saved the document or not.

Figure 11-2:
Create a
history for a
written
document.

- *If you don't want to create a history for the document:* Select the No, Do Not Record History radio button.

- *To specify whether to print an envelope for the contact:* You have to hand it to ACT!: The program really tries to be as accommodating as possible. After you work your fingers to the bone creating your latest tome, ACT! gently asks you whether you want to print an envelope. If you select No, you're done with the letter-writing process.

After you complete the special order for your mail merge, all that's left to do is to click the OK button, close your word processor, and return to ACT!. If you select Yes to print the envelope, the Print dialog box appears.

We're Off to See the Mail Merge Wizard

Now that you've created a document template — or edited one of the existing ACT! templates — you're ready to fill in your template with contact information. ACT! provides you with the Mail Merge Wizard to take the guesswork out of this procedure. When you create a mail merge to one or more contacts, follow these four basic steps:

1. Select the contacts to whom you're sending the letter.

2. Select the template that includes both the contact fields that you want to merge into the letter and the body of the letter itself.

3. Choose to send the output to your word processor, printer, fax machine, or e-mail program.

4. Perform the mail merge.

Luckily, ACT! takes the laborious task of mail merging and simplifies it via the Mail Merge Wizard. Throughout the process, you encounter just a few easy-to-navigate windows. Trust me — there's no chance of losing your way because ACT! holds your hand during the entire journey.

To perform a mail merge, follow these steps:

1. **Select the contacts to be the recipients of your mail merge.**

   To do so, either use a lookup to select certain contacts (such as all contacts in a specific state, city, or company) or select contacts from the Contact List.

   If you're creating one of those charming Christmas newsletters telling all about your two kids who just graduated from Harvard Medical School and your recent month-long excursion to purchase two Mercedes — leave me off the list!

2. **From any ACT! view, choose Write⇨Mail Merge.**

   ACT! acts a bit theatrical here, what with all the talk about wizards and all. The Mail Merge Wizard opens with a screen that announces that you are starting the Mail Merge Wizard. Like the coming attractions, you can skip the first screen (just click Next) to go directly to the second wizard screen.

3. **Decide how you want to send the merge.**

   Decisions, decisions! The four choices on today's menu are

   - **Word Processor** saves all the merged documents into a single word processor document. This choice is good if you want to review your merged documents before printing them.

   - **E-mail** sends all the merged documents as e-mail messages.

     If you choose to send out a mail merge via e-mail, each recipient receives an e-mail specifically addressed to that person. No one sees a list of the other recipients.

   - **Printer** is a good choice if you're sure that your contact information and that your template is perfect, as in *error-free*. This choice is also popular if you like to chop down trees in the Amazon. This option sends all the merged documents directly to the printer.

   - **Fax** sends all the merged documents as fax transmissions. If this option is grayed out, you don't have ACT!-compatible fax software installed on your computer.

4. **Pick your template and click Next.**

   Indicate the template to use in your mail merge by clicking the Browse button and selecting the name of the document template that you want to use.

The Mail Merge Wizard continues and demands to know, in a loud booming voice, what contacts you want. All right, you caught me in one of my Judy Garland flashbacks. You can't actually hear the question, but it comes across loud and clear in Step 4 of the Mail Merge Wizard, as shown in Figure 11-3.

Figure 11-3: Choose the contacts to include in a mail merge.

5. **Choose to whom you want to send the mail merge and then click Next:**

   • *Current Lookup* merges your document with the contact records that you choose in Step 1.

   • *Current Contact* sends the merge only to the contact currently showing in the Contact Detail window.

   • *All Contacts* goes to everyone in your database.

   • *Selected Group* enables you to merge your document with a specific contact group.

   • *Selected Company* enables you to merge your document with all the associates of a given company.

   Depending on the send choice you pick in Step 3, you're pretty close to the finish line. You can just click Finish in the recap screen that appears.

   • *If you chose the word processor option,* you can now spend the next two hours reviewing 1,001 personalized letters to your dearest friends and relatives, ensuring that all the information therein is accurate.

   • *If you chose the printer option,* you hear the happy sound of your printer spitting out 1,001 personalized letters to your dearest friends and relatives.

• *If you chose the fax option,* your faxing software opens, and you're ready to fax.

6. **You have a little more work ahead of you if you chose the e-mail option.**

   Try not to be discouraged. Your e-mails are going to arrive at their intended destination long before those people choosing one of the other options even finish stuffing envelopes or decipher the new area code rules for a fax transmittal. Besides, you're treated to the options that you see in Figure 11-4.

Figure 11-4:
E-mail merge options.

   • Type the subject line of your e-mail.

   • Create a history of your e-mail by including the subject or the subject and message of your e-mail on the History tab. You also have the options of attaching the entire e-mail message to a history or simply creating no history at all.

   • Send an attachment along with your e-mail.

   • Specify that each recipient of your e-mail send you back a Return Receipt.

7. **Click Next to continue and set your options for the contacts who have missing e-mail addresses.**

   I hope you feel appropriately ashamed by the fact that you made ACT! work so hard while you simply sit back. ACT! now patiently asks you one final question regarding your e-mail addresses. As you can see in Figure 11-5, you have several choices as to how to handle the MIAs.

8. **After you choose all your options, click Finish.**

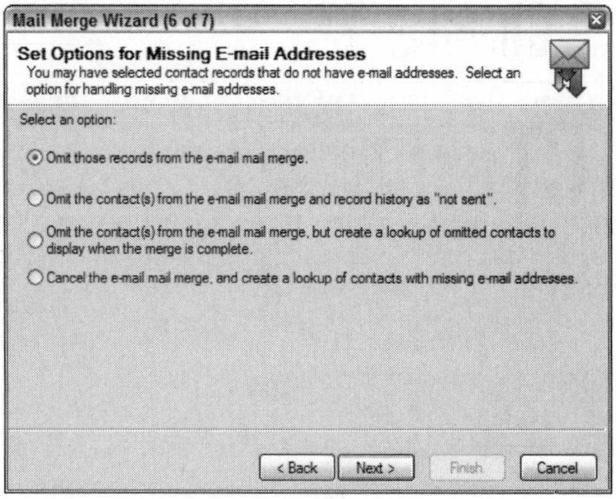

Figure 11-5:
Determine
the
recipients of
your mail
merge.

Congratulations! You have now completed in a very short time what used to take hours and hours of work. Well done!

Chapter 12

ACT! E-Mail

· ·

· ·

*I*n this chapter, I show you how to integrate ACT! with your existing e-mail client. ACT! enables you to send e-mail through it to an individual contact in your database, to a selected group of contacts in your database, and to people who are not in your database. You also discover the various preference settings that are crucial in order to e-mail successfully.

Getting Started with ACT! E-Mail

To fully understand the e-mail portion of ACT!, you must understand the concept of the e-mail client. An *e-mail client* is an application that runs on a personal computer or workstation and enables you to send, receive, and organize e-mail. A senior executive at SAGE Software once told me, "ACT! is not in the business of designing e-mail clients." What that means is that ACT! isn't built to replace your existing e-mail client; rather, ACT! works on top of it. It also means that if you really want to send out a lot of e-mail using ACT!, you probably want to investigate one of the add-on products that I mention in Chapter 24.

As of this writing, ACT! 2006 supports the following e-mail clients:

✔ Internet Mail (an internal stand-alone e-mail client that supports the use of your SMTP and POP3 settings)

✔ Outlook

✔ Outlook Express

✔ Eudora

✔ Lotus Notes

For years, ACT! users could not use America Online (AOL) as their e-mail client if they wanted to integrate with ACT!. Programs such as Yahoo!, Hotmail, and AOL use the IMAP protocol. ACT!, like most e-mail clients, requires the SMTP/POP protocol favored by most Internet service providers (ISPs). (Don't sweat all the acronyms; just stick with me here.) However, I know a work-around for those of you who can't — or won't — give up your AOL. Outlook lets you configure an IMAP e-mail account. When prompted, set the Incoming mail server (IMAP) to `imap.aol.com` and the Outgoing mail server (SMTP) to `smtp.aol.com`.

The two most commonly used e-mail clients are Outlook and Outlook Express in the Windows environment. For business purposes, Outlook is probably the e-mail client of choice. With more features than Outlook Express, it's more attuned to the business environment. Outlook comes bundled with most versions of Microsoft Office and is a common fixture on most office computers. Outlook Express comes as part of the Windows operating system. Because it's a much more basic program, Outlook Express isn't as often used for business e-mailing.

Setting Your E-Mail Preferences

If you initially set up your database using the Getting Started Wizard (see Chapter 3, where I show you how to work your way through the wizard), you already specified your e-mail client. If you're working on an existing database, here's what you must do to configure ACT! for e-mail:

1. **Test to make sure that your e-mail is functioning correctly outside of ACT!.**

   Before you configure your e-mail preferences in ACT!, I recommend testing your e-mail to make sure that it's working correctly. Send a test e-mail to your significant other using Outlook or Outlook Express. Doing so helps eliminate problems if you have trouble e-mailing in ACT! for some reason.

2. **Choose Tools⇨Preferences and then click the E-Mail tab.**

   The E-mail Preferences dialog box appears, as shown in Figure 12-1.

3. **On the E-Mail tab, click the Composing Options button.**

   The Composing Options dialog box opens, as shown in Figure 12-2, where you set preferences for your ACT! e-mail.

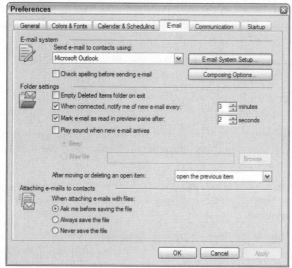

Figure 12-1:
The E-mail
Preferences
dialog box.

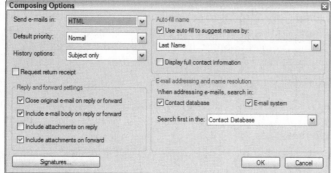

Figure 12-2:
Set e-mail
composing
options
here.

4. Choose from the following options:

- *Send E-Mails In:* Lets you select HyperText Markup Language (HTML) or plain text for the default format type of new messages.

- *Default Priority:* Allows you to select a Low, Normal, or High priority as the default preference for all your new e-mail.

- *History Options:* Allows you to select the history type that's recorded after you send an e-mail. You can choose to have nothing, only the subject, the subject and full body, or an attached copy of your message recorded on the History tab.

- *Request Return Receipt:* Prompts the recipient of your message to automatically send a notification when he or she receives your e-mail.

- *Close Original E-Mail on Reply or Forward:* Closes the original message window when replying to or forwarding e-mail.

- *Include E-Mail Body on Reply or Forward:* Instructs ACT! to include the original message text when you reply to or forward a message.

- *Include Attachments on Reply:* Instructs ACT! to include the original attachment when you reply to a message that includes an attachment.

- *Include Attachments on Forward:* Same as the preceding bullet, except that this option applies to messages with attachments that you forward.

- *Use Auto-Fill to Suggest Names By:* Instructs ACT! to automatically complete the rest of a recipient's name after you type the first several letters of it. You can choose to base this automatic completion on a first name, last name, company, or e-mail address basis.

- *E-Mail Addressing and Name Resolution:* Determines whether you want the auto-fill to search through the contact database (ACT!) and/or the e-mail system database (Outlook or Outlook Express) to find recipient names. You can also indicate which database you like to have ACT! search through first.

5. Click the Signatures button.

The E-Mail Signatures dialog box pops open. Here you type your signature and any other information that you want to appear in your new e-mail messages.

If you want to include a hyperlink to your Web site or email address or if you want to include some sort of a graphic in your signature, create that HTML code in a program such as FrontPage and paste the code into the E-Mail Signatures dialog box.

6. Click OK when you finish setting your signature preferences.

The signature appears every time that you originate a brand-new e-mail from the ACT! E-mail window to a contact or contacts. When you click the contact's e-mail address or choose Write⇨E-mail Message, ACT! automatically uses the `emailbody.adt` template discussed in Chapter 11 rather than the signature that you just created.

7. After you set all your Composing Options preferences, click OK.

The Preferences dialog box reappears.

8. Click the E-mail System Setup button.

The E-mail Setup Wizard opens, as shown in Figure 12-3.

Figure 12-3:
The E-mail
Setup
Wizard.

9. **Select your preferred e-mail client and then click Next.**

- *Internet Mail:* If you select Internet Mail, you have a bit of work to do, as you can see in Figure 12-4. You're prompted to fill in several screens full of information including your user name, e-mail address, password, and the SMTP and POP3 assigned to you by your e-mail service provider. (You might also be asked for your shoe size and blood type.) If you don't have this information you'll have to call your ISP to get it.

- *Outlook:* If you select Outlook, you're asked whether you want to use your default Outlook settings and to choose from the signatures that you composed in Steps 5 and 6.

10. **On the final screen of the E-mail Setup Wizard, click the Finish button.**

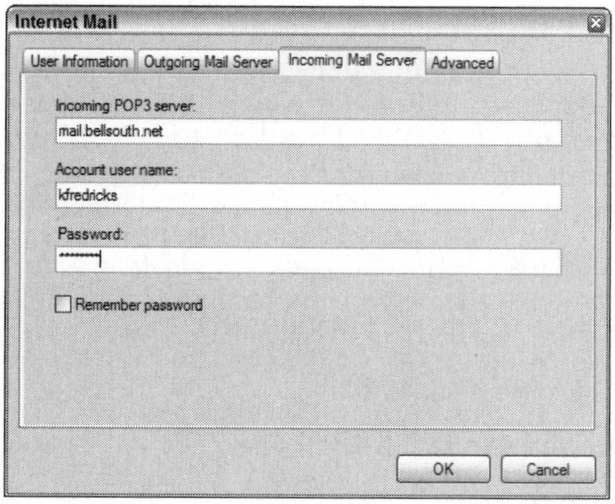

Figure 12-4:
Setting up
Internet
Mail.

E-Mailing Your Contacts

A benefit of sending e-mail from within ACT! is that a history of the event is added to your contact's History tab each and every time that you send an e-mail. E-mail is an increasingly popular form of communication, so having a history of all the e-mail that you send to each of your contacts helps you keep track of it all. You can send e-mail messages to one or more contacts and attach contact records, group records, or files to your messages.

Depending on how you like to reach your contacts, you can send e-mail to them using ACT! in a variety of ways. You might send a one-time e-mail to an individual contact, or you might send a form e-mail to either an individual or a whole group of your contacts. You might also want to send a spur-of-the-moment message to one contact — or even thousands of your contacts. Explore the possibilities.

E-mailing an individual contact

To send an e-mail to the current contact, follow these steps:

1. **Create a new e-mail message with one of three methods.**

   Although these three methods all result in a new message (see Figure 12-5), they work in slightly different ways.

   - *Click in the contact's E-Mail field.* The contact's name appears in the To line, and the wording of the `emailbody.adt` template appears in the body of the e-mail.

   - *Choose Write⇨E-Mail Message.* The contact's name appears in the To line, and the wording of the `emailbody.adt` template appears in the body of the e-mail.

     The `emailbody.adt` template works exactly like all other ACT! templates. For a refresher course in template creation, check out Chapter 11. Because the first two e-mailing methods use a template, they can be personalized to automatically include any tidbit of the contact's information that you want. My template, for example, includes the recipient's first name in the body of the e-mail.

   - *Click the E-Mail icon on the Nav bar and then click New.* The To line is blank, and the signature you created appears in the body. This method does not use the `emailbody.adt` template.

2. **In the Subject field, type a subject.**

3. **Edit or create the message in the text box.**

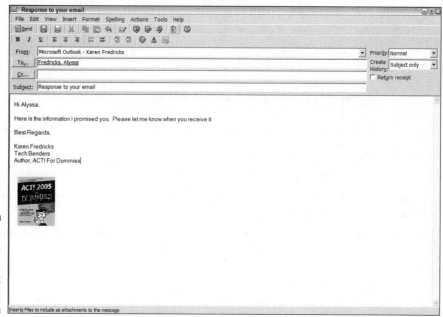

Figure 12-5:
Sending an
e-mail to the
current
contact.

4. **Feel free to pick an option or two from the New Message toolbars, depending on how fancy you want to get with your e-mail.**

When you create an e-mail in ACT!, two toolbars appear in the New Message window. If you hover your mouse over the various tools, a ToolTip appears, explaining the function of each button.

- The *top toolbar* enables you to send attachments along with your e-mail. You're probably already familiar with the concept of file attachments. ACT! also allows you to send either a single contact record, a group of contact records, or a company to recipients (if they're using ACT!).

- The *bottom toolbar* enables you to make changes to the text formatting exactly as you do in any word processor. Notice also two buttons (refer to Figure 12-5) that allow you to insert either a graphic or a hyperlink into your e-mail message.

If the bottom toolbar is grayed out, you probably set your e-mail preference to plain text. Try switching it over to HTML if you want to add a splash of color to your e-mails — or at least if you want to be able to use the formatting toolbar!

5. **(Optional) Change the default options for Priority, Create History, and Return Receipt (upper-right).**

See Step 4 in the section "Setting Your E-Mail Preferences," where I explain these options.

6. Click Send.

Off your mail goes. Depending on the Create History option that you chose, a message appears on the contact's History tab.

Sending mass e-mails

ACT! makes a distinction between sending e-mail and sending *merged* e-mail. Merged e-mails all share the following characteristics:

✔ When you send a merged e-mail, ACT! relies on a template.

✔ When you send a merged e-mail, you must include at least one contact field in your template.

✔ E-mail merging in ACT! allows each individual contact name to appear in the To line rather than having to send the mail using the Bcc (blind carbon copy) field.

Important things to consider when sending a mass e-mail

Before jumping headfirst into the world of mass e-mailing, consider the following important points:

✔ **Test your e-mail preferences.** You should test your e-mail preferences before sending your missive out to thousands of people. If you don't, you might find yourself with a thousand e-mails in your outbox that can't be sent. Try sending a sample e-mail to a friend or colleague.

✔ **Test your e-mail template.** Again, testing your message before sending it across the universe is always a good idea. Try sending the message to a co-worker or colleague first. Having correct spelling and punctuation isn't a bad idea, either. Make sure the graphics can be viewed correctly as mentioned in Chapter 11.

✔ **Check with your ISP.** Many ISPs have implemented safeguards against *spam*. Before you send an e-mail to all the contacts in your database, call your ISP to find out how many e-mails you can send at a time. If your ISP limits the number of e-mails you can send at one time, you need to send your mailings in smaller groups or purchase an add-on product that sends your e-mail in batches. You can discover more about these products in Chapter 24.

✔ **Read up on the Can Spam laws.** Laws are in place that require your e-mail to contain various elements, including your correct contact information and a way for recipients to opt out should they not want to hear from you.

Sending non-merged mass e-mails

If you're not entirely comfortable with the concepts of e-mail blasting, you might want to start out by sending an e-mail to your contacts rather than attempting an actual e-mail merge. This way is great for less computer-oriented ACT! users to reach a large number of contacts.

You can send non-merged e-mail at the spur of the moment because it doesn't involve the creation of a template. However, you cannot customize the To or Subject portions of the e-mail with any of your contact's specific information.

To send an e-mail to any number of your contacts, here's all you have to do:

1. **Create a lookup (Chapter 6 shows you how) to find the contacts to whom you want to send the e-mail.**

   For example, if you want to send an e-mail to all customers in the Southeastern Region, create the lookup and then narrow it to include only those contacts that have an e-mail address.

   Narrow your lookup by choosing Lookup⇨E-Mail Address. Then select Narrow Lookup for the current lookup and then click Non-empty Fields. *Voilà!* Your lookup is narrowed to include only those contacts having an e-mail address.

2. **Click the E-Mail icon on ACT!'s Nav bar.**

   The ACT! E-Mail dialog box opens.

   If you set your e-mail preferences to either Outlook or Outlook Express, you now see a mirror image of either your Outlook or Outlook Express folders.

3. **Click the New icon on the e-mail window's toolbar.**

   The New icon is easy to spot — it's the icon that says *New* on it!

4. **Click the To, Cc, or Bcc button.**

   The Select Recipients dialog box opens, as shown in Figure 12-6. Here's where you choose multiple contacts who all receive your e-mail blast.

5. **In the Address Book drop-down list, select the address book that you want to use.**

   You can select to use either the currently opened ACT! database or your Outlook e-mail addresses.

6. **In the Select From drop-down list, choose All Contacts, Current Lookup, Groups, or Companies.**

   - *All Contacts:* Provides you with a list of all your contacts

   - *Current Lookup:* Limits the list of recipients to contacts in your current lookup

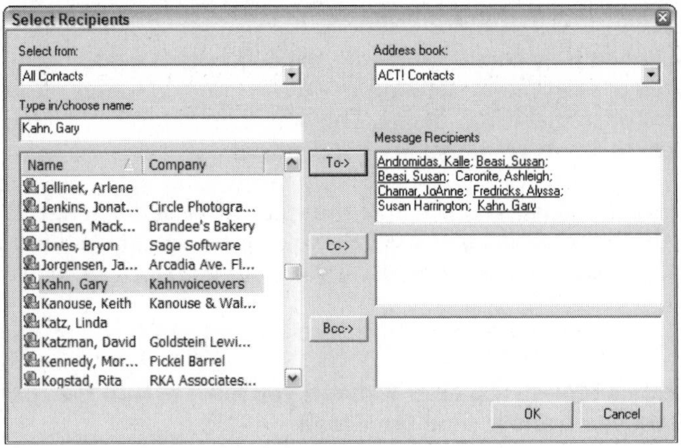

Figure 12-6:
Select
recipients
for an e-mail
blast.

- *Groups:* Displays a list of the groups in your current ACT! database

- *Companies:* Displays a list of the companies in your database

7. Select one or more names from the list on the left.

- To select a *single* name, click it.

- To select a *contiguous list* of names, click the first name in the list, press Shift, and then click the last name in the list that you want to select.

- To select *multiple (noncontiguous) names* in the list, click the first name that you want to select and then press Ctrl while clicking any and all names that you want to select.

8. Click the To button.

The names that you select appear in the Message Recipients box.

Unless you want all the recipients of the message to know the names of everyone else who received your e-mail, click the Bcc button rather than the To or Cc buttons.

9. Click OK.

You return to the New Message window. The names of all your intended recipients now appear in the To (or Cc or Bcc) area of your e-mail message.

10. If you like, change any of the e-mail options.

Go for it! Insert a link to your Web site or attach a file. You find plenty of options in the New Message menu.

11. Verify that all your intended recipients have a valid e-mail address.

ACT! automatically checks to ensure that an e-mail address exists for each of your recipients. If you look at Figure 12-6, you'll notice that some of the names in the Message Recipients field are underlined; those represent the contacts with valid e-mail addresses. If a name does not have a valid e-mail address, it's not underlined. When you send the message, you're prompted to add any e-mail addresses that ACT! doesn't find.

ACT! isn't perfect — although it comes pretty darned close! The e-mail checker finds contacts with blank e-mail addresses as well as those missing key pieces of information, such as the @ character. If you don't know someone's e-mail address, leaving it blank is better than inserting something cute like N/A that can confuse — or at least slow down — the checker.

Don't know whether an e-mail address is correct? Right-click any underlined name and choose Properties to sneak a peek at the e-mail address you have on record for that contact.

12. **Click Send.**

   You might want to pat yourself on the back, content with the knowledge that you have mastered the art of sending an e-mail blast.

Sending a templated e-mail to a party of one

Using ACT! to create an e-mail merge enables you to send personalized templates for each recipient. The cool thing about ACT! templates is that you can use them for either snail mailing or e-mailing. In Chapter 11, I show you how to produce a mass mailing. The Mail Merge Wizard provides you with the option to e-mail as well as snail mail.

If you want to send a thank-you e-mail to just one of your contacts and don't want to go through the entire wizard again, here's a few shortcuts.

1. **From any ACT! screen, choose Write⇨Other Document and chose the template that you want to use for the body of your e-mail.**

2. **Generate the e-mail message.**

   • *In Word:* Choose ACT⇨Send E-mail. You have the choice of sending the template as an attachment or as the body of the e-mail. After you make your selection, select the name of your recipient and click OK.

   • *In the ACT! word processor:* Choose File⇨Send⇨E-mail.

Figure 12-7 shows how the message was personalized to include both the contact's name and pertinent information.

Mail merge must include at least one mail merge field. If you aren't personalizing your e-mails, you need to choose a different method of e-mailing. Also keep in mind that you'll probably want to create a lookup of the contacts you want to e-mail *before* starting the e-mail merge so that your e-mail will reach the correct recipients!

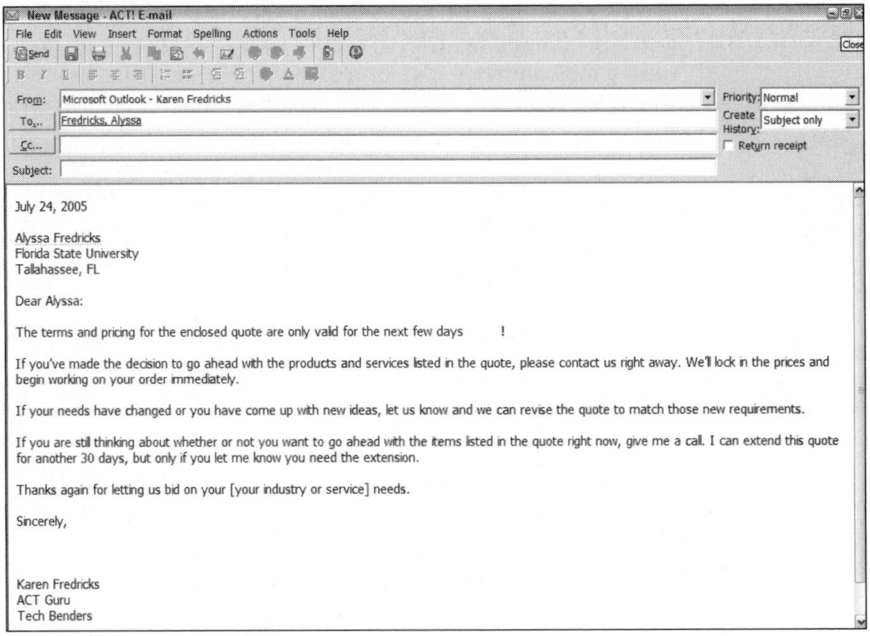

Figure 12-7:
Sending a
personal-
ized e-mail
template.

Editing e-mail addresses

The one critical ingredient of sending an e-mail is having an e-mail address. No doubt you've already added many e-mail addresses to your ACT! database, but I'm guessing that you haven't yet discovered a good way to correct or change existing e-mail addresses.

ACT! is designed to launch the e-mail window when you click the E-Mail field in the Contact Detail window. This feature allows you to easily send e-mail in ACT! but makes editing existing addresses difficult.

To edit an E-Mail address, try one of these methods:

✔ Use the Tab key to move the cursor to the E-Mail field. After the cursor is in an E-Mail field, you can edit it by clicking the E-Mail field's drop-down arrow.

✔ Move the mouse pointer over the E-Mail field and right-click. You can now edit the E-Mail field.

✔ Hold the cursor over the E-mail field and wait a few seconds; the cursor changes from a hand to a vertical line.

Working with Incoming E-Mail

When you're proficient at sending e-mail, you need to know how to read an e-mail message. Although you can continue to view your mail using your existing mail client, you want to familiarize yourself with the ACT! e-mail client. After you open up ACT!'s e-mail by clicking the E-mail icon on the Navigation bar, you might want to perform one of the following tasks:

✔ **Open a message.** Double-clicking the message does the trick.

✔ **Read messages in another folder.** Simply click the folder in the Folder List.

✔ **Sort your e-mail messages.** You can change the order by clicking any column header.

✔ **Create a new contact record from an incoming e-mail (if the contact isn't already in your database).** Right-click the message and choose Create Contact From Sender.

This is a particularly timesaving feature of ACT! and ensures that potential contacts don't get lost in the shuffle.

✔ **Attach the e-mail to a contact's History tab.** Just like you can create an automatic history record each time that you *send* an e-mail to a contact, you can also create a history each time that you *receive* an e-mail from a contact.

   a. Choose Actions⇨Attach⇨Attach to Contact.

   b. On the Attach E-mail to Contact dialog box that appears, click the name of the contact(s) to associate with the e-mail message.

   c. Click the To button and then click OK.

   ACT! places a note on the contact's History tab indicating that you received an e-mail from the contact.

✔ **Schedule a follow-up.** Right-click the message and choose Create Activity from Message.

You can now schedule a follow-up; the subject of the e-mail automatically appears in the Regarding area of your activity.

Part IV
Advanced ACT!ing

The 5th Wave   By Rich Tennant

@RICHTENNANT

"Look— you've got Project Manager, Acct Manager, and Opportunity Manager, but Sucking Up to the Manager just isn't a field the program comes with."

In this part . . .

*O*n the surface, ACT! is a deceptively easy program to master. However, those of you who are so inclined — or didn't run fast enough — might want to add ACT! database Administrator to your current job description. The database Administrator is in charge of adding new fields to the database and making sure that they are artistically placed onto your layout. Need to take your database with you? You'll be able to synchronize your database with a little help from this section. Best of all, when things go wrong, guess whom everyone will turn to? Not to worry, though — just turn to this section for help.

Chapter 13

Creating Contact Fields

• •

• •

I am a firm believer that a little knowledge is a dangerous thing. Although adding a field to your ACT! database is not a hard thing to do, it is something that should be well thought out and planned in advance. This is particularly true if you plan on sharing your database with other users. Planning is important because you usually have a goal in mind for your database. If your goal is to create a report with three columns — one for the contact name, one for the birthday, and one for the Social Security number — you need to make sure that all those fields exist in your database. Planning also prevents you from adding thousands of contacts to your database, only to find you have to modify each record to include information that was omitted the first time around!

To add a field to your database, you must be a Database Manager or Administrator; the makers of ACT! made this a requirement so that you understand the importance of this responsibility. So unless you have administrative rights to the database, you don't even have to read this chapter! I suppose you still could, just for curiosity's sake, but it isn't necessary.

In this chapter, I show you (all of you who have Administrator- or Manager-level rights to your databases anyway) not only how to add new fields to an ACT! database but also how to set the various field parameters to help users use the database more effectively and efficiently.

Before getting started, I want to briefly outline the three steps involved with adding fields to a database:

1. Understand why you want to add fields and what purpose these fields will serve.

2. Determine what fields you're going to add and what drop-down lists will be available in each.

I can't stress enough the importance of this step. Plan ahead! Or you might end up with a big mess. . . .

3. Add the fields.

And, *voilà!* You're done. (Okay, this one has a whole bunch of steps, but you get what I mean.)

Understanding the Concept of Fields

For most of you, adding a field to your database will be easy. After all, you're good at following directions. However, for some of you, knowing *why* to enter a field can prove to be more challenging.

To explore the question of why, I first want to reiterate the basic concept of fields. What the heck is a field? A *field* is a single piece of information. In general, a field contains just one piece of information. For example, you have only one business ZIP code; therefore, you have one business Zip Code field. Alternatively, you probably have several phone numbers: home, business, toll-free, cellular, fax, beeper . . . and the list goes on. Each of these phone numbers requires a separate field.

A good field holds one fairly specific piece of information. A bad field contains too much information. For example, having a separate field for your street address, city, state, and ZIP code is a good thing. These separate fields allow you to perform a lookup based on any of the criteria: You could find clients by ZIP code, city, or state. An example of a bad field is lumping all the address information into a single field; in this example, you'd then lose your ability to perform a lookup by ZIP code, city, or state. (Need a refresher on performing lookups? Head to Chapter 6.)

Consider the following basic rules when determining the criteria for adding a field to your database:

✔ **A field contains an important tidbit of information.**

✔ **A field can be used to perform a query or sort.** For example, you might want to send a mailing to all your customers in New York and sort your mailing by ZIP code. To do this sort, you need separate fields for contact type, state, *and* ZIP code.

✔ **A field can be used to insert information into a report or template.** If you want to create letters thanking one person for buying a purple polka dot vase and another for buying a leopard-print vase, you need a vase type field.

Do Your Homework!

Okay, I admit it — I'm a former secondary school teacher, and I guess that background just naturally spills over into my ACT! consulting. Well class, pretend you're back in school because you're going to be assigned some homework. To be politically correct, I could have said you're now entering the *pre-planning stage of your ACT! implementation.* But I still consider it important homework that you must complete *prior* to jumping in and adding new fields to your database, so your assignment is as follows:

1. **Jot down all the fields that you want to see in your database.**

   Most of the fields you want to see such as company, name, phone number, and address are already included in ACT!. What you need to decide here is what fields, if any, are specific to your business.

2. **Scurry around the office and collect any documents that you want ACT! to create for you. This includes both forms and form letters.**

   You're going to have to get a little high-tech here, but I think you can handle it. Get out your trusty highlighter and highlight any of the information in each document that is contact specific. For example, each contact has its own unique address. Maybe you're thanking particular contacts to meet to discuss purchasing widgets (as opposed to gadgets, which you also sell). This means that you need a Product field.

3. **Think how to populate the fields with drop-down lists. Then, on the list that you started in Step 1, jot them down to the side of each of the fields.**

   For example, if you run a modeling agency, you might need a field for hair color. The drop-down choices could contain red, blonde, black, and punk pink.

4. **Sketch out any reports that you want to create from ACT! and add the column headings to the now rather long list that you created in Step 1.**

   The idea here is to get your thoughts down on paper so that you can visualize how you want your ACT! report to look. If you already have a sample of your report in Excel, you can use that. If not, get out your trusty pencil and outline on a piece of paper what you like your report to actually look like.

5. **Get out a red pen. At the top of your paper, write 100% and Well Done and then draw a smiley face. Hang your list on your refrigerator.**

   Okay, that last step isn't really necessary, but now you're well on your way to having the database of your dreams!

Dust off your thinking cap as you create your list. Sometimes one field will do the job, and other times you might need multiple fields. For example, suppose you sell widgets that are red, white, or blue. In one scenario, a customer needs to buy only one widget; in this case, you create a product field with three choices in the drop-down list — red, white, or blue. Or perhaps you manufacture a different kind of widget; in this case, a customer would hopefully buy one of each color. This time, your purposes would be better served by creating three fields — one for each type of widget.

Adding a New Field to Your Database

Believe it or not, after completing your homework (see the preceding section), you're done with the hard part of the task. The actual addition of fields is relatively easy; just follow the steps.

Only an ACT! user with Administrator or Manager privileges can add new fields to an ACT! database. If the Define Fields option is grayed out in Step 1, you aren't logged in as one.

1. **In any ACT! view, choose Tools⇨Define Fields.**

   The Contact Detail window is generally a good place to start for most of your customization projects. The Define Fields dialog box appears, as shown in Figure 13-1. The View Fields For drop-down list indicates that you're editing or adding new contact fields to the database. You can also add new group, company, and opportunity fields to your database by switching the View Fields For list to the appropriate choice.

Figure 13-1:
The Define Fields dialog box.

ACT! does not allow you to add new fields or edit existing fields while other users are logged on to the database. If you see the warning shown in Figure 13-2, you know that other users are indeed currently logged on to the database. What to do? Storm over to their workstations in a huff and demand that they exit out of ACT! immediately. If that doesn't work, consider bribery. Conversely, as long as you are editing fields, other users cannot access the database. If you look in ACT!'s title bar, you even notice that (Locked) now appears. To avoid frustration on everyone's part, you might want to explain this concept to the users of your database.

Figure 13-2:
Another user is using the database.

2. **Start by renaming one of the 10 user fields. You find all your fields listed alphabetically by field name. Select one of them.**

   This is where you need to drag your homework off the refrigerator and type in one of the fields that you had planned to create in the Field Name box. ACT! supplies you with ten user fields that you can customize to better serve the needs of your business. After all, *Social Security Number* is a lot more meaningful than *User 2*.

3. **Click the Edit Field option in the Field Tasks section.**

   You're rewarded with a friendly looking window that looks exactly like the one shown in Figure 13-3.

   When you run out of user fields to rename, feel free to click the Create New Field option in the Field Tasks section.

   ACT! rewards you with a blank, new field in the Field Name box and assigns it the name *New Field* until you can think of something better to call it. At that point, the following steps are identical to the steps you follow for editing a field.

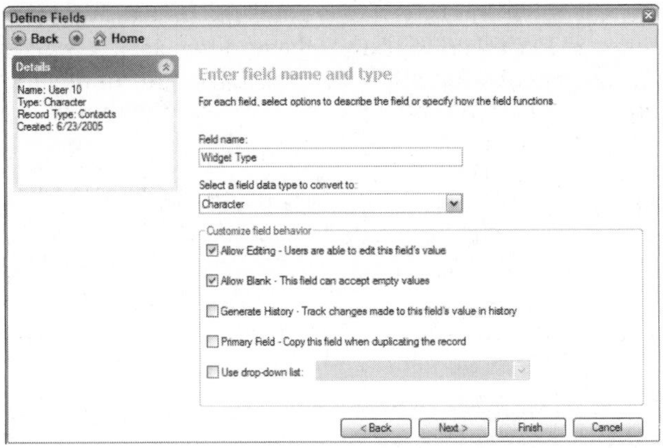

Figure 13-3:
Defining an
ACT! field.

4. **Type a field name.**

   Try not to get too fancy or long-winded when naming your fields. Using special characters such as <, >, $, or : can cause problems when creating queries and mail merges, so I recommend that you not use them. You can use spaces in the field name, but don't end a field name with a space. And because long field names can be hard to place into mail merge templates and layouts, you're better off keeping field names as short as possible.

5. **From the Select a Field Data Type to Convert To drop-down menu (refer to Figure 13-3), choose a field type for the field that you're adding.**

   You can create a variety of different types of fields. Actually, there are 18 different field types, but who's counting? If you're renaming one of the user fields, your choices include:

   • *Character:* This is probably the most common of the field type choices; a *character field* can contain both numbers and characters. It's kind of a one-size-fits-all kind of field.

   • *Currency:* As its name implies, this is for fields relating to cold, hard cash. The field comes equipped with a dollar sign, appropriate commas, optional decimal places, and a sunroof (optional).

   • *Decimal:* This field accepts only numbers, a decimal point, and more numbers.

   • *Initial-Caps:* At first glance, this seems like a nifty option. The idea behind the Initial Capitals option is that you can turn *KAREN FREDRICKS* into *Karen Fredricks.* Seems like a great idea on paper. In reality, however, you end up with *Ibm Corporation* and *Marcus Welby Md.*

   • *Lowercase:* i suppose you might want to type in all lowercase. i just can't imagine why.

- *Memo:* This is where you can store a large amount of information that you don't want to risk burying away amidst your other notes. For example, you might want to include your driving directions in this area.

- *Number:* This option enables you to enter only numbers into a field. Say you want to find all your customers that have more than 30 employees. You can easily search for a number greater than *30,* whereas you can't possibly search for a number greater than *thirty.*

- *Upper Case:* I NEVER TYPE IN ALL UPPERCASE BECAUSE I FEEL LIKE I'M SCREAMING. BESIDES, I'M AFRAID I MIGHT DEVELOP POLYPS ON MY FINGERTIPS.

- *URL Address:* Use this field type if you need to associate another Web address with your contacts.

ACT! already comes equipped with e-mail and Web site fields for your viewing pleasure. And, you can add several additional e-mail addresses to the existing ACT! E-mail field.

If you're creating a brand-new, field ACT! gives you all of the choices on the menu above plus a couple of brand-new ones:

- *Address:* Talk about a timesaver! When you designate a field as an address field, ACT! automatically creates seven fields: three for the street address, and another four for the city, state, ZIP, and country.

- *Annual Event:* Like it or not, some events take place once a year. Use this field to find birthdays, anniversaries, and yearly renewals regardless of the year.

- *Date:* A really cool thing happens when you make a field a Date field. When the time comes for you to enter information into a Date field, you see a tiny little calendar that enables you to select a date. The calendar is cute, but more importantly, it supplies a useful purpose. If you create a field for a birthday and make it a Character field, the other local yokels using the database might get creative and input anything from Jan 1 and January 1st to 01/01 and 1/1. Finding all birth dates in the month of January would become an exercise in futility.

- *Date/Time:* When you want to be really exacting, create a Date/Time field to record the exact date and time of an event.

- *E-mail:* It used to be that everyone you know had several phone numbers. Now, the chances are pretty good that your contacts have numerous e-mail addresses. Here's your opportunity to include as many as you like.

- *Phone:* In Chapter 4, I show you all those nifty things that ACT! does to speed up the data input process. If you designate a field to be a Phone field, you automatically get a year's supply of dashes.

- *Picture:* A picture is worth a thousand words, and here's where you can stick a picture of each client or a picture of each product that they bought.

- *Time:* If time is of the essence, this is where you can input a time.

- *Yes/No:* This actually creates a check box field that you can mark. Call me old-fashioned, but I think *Check Box* would have been a more appropriate name. To further confuse the issue, a query on this field looks for True or False values.

6. **Assign any of the five optional attributes for the field being added and click Next. Feel free to choose several attributes if you wish.**

   Depending on the field type you select, all these features might not be available. For example, if you choose the Date field with the cute little calendar, you won't have the drop-down list option.

   - *Allow Editing:* This enables any of your users to add new data to a field.

   - *Allow Blank:* If you want to require that a field must be filled in, you need to remove the check mark from this field. Use this option if you want to require a user to enter information into a certain field.

   - *Generate History:* This neat little feature generates a history on the History tab when you change the contents of the field.

   - *Primary Field:* When you duplicate a contact record, the primary fields are the fields that are duplicated.

   - *Use Drop-Down List:* When you choose this feature, you can either pick an existing drop-down list or create a new, unique drop-down list. I cover creating drop-down lists later in this chapter in the "Creating a drop-down list field" section.

7. **Customize your field further by choosing from the following optional selections and then click Next.**

   The next Define Fields screen — Customize field behavior — opens, offering you a few more choices for your editing pleasure.

   - *Default Value:* If 80 percent of your database consists of customers, you might assign *Customer* as the default value of the ID/Status field.

   - *Field Format:* If you want dashes or another symbol to appear automatically in a field, here's the place to do it by inserting the symbol where you want data to go. For example, a Social Security number looks like ###-##-####.

   - *Field Length:* You might want to limit the number of characters that a user can enter into a given field; for example, you can limit a field looking for values of Yes or No to three characters.

Trim the field length whenever possible. If the longest value in a field is Yes and the field length is 75, you've created a lot of dead space. Cutting down the field length helps reduce the size of your database — and ultimately increases performance.

8. Set optional triggers.

Adding a trigger to a field causes something magical to happen when entering data into a field. For example, you might want an Excel spreadsheet to open when you move your cursor into the field, and an activity series to start when you leave the field. In Figure 13-4, you see three ways to start a trigger: when changing a field, when entering a field, and when leaving a field.

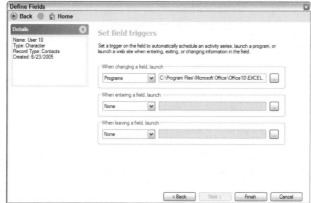

Figure 13-4: Attaching a trigger to a field.

For each type of trigger, you can assign one of three possibilities:

- *None:* If you want nothing to occur, choose this option.

- *Program:* Clicking the Browse button allows you to navigate to virtually any file in your computer. You can browse to a program, a URL, or even to a specific file.

- *Activity Series:* Clicking the Browse button takes you to a list of the activity series that you created. If you haven't created any activity series, pay a visit to Chapter 8 to find out how.

9. Click Finish.

Many of the neat add-on products that complement ACT! are designed as field triggers; when you purchase the add-on, you might need to link the product to a specific field. Check my Web site at www.techbenders.com/act4dummies.htm to find out more about some of these special trigger products.

Working with Lists

The sure-fire way to destroy a database is by adding information in an inconsistent manner. Drop-down lists help ensure that users input data in a uniform way. As an extra, added bonus, drop-down lists also save you time; when you type in the first several letters of an item in your drop-down list, ACT! responds by completing the word for you.

In ACT!, you find three major list types. Two of them, the Product List and the Process List, are associated with your Opportunities. The other list type, Drop-Down, is associated with your contact, group, company, and opportunity fields. Although you can add new items to a list as you are using it, managing your lists in one central location — the edit fields area — is easier.

Creating a drop-down list field

Associating a drop-down list with a field requires two things:

✔ Specifying that the field is to contain a drop-down list

✔ Adding items to the drop-down list

Although which one comes first doesn't matter — the field or the drop-down list — I start by creating the field that is to contain a drop-down list:

1. **From any ACT! window, choose Tools⇨Define Fields.**

   The Define Fields dialog box opens in all its glory (refer to Figure 13-1). You might even notice three items in the List Tasks area. Hold that thought — I discuss those in the next section.

2. **Click the field name that you want to contain a drop-down list and then click the Edit Field option in the Field Tasks area.**

   The first of the Define Fields dialog windows open.

3. **Select the Use Drop-Down List check box.**

   If you want to use an existing drop-down list, here's your golden opportunity. For example, the last time I checked, there were 50 U.S. states; those states are the same for my mailing, business, and home addresses. You could have one State drop-down list and associate it with the mailing, business, and home state fields.

4. **Click Finish.**

Whew! That was pretty easy. If you're using an existing drop-down list, you're finished. However, if you need to build a drop-down list from scratch, you have more work. Fortunately, ACT! returns you to the Define Fields dialog box, which is right where you need to be to create or edit a drop-down list.

Creating a drop-down list

This might seem like a case of "Which came first, the chicken or the egg?" In the previous section, I tell you how to associate a field with an already created drop-down list. For example, if you create a mailing list address, you can use the existing State drop-down list to avoid having to type in all the states into a new drop-down list. In other cases, you need to go back and create the drop-down list. Here's what you need to do:

1. **From any ACT! screen, choose Tools⇨Define Fields (refer to Figure 13-1).**

   If you just created the drop-down field, you can skip this step because you're already there!

2. **Select Manage Drop-Down Lists from the List Tasks area.**

   The Create, Edit, or Delete Drop-Down Lists window appears.

   - *To create a drop-down list:* Click Create Drop-Down List from the Drop-Down List Tasks area.

   - *To edit a drop-down list:* Select the drop-down list and then click Edit Drop-Down List from the Drop-Down List Tasks area.

   The Enter Drop-Down List Name and Type window opens, as shown in Figure 13-5.

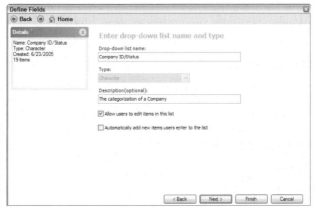

Figure 13-5: Configuring a drop-down list.

3. **Configure the following drop-down list options and then click Next:**

   • *Drop-Down List Name:* To make things less complicated for your-self, use a name that very closely resembles the name of the field that will be associated with the drop-down list.

   • *Type:* Choose what type of field goes in the list — for example, character.

   • *Description:* If you have a lot of drop-down lists, you might need to give your list a bit of further explanation.

   • *Allow Users to Edit Items in This List:* Users have the ability to edit the drop-down list while they enter contact information.

   • *Automatically Add New Items Users Enter to the List:* This lets your users define the items that will be used in a drop-down list by auto-matically adding each item they enter into the drop-down list.

Be very cautious about including those last two options. Allowing users to edit items in the drop-down list can carve away at the standardization that you've strived so hard to maintain. If you decide to allow users to automatically add new items to a drop-down list, you might want to do so only temporarily. Although this option is a great way to build a drop-down list from scratch, you run the chance of creating a mess. Make sure that all users have a good idea of the kind of items that should — and shouldn't — be added to the drop-down lists. And, more impor-tantly, make sure they peruse the existing entries in the drop-down list before adding new items to avoid duplication.

4. **From the Enter Drop-Down List Values window, choose one of the fol-lowing options:**

   • *Add:* When you click the Add button, your cursor jumps down to the bottom of your list of drop-down items. Type in the new drop-down item and an optional description, and you're all set.

   • *Delete:* This permanently removes the selected item from the drop-down list. However, previously entered information based on the removed drop-down item still remains in your database.

5. **Type in the drop-down list item and an optional description.**

   Chances are that you don't need to include descriptions in your drop-down list. Once in a while, though, they can prove to be priceless. The State drop-down list consists of the two letter state abbreviations; the description includes the full name of the state for those of us who can never remember whether MA stands for Maine, Maryland, or Massachusetts! You can see what I mean in Figure 13-6.

6. **Click Finish when you finish adding all the items you want to your drop-down list.**

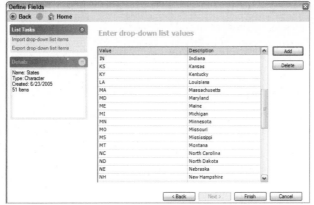

Figure 13-6:
Adding
items to a
drop-down
list.

Managing the Product List

In Chapter 19, you can find almost everything you need to know about the exciting world of Opportunities — and believe me, there are a bunch of cool things. However, in this chapter, you discover how to modify your opportunity fields — and the drop-down lists associated with them. You'll also find out how to input a list of the products or services that you routinely sell to your customers or clients.

Don't think that because your company doesn't sell widgets — or some similar item — that you can't use the Product List. Perhaps a better name for this field would have been Products/Services. At any rate, if you are gaining financially from your customers, use the Product List to help you analyze your profit centers.

To modify your Product List, follow these steps:

1. **From any ACT! screen, choose Tools⇨Define Fields (refer to Figure 13-1).**

   The Define Fields window opens.

2. **Click Manage Product List.**

   The Manage Product List dialog box opens, as shown in Figure 13-7.

3. **Click the Add button.**

   A New Product item appears at the bottom of the list of your product names.

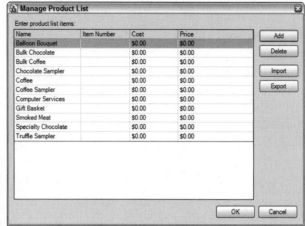

Figure 13-7:
Editing the
Product List.

4. **Fill in the appropriate fields.**

   You can move through the various fields by pressing Tab.

   a. Assign a name to your product.

   b. Enter an item number if you use them.

   c. Add the cost that you pay for the item if applicable.

   d. Include the price you're going to charge your customers for the item if you adhere to a set price structure.

   If your costs and prices fluctuate, feel free to leave those fields blank. You can always change them each time you enter a new sales opportunity.

5. **Click OK to close the Manage Product List dialog box and then click Close to close the Define Fields window.**

Managing the Process List

The ACT! program was originally developed as a sales tool for busy sales people. Today, the product has evolved to the point that just about any industry and individual can benefit by using ACT!. However, the tradition of sales tracking remains, and the Process List is just one of those examples. ACT!'s Process List allows you to set up the steps that everyone in your organization follows when trying to close a sale. You can even associate a probability with each step. It is rumored that you need to contact someone 12 times before you convert them from a prospect to a customer; here's where you can be reminded of where you are in that process.

To edit or create a Process List, follow these steps:

1. **From any ACT! screen, choose Tools⇨Define Fields⇨Manage Process List.**

   The Create, Edit, or Delete Opportunity Processes dialog box, as shown in Figure 13-8, appears. If you already set up a Process List, you see it listed by name, description, and the current stage number in the Process List.

2. **Select one of the following three options and click Next:**

   • *Create New Opportunity Process:* Creates a brand-spanking new Process List.

   • *Edit Opportunity Process:* Allows you to edit an existing Process List.

   • *Delete Opportunity Process:* Deletes an existing Process List. Rather than deleting an existing list, you might decide to make it inactive. You see that option on the next screen.

3. **Double-click a name, description, or probability to change it.**

   If you're editing an existing Process List, modifying an entry by double-clicking is easy. The steps from the previously created Process List appear, as shown in Figure 13-9. If you're creating a new Process List, your processes are empty. Don't worry though — you can fill them up easily enough.

4. **Click the Add or Delete button to further configure your Process List.**

   The stages are numbered. ACT! automatically numbers the stages in a Process List, saving you the effort. If you want, you can change the order by choosing one of the options to move an option either up or down on the list. When you move an option, all subsequent stages automatically renumber.

5. **Click Finish when you're done.**

Figure 13-8:
Creating or editing a sales process.

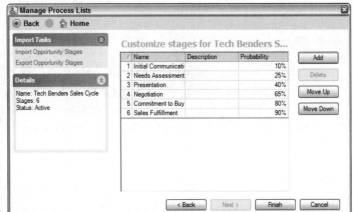

Figure 13-9:
Customizing the stages in a sales process list.

In ACT!, you can often skin a cat or solve a problem in more than one way. You can access the Product and Process lists from two other areas of ACT!:

✔ From any ACT! screen, choose Contacts⇨Opportunities⇨Manage Product (or Process) List.

✔ Scroll down to the bottom of the Product or Process List when creating a new — or editing an existing — opportunity. From there, you can select Edit List.

A Few More Customization Options

Managers and Administrators have all the fun when it comes to ACT! because they can customize a database to their heart's content. In this section, I point out a few commonly overlooked areas that can be customized.

Adding custom activity types

Out of the box, ACT! gives you five activity types: call, meeting, to-do, personal activity, and vacation. You can modify this list of activity types by creating a custom activity type. To add a custom activity type, just follow the bouncing ball:

1. **Choose Schedule⇨Manage⇨Activity Types.**

   The Manage Activity Types dialog box appears, which bears a striking resemblance to Figure 13-10.

2. **Click Add.**

   The Add Activity Type dialog box appears, as seen in Figure 13-11.

   a. Type the name for the activity type in the Name field.

   b. Select the Active - Allow New Activities of This Type check box if you want to allow users to schedule activities of this type.

3. **Create the result options to use when the task is completed.**

   Every ACT! activity has results associated with it. These result choices appear when you clear an activity; once you clear the activity the result you selected is automatically entered into the history tab of the contact associated with the activity. When you create an activity type, two types of results are automatically assigned to it: Completed and Not Completed.

Although you cannot delete these two options, you can edit them. You can also add new result types. When you add a new result type, it becomes available as an option when you clear an activity.

• *To add a new result type:* Click the Add button.

• *To edit a result type:* Click the Edit button.

4. Click OK in the Add Activity Type dialog box.

The activity type appears in the Activity Types list the very next time you schedule an activity.

Don't ask me why, but for some unknown reason, you can't delete an activity type after you create it. However, you can edit the activity type and even change the name of the activity type. Go figure!

Editing priority types

If there is a square inch of ACT! that can't be customized, I haven't found it yet. Even the priorities you use when scheduling activities can be tweaked. ACT! includes five basic priority types: High, Medium-High, Medium, Medium-Low, and Low. However, only three of the priority types (High, Medium and Low) are active. A priority must have Active status in order for it to appear when you schedule an activity. And although you can't add a new priority type, you can rename an existing one if you so desire.

1. From any of the ACT! screens, choose Schedule⇨Manage⇨Priorities.

The Manage Priorities dialog box opens, as seen in Figure 13-12.

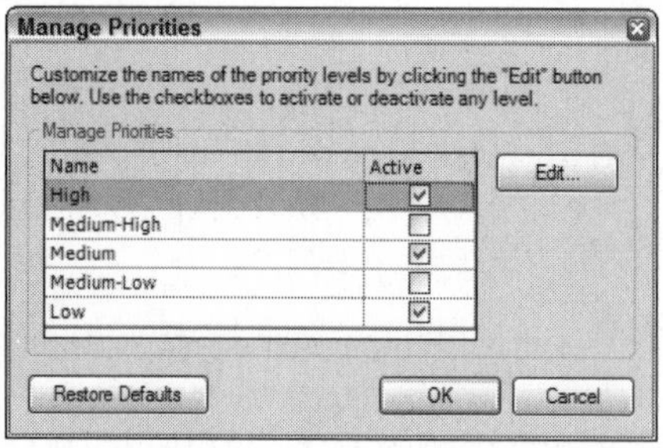

Figure 13-12:
The
Manage
Priorities
dialog box.

> **Manage Priorities**
>
> Customize the names of the priority levels by clicking the "Edit" button below. Use the checkboxes to activate or deactivate any level.
>
> Manage Priorities
>
> | Name | Active | |
> |---|---|---|
> | High | ☑ | Edit... |
> | Medium-High | ☐ | |
> | Medium | ☑ | |
> | Medium-Low | ☐ | |
> | Low | ☑ | |
>
> Restore Defaults   OK   Cancel

2. Select the priorities you want to activate by selecting the check box in the Active column.

3. Highlight a priority and then click the Edit button to change the name of a priority.

4. Click OK when you finish editing the Priority List.

Chapter 14

Customizing Layouts

Many ACT! users are confused about the concept of the layout. In fact, some of you might have ended up renaming a layout label when you wanted to rename fields. A *field* is a place to store information. The *layout* is how you actually see those fields. Your layout determines both the order of the fields and the format of each field. A layout is the name for a file that determines which fields you see and in what order those fields appear. After you add new fields to your ACT! database, the next step is to stick them into an existing layout (or design a new one).

The layout confusion is further compounded by users who share their database across a network. Problems occur if the users access different layouts. Depending on the layout that they use, some users might not be able to see all the fields of the database.

In this chapter, I show you how to use the Layout Designer to modify an existing layout. Here you master adding or replacing fields and tabs on your layout, reordering all the fields when you finish, and finally, adding a few artistic touches to your masterpiece.

Only database users with the Administrator or Manager level security have access to the Layout Designer. If you are a Standard, Restricted, or Browse level user, you get to sit back, put your feet on the desk, and direct the Administrator or Manager as to how you want to have the layout designed. Be careful what you wish for, however; if you are an Administrator or Manager, you get to do all the dirty work, so keep reading!

Modifying an Existing ACT! Layout

Before you begin modifying an existing layout, think about how you want your fields arranged on your layout. Why not try out all the layouts that come with ACT!? This way, you can get a feeling for the one that's most comfortable for you. Don't worry about colors or the names on the tabs — you can change all that.

Arranging fields the way you want them

Ah, the age-old question of form versus function. This hint might sound like a no-brainer, but many ACT! users never realize the importance of changing the field locations in their layout. For example, you might choose a layout that has the main business phone number on the top portion of your layout, the home phone number on a different tab along the bottom, and the mobile phone number in a third location. If you're constantly flipping between tabs to find phone numbers, move them together into one strategic place on your layout. This organization might not make your layout *look* better, but you'll certainly *feel* better! The point is to design your layout in such a way that data input becomes easy — and possibly even fun!

Here's what you do to modify an existing layout in terms of field selection and placement:

1. **Choose the layout that's closest to the one that you want to have.**

   If you need help with switching layouts, take a peek at Chapter 2.

2. **Choose Tools⇨Design Layout⇨Contact.**

   You're also given a choice of group and company. That's because you can also design — or redesign — your group and company layouts in exactly the same way as you do for your contact layout.

   The Layout Designer opens. Each field consists of two elements (see Figure 14-1):

   - The *field label,* which is an optional element, usually appears immediately to the left of a field.

   - The *field* itself is identified by the down arrow that appears at the field's right edge.

3. **Maximize the Layout Designer.**

   Okay, this step isn't a necessity, but it sure makes your design chores a whole lot easier! I'm always amazed when I see someone struggling with layout on a small portion of the monitor.

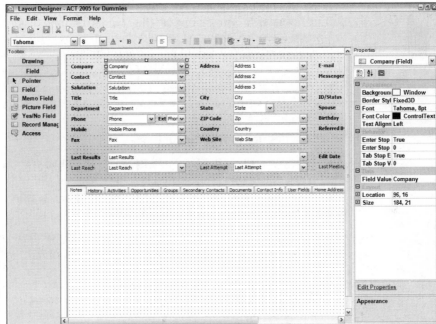

Figure 14-1:
The ACT!
Layout
Designer.

4. Make sure the toolbox and Properties window are both open.

These are two important elements that you need to have open in order to create or modify a layout. The toolbox sits on the left side of the Layout Designer, and the Properties window sits on the right side. Feel free to move them out of your way if you like, but trust me — you're going to need them momentarily! (Read more about these features in Chapter 10.)

If the toolbox and/or the Properties window are nowhere to be seen, try giving the View menu a click to open them. You see both of them listed right there; a check mark next to either Toolbox or Properties Window means they are alive and well — and living on the Layout Designer.

If the Properties window gets in your way on occasion but you don't want to keep heading up to the View window every time you want to open or close it, press F4 to speed up the process.

5. Choose File⇨Save As and give your layout a new name.

I recommend saving and naming your new layout with an easily recognizable way. That way you can later go back to your original layout (if you totally annihilate this one) and easily identify your layout.

The name of your layout appears in the Layout Designer title bar (refer to Figure 14-1).

Save changes to your layout early and often. The Save icon on the Layout Designer is represented by the standard floppy disk icon. Click it to save your work. Relying on the old Undo standby (Edit⇨Undo) is an option, but saving your layout early and often is always a good idea!

When you save a contact layout, ACT! automatically assigns it the extension .cly. When you save a group layout, ACT! gives it the .gly extension. And when you create a company layout, the file is given the .aly moniker.

6. Select the Pointer tool in the toolbox.

The *Pointer tool,* the tool that you'll probably use most often, enables you to select fields so that you can move, change, or remove them.

7. With the Pointer tool, select the fields and field labels that you want to move — or remove — from the layout.

Removing unused fields can simplify a layout and make room for other fields that you want to add. I recommend removing what's unwanted before moving on to other aspects of the layout design process.

Make your selections by any of these methods:

- Click any field or field label to select it.

- Click any field and then press Shift or Ctrl while clicking additional fields to select multiple fields and labels.

- Create a box around the desired labels and fields by holding down the left mouse button and then dragging to create a selection box.

When you select a field, a border of small boxes (called *handles*) appears around the field indicating that it's selected. In Figure 14-1, the Company field is selected.

8. If you want to remove fields, press Delete.

The unwanted fields go away.

Removing a field from the layout doesn't remove the actual field from the database. The field remains in your database but isn't visible in the layout. See the "Using layouts to restrict access to key fields" sidebar for more details.

9. To move fields around, select them with the Pointer and then drag them to a new location on your layout.

If only rearranging the living room were this easy! The idea is to drag the selected fields and their corresponding labels to the place on your layout that seems the most logical to you. When you hold your mouse over selected fields, your cursor transforms into a plus sign, indicating that you're ready to move the field.

If you need to make only a minor adjustment to the field location, you might try using your keyboard's arrow keys for really fine-tuning your layout.

You can move a group of fields by selecting them and then pressing Ctrl+X. Move your cursor to the new spot on your layout where you want to place the cells and press Ctrl+V to paste the fields. *Voilà!* — you move the group of fields *en masse*.

Adding new fields to the layout

In Chapter 13, you find out how to modify existing fields or to create new ones from scratch. When you rename an existing field in ACT!, you then tweak its label to reflect the change in field name. Typically, you start by renaming one or all of the ten user fields. At that point, your work is almost over because the field is already included in your layout. To change a field label, simply double-click it; you'll end up in the label edit mode, at which point you can type in the new field label.

Make sure that the labels in the Layout Designer match the actual names of the fields. For example, I might have a field called Men's Room but give it the label Ladies' Room — and end up with very unexpected results!

Adding a new field from scratch to your ACT! database is a bit more complicated because after you create the new field (see Chapter 13), you now need to find a place for it on your layout. However, if you follow the upcoming steps, you'll find that adding the new field to your layout is certainly not an insurmountable task:

1. **Click the Field tool in the Layout Designer toolbox, hold down the left mouse button, and then drag the cursor to the right to define the field's initial size and position on your layout.**

   The Select Field dialog box opens, presenting a list of all the fields that do not currently appear on your existing layout. The fields are listed alphabetically. If you add an address block, all the related fields appear together, which allows you to easily add them all to your layout in one fell swoop. For example, notice in Figure 14-2 that all the credit card address fields are lined up together.

   Chapter 13 talks about setting up new fields. In general, I recommend setting up your new fields first and then placing them on the layout. However, if you add your new fields to your layout and find that you forgot to add one of your key new fields, don't worry. Just click the New Field button, conveniently located at the bottom-left corner of the Select Field window, to add a new field on the fly.

Figure 14-2:
Adding
a new field
to an ACT!
layout.

Clicking the Field button allows you to add the vast majority of new fields that you've added to your database. However, a few other field types lurk in the Field section of the toolbox. These include

- Memo
- Picture
- Yes/No
- Record Manager
- Access

The Memo and Picture fields are super-sized fields that need to be made larger than your other fields. The Yes/No fields are tiny little ones that are only large enough to hold a check mark. Don't worry if you're having trouble guesstimatin the size of those fields because ACT! automatically resizes them for you. Chances are that you'll never have to add the Record Manager or Access fields to your database because they're already included in your original layouts — and you can't add additional fields of those types.

Even though the field is called a Yes/No field, it's actually a check box field that you click to indicate yes or no.

2. **Select the field that you want to add to the layout, deselect the Include a Label check box if you don't want the field to have a label, and then click the Add button.**

   The field is added to your layout. You can add as many fields to your layout as you like, but you're allowed to use each field only once.

3. **When you're done adding fields, click the Close button in the Select Field dialog box.**

Changing the tabs

Just like you can add, move, or remove the individual fields of your database on your layout, you can also add, move, or remove the tabs that are on your layout. Using tabs is a great way to organize the fields in your database. For example, you might have a Products tab that lists the various products that you are tracking — or a Personal tab that includes contact info: his or her birthday, anniversary, blood type, IQ, and shoe size. The whole point of being able to customize your layout is to make it comfortable for you. If you find yourself constantly hunting for a field, chances are that your fields are not arranged in a logical fashion. If that's the case, consider editing the tabs on your layout:

1. **From the Layout Designer, choose Edit⇨Tabs.**

   The Edit Tabs dialog box appears (see Figure 14-3), where ACT! gives you several tab customization options.

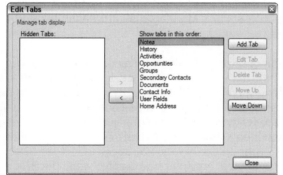

Figure 14-3: Editing tabs in an ACT! layout.

2. **Hide any system tabs you no longer want to display in your layout.**

   The single left- and right-pointing arrows in the Edit Tabs dialog box allow you to hide a system tab. Although the system tabs — Notes, History, Activities, Groups, Opportunities, Secondary Contacts, and Documents — can't be deleted, you can hide them by moving them into the Hidden Tabs area on the left side of the Edit Tabs dialog box.

3. **Customize your tabs according to your own sense of design and order.**

   • *Add Tab:* Add an additional tab to your layout. Enter a name for the new tab in the Add Tab Layout dialog box and then click OK. You now need to go back and add some fields to that shiny new tab.

   • *Edit Tab:* Give a tab a new name.

- *Delete Tab:* Remove a tab other than a system tab from your layout.

  When you remove a tab from a layout, all the fields located on that tab are removed as well. Consider moving — or removing — all the fields from a tab *before* you delete the tab itself!

- *Move Up:* Move a tab so that it appears *before* another tab.

- *Move Down:* Arrange a particular tab so that it appears *after* another.

4. **Click Close when you're happy with the names and order of your tabs.**

Changing the order of things

You can — and should — use the Tab key to progress through your fields as you input contact information into your database. When you start with an ACT! layout right out of the box, you can tab through the fields in a logical order — that is, from top to bottom. However, you might prefer to move horizontally across the layout rather than vertically from top to bottom. Or, you might find that after adding a few fields, you can no longer tab through your fields with the greatest of ease. Modifying layouts generally renders the field entry order non-sequential.

Although having out-of-sequence field ordering doesn't damage your database, it does make inputting data difficult. Each time you press the Tab key, your cursor skips to the next *numbered* field instead of to the next field that you see on your layout. This could be a real bummer if not for the fact that you can reorder your fields when necessary. A *tab stop* is associated with every field on your layout; the Tab Stop number determines the order of the fields.

Although an important step, consider waiting to change the field order until you are absolutely, positively, 100 percent certain that you're happy with how you placed the fields on your layout. There is no magic way to simply number the fields consecutively from 1 to 100; unless you want to waste a lot of your time by redoing your work, you might save this step until after you live with your layout for a while.

1. **Choose View⇨Tab Stops⇨Show Tab Stops in ACT!'s Layout Designer.**

   The tab stop appears in the Layout Designer, as shown in Figure 14-4.

   When you enter the land of Tab Stops, you'll probably notice two things: Little red numbers now appear to the right of each field, and you no longer have the toolbox and Properties window to play with.

   When you add a new field to your layout, ACT! automatically assigns the field the next available field number. When changing the field number order, focus on those fields because that's where the numbering is out of whack. If you remove a field number and don't assign it to another field, ACT! automatically assigns that number to the next field that you add to your layout.

2. Select any fields for which you want to change the field order.

If you select the fields whose field entry order you want to change (refer to Figure 14-4, where the fields are not numbered sequentially), the number disappears.

3. Select the fields a second time to reassign the field the next available number.

When you select the field again, the next available number is assigned to the field. Feel free to select the fields in any order you want. After all, this is your layout!

4. Right-click a field, choose Set Index, and type in a field number to advance several fields at a time.

This is a great party trick in the event that you need to squeeze a field or two in among all your existing fields and don't want to have to click and re-click each and every field in your layout. Say, for example, that your fields are numbered sequentially from 1 to 61, and you want to stick a new field smack under field 1. Whew! You're looking at a lot of click time. But wait! If you right-click field 2, choose Set Index, and change the field number to 3, you see all the fields from 2 through 61 magically increase by one digit.

I wish I had a great tip for decreasing the field numbers in the event that you remove a field. Unfortunately, I don't. And, I wish you could undo the field numbers if you increase them by accident. You can't. All I can tell you is to be careful when setting the field index because it can't easily be reversed.

5. **Choose View⇨Tab Stops⇨Show Tab Stops to leave the tab stop area.**

6. **Choose View⇨Enter Stops⇨Show Enter Stops to begin editing the enter stops.**

   Just like the tab stops control the order that your cursor follows as you tab through your layout, the *enter stop* controls the path your cursor takes as you press Enter. Think of the enter stop as a bypass, allowing you to skip merrily from one area of your layout to the next.

   The enter stop looks and feels pretty much like the tab stop with two major differences: The Enter Stop dialog box is tastefully decorated in green instead of red, and you use a whole lot fewer of them. In general, you want to place an enter stop at the beginning of each group of fields. You might want to have one at the beginning of the address, one at the start of the phone numbers, and a third one conveniently located on the first of the personal fields.

7. **Choose View⇨Enter Stops⇨Show Enter Stops to return to the Layout Designer.**

Beautifying Your Layout

I'll admit that I count myself among the artistically challenged of this world. If you read and assimilate everything in the beginning of this chapter, you're now pretty much equipped to go forth and design a nifty new layout. But before tackling that new design project, you might first want to give some thought to some of the things that can make your layout a bit more aesthetically pleasing.

Doing minor touch-up work

At this juncture, you leave the area of function behind you and move on to some of the more aesthetically pleasing aspects of layout design. You can also decide whether your layout needs a major or minor makeover. The Edit Properties dialog box (see Figure 14-5) allows you to make changes to the font, font size, and other attributes, and to the basic border style. Right-click the label or field you want to change and choose Edit Properties. This is great for simple touch-up work but is rather limiting if your layout needs an extreme makeover. For help with that, see the following section.

Figure 14-5:
The Layout
Designer
Edit
Properties
dialog box.

Creating an extreme makeover

Use the Properties window if you want to create some major changes. There are two great advantages to using the Properties window over the Edit Properties dialog box. First, you can edit more than one field at a time. Secondly, you have a whole lot more choice about which elements you can edit.

If you click around in the Layout Designer, the choices in the Properties window change accordingly. For example, if you click in a field, you can change the various color and font attributes; if you click in a label, you can edit the text of the label.

If you're having trouble reading the various options on the Properties window, resize it so that you can read it better. Simply place your cursor over the left edge of the window; when your cursor changes to a double pointing vertical line, drag to the left to expand the window.

Changing a field label

In most cases, the field name and the field label are exactly the same. Having a field label differ too radically from the name of the actual field proves to be quite confusing when you wander into the area of template and report creation. However, sometimes you might want to tweak the field label so that it fits on your layout better. For example, a field named *Cellular Telephone Number* might be shortened to a more readable label *Cell*.

You can change a field label with two different methods:

✔ **Double-click the label.**

The label turns into a text box with a blinking cursor. Delete any unnecessary letters and type the new label.

✔ **Type the new field label in the Text section of the Properties window.**

Adding color to your drab life

ACT! comes with close to a zillion colors that you can add to your layouts. Okay, you caught me; there might be a few less than a zillion, but I think just about every color of the rainbow is represented. To use one of those nifty colors, follow these steps:

1. **Click in the background of your layout in the Layout Designer.**

2. **Select a background color from the Properties window.**

   You can now change the background color by clicking the Background Color drop-down arrow and selecting a color that matches your mood — or the décor of your office. Like magic, your background color changes. If it doesn't, it's probably because a graphic is hiding that beautiful background color. If that's the case, go on to the next section.

Some of you may be a little hard to please and find that the colors provided in ACT! just don't match the décor of your home or office. If you want to add your own custom-blended color to your layout, mix your very own custom color via the Custom Color tab. When you create a custom color, the Properties window displays the RGB (red, green, and blue) number associated with the custom color. Feel free to change those numbers if you've worked with graphic programs in the past and want to match your layout to a specific color.

Changing the colors of your fields and labels is just as easy. Just select the fields or labels and change the color option in the Properties window exactly like you do for the layout background.

You can select as many fields and/or labels as you like and then change the color for your entire selection at the same time.

Got a few fields that you want to make sure are used by your users whenever possible? Make a field mandatory by turning off the Allow Blank option in the Define Fields dialog box. This option can be an annoying one if you just don't have the information needed to fill in the field at the time of your data input; ACT! demands that you supply the missing information before you leave the record. An alternative might be to highlight the critically important fields in a stunning shade of yellow so that users recognize their importance without being asked to supply information that they might not have.

Adding the Finishing Touches

Whew! After you add, delete, move, and color your fields, you're ready to sally forth into the world and start using your new layout. But wait! If you look carefully at your layout, things might look a bit, well, cockeyed. (That's an official computer term to indicate that your fields seem out of whack because they consist of various sizes and aren't aligned properly.) If I didn't like you so well, I'd tell you to grab your mouse and start adjusting those whacko fields by dragging them into submission. Several hours later, after much dragging, resizing, and probably quite a bit of cursing, you'd probably end up in pretty much the same place as you started. But because the point of this whole book is to show you how to do things the easy way, you might want to read the following sections instead.

Lining up fields and labels

One way to give your layout a truly polished look is align all fields and labels. When you move a field to a new location on your layout, there is a strong possibility that the field is slightly out of line, both vertically and horizontally, with the other fields. Of course, you can always try to "eyeball it" by dragging the field around, trying to get it into just the perfect spot. This method can be very time consuming, aggravating, and hard on your carpal tunnel. I have a much easier — and precise — way to accomplish your goal:

1. **Select the errant field that is out of alignment.**

2. **Click the *anchor field* (the field that is properly aligned).**

   If you look closely, the selection boxes around the errant field are white, and the selection boxes around the anchor field are black. This is your indication that the anchor field stays in place, and the other field lines up with it.

   You can align several fields at a time by selecting them and right-clicking the anchor field. The field you right-clicked now becomes the anchor, and all the other selected fields line up with it.

   Hold down your Shift or Ctrl key while clicking the fields in your layout to select more than one of those puppies at a time.

3. **Right-click any of the selected fields and choose an alignment option.**

   As you can see in Figure 14-6, you're given a whole bunch of options from which to choose. Here are the two you'll probably use most often:

Figure 14-6:
Aligning fields and labels.

Bring to Front
Bring Forward
Send to Back
Send Backward
Cut
Copy
Paste
Delete
Align Lefts
Align Center
Align Rights
Align Tops
Align Middles
Align Bottoms
Align to Grid
Select All

• *Align Lefts:* Typically your fields look the best lined up along the left edges looking vertically down the layout. To do this, you want to select your fields from top to bottom before aligning.

• *Align Tops:* When you have two or three columns in your layout, you want your fields to align along the top edges as well. Select your fields horizontally, from left to right, before choosing this option.

If you choose the incorrect alignment option, you might end up with a mess in which all your fields are now on top of one another. Quick! Reach for the Undo button. Don't see it? Choose Edit➪Undo.

4. **Click anywhere in your layout to remove the selection boxes.**

Resizing fields

You'll probably find yourself in a number of situations in which you need to resize one or more fields. Typically, you want to make several fields smaller to squeeze more fields into your layout. You might want to make several fields larger to add more data into those fields. Or, you might find that a new field you just placed on your layout isn't the exact same size as the other fields. Again, you can manually resize your fields one at a time. You can also knock your head firmly against the wall several times, but I don't recommend either activity.

✔ **To resize several fields at once:** Select all the fields that you want to resize *en masse.* Then place your cursor on one of the selection boxes on either the left or right edge of the selected fields. When your cursor turns into a single horizontal arrow, drag the selection box to the left or right, depending on whether you're making the fields larger or smaller.

✔ **To resize against the anchor:** Select all the fields that you want to be the exact same size as an anchor field. Press the Ctrl key, click the anchor field once, pause, and then click it a second time so that the selection boxes are now black. Choose Format➪Make Same Size➪Width.

Adding a logo or a graphic

Perhaps the best way to truly personalize your layout is by adding your very own logo to it. Adding a graphic to the layout means that the graphic appears on each and every one of your contact records. Don't confuse this with using with a Picture field; a Picture field varies for every one of your contacts. You can add your *chef-d'oeuvre* to your layout by following these easy steps:

1. **From the Layout Designer, click the Drawing tool from the toolbox and then choose the Image tool.**

2. **Using your mouse, draw a shape on your layout to match the graphic you want to insert.**

The Open dialog box opens.

3. **Navigate to the graphic you want to insert, select it, and click Open.**

   The graphic now appears on your layout. You can drag the graphic to a new, improved location by placing your cursor on any of the edges of your graphic. When your cursor turns into a plus sign, drag the graphic to the appropriate spot on your layout.

Your graphic appears exactly the same size as it was originally created. If the graphic is too large or small to fit your layout, resize it using a graphics program. You might find, however, that the frame that you drew in Step 2 doesn't exactly fit your graphic. You can resize it by placing your mouse on one of the white squares that borders the graphic and dragging the border to match the size of your graphic.

Creating a circle in a square

Admittedly, no one would ever confuse me with Picasso. However, some of you might be of a more artistic persuasion, or just want to take advantage of some of the drawing tools to add a little clarity to your layout. By creating a square that is slightly larger than a grouping of several of your fields, you in essence create a frame that serves to highlight those fields.

If you click the Drawing tool in the toolbox, notice the Rectangle and Ellipse options; these are just fancy words for *square* and *circle*. At any rate, by clicking either of these options, you can draw a square or circle (okay, a rectangle or an ellipsis) on your layout. After they're drawn, you can head over to the Properties window and change the color of your newly created shape. This is a great way to emphasize a group of fields, particularly if your layout is starting to look cluttered.

Did your newly created circle or square plunk itself down on top of your existing fields? Although this leads to an interesting work of art, you probably prefer to have the graphic behind the fields. Don't panic; simply right-click the graphic in question and choose Send to Back.

Adding text boxes

If a picture is worth a thousand words, a text box might just be worth a million. Inconsistent data input is a sure-fire way to decrease the productivity of your database. This lack of uniformity is often caused not by lack of knowledge but rather by lack of communication. Adding a text box to your layout is a great way to help users input key pieces of information in the right place and to help organize the groups of data on the layout. Use your text boxes to create a heading for a group of fields or to include data input instructions to your users.

1. **From the toolbox, click the Drawing tool and then choose the Text tool.**

   Your cursor now looks like a plus sign instead of the normal arrow.

2. **Find the spot on the layout to add a text box, hold down your left mouse button, and drag the cursor to create a box.**

3. **Enter the text in your new text box.**

   Guess that's why they call it a text box. Feel free to write a book here if you wish. When you're finished, just click one of the text box borders and watch in awe as little white squares appear all around your text box. Feel free to grab any one of those boxes and expand your horizons — or in this case your text box — to accommodate your verbiage.

4. **Use the Properties window to customize your text box.**

   Here's where you can really have fun. As long as the new text box is selected, you can change the text, font attributes, font color, and background color of the text box.

I'm a firm believer in doing things the easy way whenever possible. If you find yourself longing to have several text boxes all formatted the same way, create the first text box, customize it just the way you like it, and then clone it by right-clicking it and choosing Copy. At that point, you can paste it on your layout — and the only thing you have to change is the text.

Building a table

If you find yourself running out of room on your layouts because you needed to add so many customized fields, here's a workaround. As an alternative to the traditional concept of listing all your field labels next to your actual fields, arrange your fields in table format, as shown in Figure 14-7. The idea here is to save room and allow you to easily fill in vital information.

Consider building a table if you have several products and need to track the purchase date, serial number, and expiration date for each one. Or maybe you're a realtor and want to list the dimensions of several rooms. Not all databases can take advantage of a table format, but those that can will benefit from freeing a lot of space on their layout.

Company	Appt Date	Code	Comm Rate	Excess Comm	Class Date
Excess Flood					
Bankers Flood					
Reliable HO					
Reliable WC					
Surety Company					
Citizens					
Fulcrum					
Focus Financial					

Figure 14-7: A layout formatted as a table.

Chapter 15

Zen and the Art of Database Maintenance

- -

- -

*I*n this chapter, I show you how to take care of your motorcycle . . . er, I mean your database. Would you believe that your ACT! database is very similar to a motorcycle? Both are made up of many moving parts that require maintenance. Failure to provide routine maintenance can result in big problems — for a motorcycle as well as for your database. If something does go wrong, having a backup is nice and (in most cases) necessary to keep your job. Sometimes your motorcycle gets dirty; likewise, your database is prone to clutter. You sometimes have to bite the bullet, roll up your sleeves, and do a little cleaning — and clear out old or duplicate contact records from ACT!.

Regular maintenance keeps your database running efficiently. When you don't provide routine maintenance for a motorcycle, things get corroded; likewise, when you don't provide maintenance for your database, your records become corrupted. Weird things start happening. No, you won't see a ghost, but you might not see a note that you know you created the day before. Or that note just might pop up again later — in the wrong place!

Understanding the Need to Check and Repair

I love to change the messages on my voice mail, and one of my favorite choices is, "Have you checked and repaired your database today?" Users often offer up a variety of excuses for why they don't perform routine database maintenance. These excuses range anywhere from "I didn't have time" to "I didn't know I was supposed to." Of course, many of you give these excuses *after* your database is already damaged. By then, of course, it could be too late for checking and repairing. If you are the Database Administrator, you are responsible for the maintenance of the database because the maintenance can only be done by an Administrator.

Determining the maintenance frequency

If you're a little old lady from Pasadena who uses your database only once in a blue moon, you might get away without maintaining your database. However, if the data in ACT! is extremely important to you, perform your maintenance on a routine basis. At a minimum, I recommend that your database receives a bit of tender loving care at least once a week.

My general rule is that the frequency of maintenance is directly tied to the amount of use that your database receives. There is no such thing as doing too much maintenance — only too little! Here are some situations that warrant more than weekly maintenance:

✔ **You have a multi-user database.**

When ACT! is used over a network, the database is subject to more use — and abuse. The chances of having inaccurate and incorrect information increase exponentially with the number of users entering data into the database.

✔ **You have a large database.**

✔ **You add new fields to your database.**

✔ **You make changes to the drop-down lists in your database.**

✔ **You add or delete numerous contact records to your database.**

✔ **You import another database into your existing ACT! database.**

✔ **You add — or delete — users to your database.**

✔ **You experienced a power surge, brownout, or outage.**

✔ **You had network problems.**

✔ **You suspect that your database is corrupted.**

✔ **You had a really lousy day when everything seemed to go wrong.**

A little shopping list of database horrors

Database corruption comes in many shapes and sizes. The following list describes some of the more common indications — the warning signs — of a corrupted ACT! database:

- ✔ While trying to open a database, you receive an error message or ACT! stops responding. Smoke might be seen rising from the back of your CPU.

- ✔ You receive error messages while working in ACT!.

- ✔ You can't log into the database as a particular user.

- ✔ Information appears to be missing or mysteriously appears attached to the incorrect contact record.

- ✔ You notice a significant increase or decrease in the number of contact records in your database.

- ✔ Your database acts funny or runs slower than usual.

If you notice one — or heaven forbid, more than one — of the preceding warning signs, I'm sorry to say that the time has come to either perform CPR on your fainthearted co-workers or perform some simple database maintenance. In the next section, I give you the details on performing the simple database maintenance (that is, checking and repairing). You're on your own with the CPR.

Sometimes determining whether the corruption is in the database or in the ACT! program itself is difficult. To determine this, try opening the Act8demo database that installs on your computer when you install ACT!. If the Act8demo opens and runs correctly, the problem lies with your database. If you encounter the same problems in the Act8demo database that you're having in your own database, you might need to reinstall ACT!.

Performing Routine Maintenance

The old adage, "If it ain't broke, don't fix it!" does not apply to ACT!. Proper maintenance enables your database to run efficiently and improves performance. Some of the maintenance takes on a rather behind-the-scenes approach; users don't detect that maintenance has been performed. They know, however, that the maintenance hasn't been done if they start running into problems with the database. The other type of maintenance involves actual data cleanup; astute users can detect that changes have been made to the database.

Only the Database Administrator can perform routine maintenance to ensure that your database continues to chug away without any problems. That's probably to ensure that everyone knows at whom to point if things go wrong. Some maintenance tasks require that all users log off of the database so that the database can be locked, but those can be scheduled for off-peak or even overnight hours.

In ACT!, basic maintenance is referred to as *checking and repairing*. The Database Administrator can run the Check and Repair tool regularly to ensure a healthy database, which consists of two procedures: the Integrity Check and the Re-index. These procedures are very similar to the Scan Disk and Disk Defragmenter procedures on a Windows PC. The Integrity Check scours the database for errors and repairs them if found. After any found errors are repaired, Re-index squeezes out all the little empty spaces that are left in your database when you delete contact records in order to ensure maximum performance.

Yikes! Performing the Check and Repair sounds really important so you're probably thinking that it must be really hard. Wrong! Here's all you need to do:

1. **Log in as an Administrator and make sure that all other users are logged off the database.**

   If the Check and Repair command is grayed out from ACT!'s Tools menu, you don't have sufficient administrative rights to perform that option. You might want to jog your database Administrator's memory a bit to remind him that his salary is directly proportional to the efficient performance of your database!

2. **Choose Tools⇨Database Maintenance⇨Check and Repair.**

   The Check and Repair Database window opens, as shown in Figure 15-1.

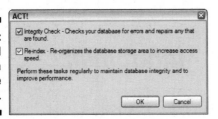

Figure 15-1: Check and repair a database here.

3. **Select both the Integrity Check and Re-index options and then click OK.**

   Your computer makes a few whirring noises, and a snazzy indicator bar appears momentarily onscreen. (Try to look important during this time so as to justify your administrative salary.) When ACT! finishes the maintenance, you receive a cheerful message telling you that everything is hunky-dory.

Backing Up the ACT! Database

You probably already know the three rules of real estate: location, location, location. Similarly, the three basic rules of computing are backup, backup, backup! With the proliferation of viruses, as well as the poor construction of many computers, backing up on a daily basis is imperative. Failure to do so can result in loss of data — as well as time and money! Having a recent backup enables you to recover quickly when the unexpected happens. (It might also ensure that you receive a paycheck at the end of the week.)

Only Administrators and Managers of the ACT! database get to back up a database. After a database is backed up, only an Administrator can restore it. Because every database requires an Administrator, you automatically landed the job if you are the only user of the database. If you need to back up the database and find that the backup option is grayed out on the File menu, you must find a database Administrator and wheedle him or her into changing your permissions. In Chapter 3, I explain the various ACT! user permissions.

If you make major changes to your database — such as importing new records, deleting old contact records, or modifying existing fields — I recommend creating a backup before you start, just in case!

When you create an ACT! database, ACT! thoughtfully automatically creates several folders for you. In addition to a database folder that houses the main database files, ACT! creates subfolders for your attachments, layouts, queries, reports, and templates. When you back up your database, ACT! compresses all the data into a single Zip file.

In addition to the aforementioned folders, ACT! also creates a backup folder. Sounds like a good idea; however, if your database is located on your local machine, chances are pretty good that the backup folder lives there as well. One of the main reasons to create a backup is to make sure that you have a copy of your database just in case something goes drastically wrong with your computer. If something bad does happen to your computer — and that's where your backup is stored — you'll find yourself without a computer, database, or backup.

In a corporate setting, the ACT! database often resides on a network drive and is backed up to a tape drive on a daily basis. However, you might be feeling a false sense of security knowing that this backup is taking place. ACT! is an SQL database — meaning that unless you have a special tool, a routine network backup will not back up your ACT! database. Feeling scared? Remind your IT person that his job security is directly related to the security of your database. Chapter 16 will give him a few alternatives.

If you use backup software or store your data on an Internet site, remember that an ACT! database consists of more than a single file. You need to store the Zip file backup that ACT! creates in order to ensure that you do indeed collect all the bits and pieces of your database.

Performing the basic ACT! backup

You must have Administrator or Manager security level to back up your ACT! database. Open the ACT! database that you want to create a backup copy of and follow these steps:

1. **From any ACT! screen, choose File⇨Back Up⇨Database.**

   The Back Up Database dialog box appears, displaying the location for the backup database, as shown in Figure 15-2.

Figure 15-2: The Back Up Database dialog box.	**Back Up Database** ☒ Back up files to: `C:\My Documents\ACT! Dummies.zip` [Browse...] ☐ Password protect file [OK] [Cancel]

2. **To back up the database to a different location from what's showing, click the Browse button, select a new location for your backup file, and then click Save.**

   ACT! automatically places ACT! in front of your database name and ends the backup file with the .zip extension.

3. **Select the option to password-protect your database (optional).**

   In case you fear spies lurking about, password-protect the backup file. However, you might not feel the urge to do so, knowing that only database Administrators can use the file.

4. **Click OK.**

   An indicator bar appears, letting you know that ACT! is creating your backup. The time required to complete your backup varies depending on the size of your database and the supplemental files that are included in your backup. When the backup is complete, a message appears telling you that your backup was completed successfully!

Backing up to various media

Backing up a database is easy. The hard part is knowing where to place your backup. For nearly 20 years, computer users relied on the floppy disk as their backup method of choice. You can kiss those floppies good-bye because they just aren't big enough to hold your backup. By default, ACT! places your backup file on your computer's hard drive. That's great if your hard drive is ultimately being backed up, but not so great if it isn't — and your computer grinds to a painful halt. Here are a couple of good alternatives to your backup housing dilemma:

- ✔ **Zip drive**: I know this sounds confusing, but you can place your backup Zip file on a Zip drive.

- ✔ **USB storage drive:** These tiny powerhouses can store the equivalent of 100 floppy disks on a device the size of your thumb.

- ✔ **CD/DVD burner:** These puppies come installed on most of the new PCs.

- ✔ **External hard drive:** The price of external hard drives has plummeted in recent years; you might want to purchase one to store backups of *all* your data files.

Restoring a backup copy of your database

A backup is no good if you don't know how to use it to restore your data. Although I hope you never have to use a backup copy, follow these steps to restore a copy of your database:

1. **From any ACT! screen, choose File⇨Restore⇨Database.**

   The Restore Database dialog box opens, as shown in Figure 15-3.

Figure 15-3: Restoring a backup.

2. **Select one of the restoration options and click OK.**

   - *Restore:* Restores all files to their original locations; this restoration option is most commonly used when data is lost or corrupted.

   - *Restore As:* Allows you to restore the database to a new location with a new filename; this option works well when you want to copy a database or move it to another computer.

   - *Unpack and Restore Remote Database:* Allows you to install a database that synchronizes back to the main database.

3. **Click the Browse button to navigate to the location where the backup file is stored; click Save and then click OK.**

   Backup files end with the `.zip` extension.

   Many of you are familiar with the .zip extension because you've worked with the WinZip software. However, don't be tempted to unzip an ACT! backup file using WinZip. The files aren't placed in the correct locations, and the backup file is probably rendered useless!

4. **Type the backup file password if prompted and click OK.**

5. **Type the Administrator's name and password and click OK.**

   Yikes! ACT! shows you the scary warning message that you see in Figure 15-4. The warning explains in no uncertain terms that if you continue, your database will be overwritten with older files. If your current database is a corrupted mess, that's a good thing; if your database is perfectly fine, that could be a bad thing!

Figure 15-4:
Scary
restore
warning
message.

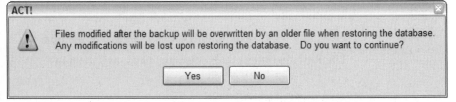

ACT!

Files modified after the backup will be overwritten by an older file when restoring the database. Any modifications will be lost upon restoring the database.   Do you want to continue?

Yes   No

6. **Click Yes to acknowledge that you want to continue.**

   Your computer whirs and hisses for a few moments and soon the restored database opens.

Performing Spring Housecleaning

The good news is that if you're reading this, you're probably the Administrator of the ACT! database; after all, if you're not the Administrator, you don't have the necessary permission to perform most of the administrative tasks. The bad news is that with the job title comes quite a bit of responsibility — and hopefully a large salary.

In addition to performing the obvious mechanical maintenance chores, you probably want to do a little bit of extra housecleaning . . . er, database cleaning from time to time. Having blank, duplicate, or incorrect contact information serves no purpose other than to make your database perform less efficiently. So bite the bullet, roll up your sleeves, and get cleaning.

Before you perform *any* type of maintenance, I strongly recommend that you back up your database so that you can retrieve any data you accidentally delete.

Weeding out duplicate contacts

Finding pesky duplicates in your database is tricky but not impossible. Because having multiple records for the same person or company is common, ACT! allows you a way to easily check for duplicate records based on predefined criteria. You can then create a lookup of the duplicate records and delete them. You can also change the criteria used to find these duplicate records.

1. **From any ACT! screen, choose Tools⇨Scan for Duplicates.**

   By default, ACT! looks for duplicate contact records based on the company name, contact name, and phone number. If the contents of these three fields are identical for two or more contacts, ACT! views them as duplicates. As you can see in Figure 15-5, you can now specify how ACT! checks for duplicate contact records in the Duplicate Checking dialog box.

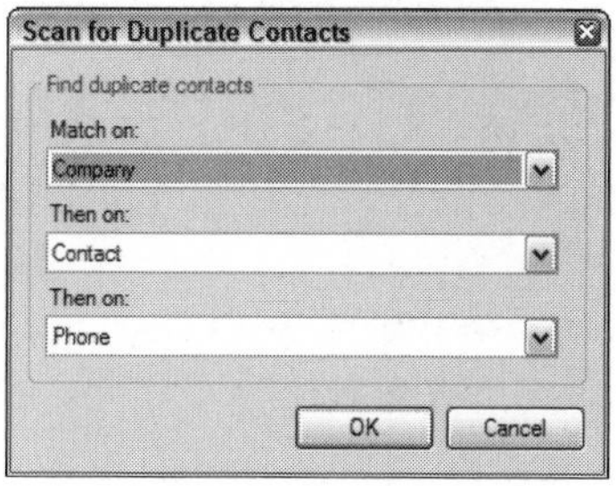

Figure 15-5: Defining duplication criteria.

Scan for Duplicate Contacts

Find duplicate contacts

Match on:
Company

Then on:
Contact

Then on:
Phone

OK   Cancel

2. **In the Find Duplicate Contacts area, choose the three fields you want ACT! to use to search for duplicate contact data.**

3. **Click OK.**

   The Contact List opens, along with a dialog box informing you that duplicates were found, asking whether you would like to combine them. From this list, you can delete records, keep records, or combine duplicate records.

4. If you want to combine duplicates, click Yes to continue at the prompt.

The Copy/Move Contact Data window opens. This is the first of six windows that you go through when merging duplicate contacts. Merging duplicates is a slow, grueling task; you have to merge your duplicates on a pair-by-pair basis.

After two contacts are merged together, there is no unmerge function. Proceed with caution!

As you progress through the wizard, you perform the following six tasks:

a. *Select a pair of duplicates.*

b. *Decide whether you want to copy the information from the first contact record to the second contact record* — or vice versa.

c. *Choose a source and a contact.* Depending on your choice, one of the contacts becomes the *source,* and the other one is the *target.* By default the new, merged contact contains all the target information. If you want to retain any source field information, click in the field and then click the Copy button.

d. *Choose whether you want to move additional information from the source to the target or have the information remain duplicated on both records.* As you see in Figure 15-6, you indicate this in the third step.

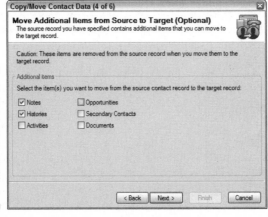

Figure 15-6:
Move
additional
information
from the
source to
the target
record.

e. *Select the additional elements that you want to merge together:* notes, histories, activities, opportunities, secondary contacts and documents. If the source contact has three notes and the target

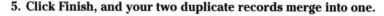

has four different notes, the final contact ends up with seven notes (if my math is working correctly).

  f. *Indicate whether to keep or delete the source record.* For your convenience, ACT! recaps the information to make your decision easier.

  If you decide to delete the source record, click Yes on the scary warning that confirms that you might be losing information.

5. Click Finish, and your two duplicate records merge into one.

You cannot undelete deleted records or contact information. If you inadvertently delete important information, run — don't walk — to your backup file and restore your information.

For many of you, merging two contact records together is only the tip of the iceberg. You need to repeat the merge process again for each pair of duplicates in your database. And, after you complete the process, you might want to start over again by changing the duplicate checking criteria.

As I stress throughout this book, having some semblance of uniformity is very important. Lack of uniformity is a great way to sabotage your database. A search for all your clients in *Ft.* Lauderdale does not include those clients in *Fort* Lauderdale. In the same way, a company or contact might be duplicated if it is entered into your database in two different ways. For example, you might have *John Q. Public* and *John Public,* or *ABC Company* and *ABC Co.* ACT! doesn't recognize any of these examples as duplicates.

You can change the criteria that ACT! uses to look for duplicate records. To find the duplicates that I mention in the preceding paragraph, you need to use a different criterion for your search. Changing your search parameters to search for duplicated phone numbers might just give you the results that you're looking for.

Removing old data

ACT! users tend to be extremely loyal; it's not unusual to run into ACT! fanACTics who have been using ACT! religiously for over 15 years. Over time, the amount of information that is stored in ACT! gets larger and larger, and that information can become less and less important. ACT! provides you with a simple tool for clearing the clutter from your database. (I just wish I had a similar tool to clear the clutter from my closet!)

1. From any ACT! screen, choose Tools⇨Database Maintenance⇨Remove Old Data.

  The Remove Old Data dialog box opens, as shown in Figure 15-7.

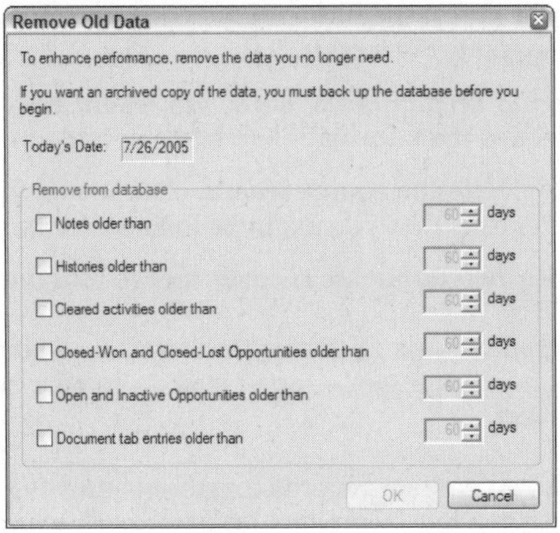

Remove Old Data

To enhance performance, remove the data you no longer need.

If you want an archived copy of the data, you must back up the database before you begin.

Today's Date: 7/26/2005

Remove from database

☐ Notes older than   60 ⬍ days

☐ Histories older than   60 ⬍ days

☐ Cleared activities older than   60 ⬍ days

☐ Closed-Won and Closed-Lost Opportunities older than   60 ⬍ days

☐ Open and Inactive Opportunities older than   60 ⬍ days

☐ Document tab entries older than   60 ⬍ days

OK   Cancel

Figure 15-7:
The Remove
Old Data
window.

2. **In the Remove from Database area, select the type of data you want to remove and indicate the number of days that you want to use to remove that data.**

   To get rid of data that is older than a year, indicate 365 days; to get rid of data that is more than two years old, indicate 730 days; and so on.

3. **Click OK.**

Like a champ, ACT! searches, scrubs, and ultimately removes any data that matches your selection criteria.

TIP

If you're still not feeling really comfortable with blowing away some of your older note, history, and activity information, you do have a few alternatives. First, you can always make an archival database so that you can refer to that information if necessary. Secondly, a number of add-on products allow you to specify even more precisely the type of notes, histories, and activities that you delete. Check in Chapter 24 to read more about the ACT! Add-on store.

Deleting a database

You might wonder why you ever want to delete your database. That's good thinking because you're right — you don't want to delete your database. However, you might have inherited several databases that you no longer use, or perhaps you created a database or two for specific, temporary purposes. Many so-called ACT! "experts" create a multitude of databases in their attempt to learn ACT!. In general, allowing users to have access to more than one database is not a good idea; chances are pretty good that one of your users ends up in the wrong database. Having a multitude of extraneous data-bases can also put extra strain on your resources and slow down your general performance.

Before deleting a database, I recommend backing it up, just in case. You might also consider moving the database to another location for safekeeping rather than deleting it. Deleting a database is ridiculously simple — **but impossible to undelete once deleted.** Proceed with caution.

Okay, are you ready? Take a deep breath and follow these steps to delete the database:

1. **Open the database that you wish to delete.**

   Be sure to close all other databases. In previous versions of ACT!, you couldn't delete an open database — only closed ones. However, when you send the all-clear to fire away, ACT! 2005 and 2006 delete the currently opened database. Govern yourself accordingly!

2. **From any ACT! screen, choose Tools⇨Database Maintenance⇨ Delete Database.**

   The Delete Database window opens, verifying that you absolutely want to delete, destroy, and make the current database disappear forever.

3. **Click Yes to bid your database *adieu.***

   Ironically, ACT! gives you two options to change your mind: No or Cancel both serves to keep your database safely in place.

Copying or moving contact data

One of the neat utilities included with ACT! is the ability to copy or move selected field information from one record to the next — for example, when an existing contact leaves a company to work at another company. When you create a new record for the individual, you realize that his previous record still contains pertinent information, such as his home phone number and birthday. By using the Copy/Move command, you can move that specific field information from his old contact record to his new one. You can then edit the original contact record with the contact details of the new, replacement one.

ACT!'s Copy/Move Contact Data function works almost exactly like the Scan for Duplicate function (in the earlier section, "Weeding out duplicate contacts"). The only difference is that unlike the duplication procedure, you're not presented with a list of contacts to start with. The onus is on you to select the two records whose field information you want to copy or move.

1. **From any ACT! screen, choose Tools⇨Copy/Move Contact Data.**

   Look familiar? It's the Duplicate Checking dialog box (refer to Figure 15-6).

2. **Click Next to proceed through the wizard screens.**

   Proceed through the wizard while remembering a few key points:

   - The *source record* is the record that contains the data that you want to copy.

   - The *target record* is the record you want to copy data to.

   - You have the option to copy or move data on a field-by-field basis.

   - You have the option to keep or delete the original source record.

Performing a global edit/replace

Another way to keep your database working well is by ensuring that all fields contain consistent information. Maybe some of your contacts have the city listed in all capitals while others don't. Perhaps some contacts are listed in *Florida* whereas other contacts reside in *FL* or *Fla.* This lack of consistency makes it extremely difficult to query your database. Like a forgiving mother, ACT! provides you with the ability to correct the error of your ways. After you pinpoint your inconsistencies, you can standardize them in one fell swoop (rather than by correcting each field on an item-by-item basis):

1. **Perform your lookup.**

   In the preceding example, you might create a lookup of *FLA* and then add *Florida* to the mix. If you need help, flip to Chapter 6 and review the section on lookups.

   Unless you're planning on changing field data for every contact in your database, make sure you perform a lookup *before* proceeding. These changes are irreversible! For example, say you notice 27 instances of *Fla* that you want to change to *FL.* If you fail to do a lookup first, you end up changing the State field for *every* contact in your database to *FL* rather than just for the original 27 that you intend to change. Unfortunately, unless you have a backup handy, you're stuck with the changes because (again!) these changes are irreversible.

2. **From any ACT! screen, choose Edit⇨Replace Field.**

   If you prefer, you can choose one of the other two options as well:

   - *Swap Field:* This option swaps the information between two fields.

   - *Copy Field:* This option copies information from one field and repeats it in a second field.

   You now see the Replace Data dialog box, as shown in Figure 15-8.

Figure 15-8:
The Replace
Data dialog
box.

Figure 15-8:
The Replace
Data dialog
box.

3. **Select your desired field from the Replace Contents Of drop-down list.**

   You can select from virtually any of your contact fields with the exception of the system fields.

4. **Enter the desired information in the Value field.**

   In this example, you type **FL** in the field. To make life even easier, ACT! supplies you with the appropriate drop-down list based on the field you indicated in Step 3.

5. **Click OK.**

6. **Read the warning that appears.**

   Generally speaking, when life — or ACT! — gives you a warning, it's a good idea to heed it. ACT! is politely asking you to verify that you intend to change all the contact records in the current lookup (see Figure 15-9). If you're not sure as to the exact number of contacts in the current lookup, click No, return to the Contact Detail window or Contact List, and read the record counter in the top-left corner.

Figure 15-9:
Last chance
warning
before
replacing all
your data.

7. **Click Yes.**

   ACT! might have to think about this for a moment depending on the number of contact records in your lookup. When it finishes, you'll notice that the field that you indicated in Step 3 has now changed for each of the contact records in your lookup.

A few more housekeeping tips

Sure, ACT! can mechanically maintain the integrity of your database. However, you, as the Administrator, can do a few things to help ensure a healthy database:

- If your organization has customized the database, limit the number of users who have permission to edit layouts and add new items to the drop-down lists.

- Periodically clear unwanted items from the drop-down lists. Insist that the users routinely pick items from the drop-down lists when entering new data.

- To avoid duplication of contacts, emphasize the importance of querying the database for an existing contact before entering a new one.

- Delete any fields not being used.

- Delete outdated attachments, layouts, reports, templates, and queries.

- Be cognizant of field length. If you have a field that holds a Yes or No value, consider trimming the field length down to three characters.

- Save contact records you rarely use to a different database and then remove them from the main database. Use a Contact Activity lookup to locate infrequently used records.

Chapter 16

Administering to Your Database

● ●

● ●

Chapter 15 talks about the maintenance procedures that should be done on a fairly routine basis. This chapter calls in the big guns and is intended primarily for those of you who use ACT! in a networked environment. And because you are working in a workgroup, you're probably using ACT! Premium for Workgroups. Many of the features, including custom defining user roles, limiting contact access, and scheduling your maintenance are found only in the Premium edition of ACT!. Other features, such as adding users and networking, can be accomplished with the Standard version of ACT! but apply to only those of you with multiple users accessing your database. Last but not least, the importing feature applies to anyone who needs to get another database or list of contact information into ACT!.

Working with the Database Users

A *Record Manager* is a contact in your database who is also a user of your database. If several people enter data into your ACT! database, I highly recommend setting up each person as a Record Manager. If you and Jane are both set up as users of the database, you need to make sure that you log in as you and Jane logs in as herself. ACT! automatically enters several key pieces of information based on how you log in to the database. For example, you're recognized as the *record creator* of each new contact that you add to the database. Likewise, if Jane enters a note, that note is associated with her name. If you generate a document from one of ACT!'s templates, your name — not Jane's — appears as the generator of that document. Most importantly, your name is associated with any meetings, calls, or to-do's that you schedule in

ACT!. Having unique, identifiable users in a database allows you to view your own activities on a calendar. Otherwise, you might find yourself driving to Podunk to visit Jane's mom on her birthday!

Only the Database Administrator has permission to add new users to the ACT! database.

Adding new users to the database

1. **From any of the ACT! screens, choose Tools⇨Manage Users.**

   The Manage Users dialog box opens, as shown in Figure 16-1.

Figure 16-1: Adding a new database user.

2. **Click Create New User.**

   In the next window that appears, you are given a choice to create the new user from an existing contact or to create a brand new user who isn't currently a member of your current database.

   Always double-check that the new user doesn't already reside in your database as an existing contact. When you set up a brand-new user, you also set up a brand-new contact, which could result in an "evil twin" situation. For example, although you know only one John Smith, he is represented twice in your database — once as a user and the other time as simply a member of your database.

3. **Choose either Existing Contact or New Contact and then click Next.**

   • *Existing Contact:* If you choose the Existing Contact option, you see a list of all the contacts in your database.

    a. You can sort the list alphabetically by either contact or company by clicking the corresponding column heading.

    b. After you sort the list, type in the first couple of letters of the contact's last name or company (depending on how you sorted the list) in the Look For text box.

    ACT! magically takes you to that name.

    c. Click Next to continue.

    • *New Contact:* If you choose the New Contact option, a dialog box opens that is similar to the Manage Users dialog box. (See Figure 16-2.)

Figure 16-2:
Enter user
information.

4. **If the new user you added is also new to your database, you need to type in his/her name.**

   If you already indicated the name of the user in Step 3, his/her name is sitting there waiting for you.

5. **Fill in the user name.**

   The user name is not case sensitive. Just make sure you remember what name you decide on. If you set up multiple users for the same database, consider sticking to a set naming convention: *Gary Kahn* or *gkahn* are good choices; you might want to avoid *Gary B. Kahn* or *Gary Kahn, Esq.*

6. **Fill in the password.**

   By now you know the drill: You type in the password once, and because that was so much fun, you type it a second time.

7. **Choose the security role of the new user and then click Next.**

ACT! provides you with five levels of security. Because you are the Administrator, you set those levels for all subsequent users.

- *Browse:* This user has the most limited role; he or she can view contacts, view calendars, and add activities. The Browse user cannot add, modify, or delete contacts; or modify or add any other data.

  The Browse role is typically assigned to users who need to look up calendar details and schedule activities. In the real world, the database Administrator typically assigns a user Browse level access if he has serious doubts as to the user's ability to add data.

- *Restricted:* This role allows users to access only areas of the application to which he or she is granted permission. The Restricted role is typically assigned to users working in a support capacity. A Restricted user can access all data that he or she creates but cannot delete any data, even if he or she created it. This role also doesn't allow users to create companies or groups.

- *Standard:* A Standard user is the default user role assigned to new users. The Standard user can see the records in a database that he creates or is given explicit access to. Standard users can add, delete, and modify records; and synchronize data. A Standard user cannot add new users to the database, perform database maintenance, back up the database, import and export data, or modify database fields and layouts.

- *Manager:* A Manager role is the second-most-powerful user role. Typically, Managers are people, such as sales managers, who manage the various users of the database and control the types of data that is entered into the database. Managers generally don't have the time — or sometime the technical knowledge — to use the various maintenance tools that I describe in Chapter 17. The Manager can access nearly all the areas of ACT! except for database maintenance and user management. The Manager is also restricted from viewing, editing, or deleting the private records of other individuals.

- *Administrator:* The Administrator can perform any database function and is the chief, the head honcho, the Big Guy — the person everyone blames if something goes wrong with the database. When a user creates a database, he or she is automatically assigned the Administrator role. This role is the most powerful role in ACT!, with access to all areas of the application and all data in the supplemental files folders. The only thing the Administrator can't do is access, edit, or delete records marked as private by another user (and get out of speeding tickets when caught doing 50 in a 35 mph zone).

Be sure to note which users you give the Administrator user level. These users are the only ones who can add users, create a backup, and perform routine maintenance on the database.

Assigning two users as Administrators of the database is always a good idea. Not only do those two people feel extra special, but it can save your little rear end. As hard as it might be to believe, the Administrator might leave the company suddenly, and without warning — taking the keys for the rest room and the password for the database with him. This means you might not be able to access the database, perform routine maintenance, add users, or make field changes. You might also find yourself looking for a new job. *Remember:* No password, no entry!

8. Select the Logon Access check box option and then click Next.

This option enables the new user to access your database. If you don't want a user to have access to your database, feel free to clear this check box. I show you how to delete and disable (but hopefully not maim!) your database users later in this chapter.

9. Select additional options that the user might be able to access.

These additional options are only customizable for Standard and Manager level users. These options aren't available to the Browsers and Restricted users in the audience, and of course, Mr. Bigshot Administrator automatically has all these options available to him.

- *Accounting Link Tasks:* Allows the user to install and use an Accounting link.

- *Handheld Device Sync:* Gives permission for the user to set up his handheld device and synchronize his ACT! data into it.

- *Remote Administration:* Lets the user of a synchronizing remote database back up, restore, and check and repair his own database. In other words, the user becomes an "almost-Administrator" for his database.

- *Export to Excel:* Permits the user to export any list view information into Excel.

- *Delete Records:* Authorizes the Standard user to delete records (contacts, companies, groups, activity series, notes, histories, opportunities, and secondary contacts) that he/she owns. By default, the Manager already has the permission to delete at will.

The above options are available only in the ACT! Premium for Workgroups edition. Sorry, the alloy wheel option is still available only for cars!

10. Click Finish.

Deleting login users

After you master adding new users to your database, you need to know how to delete users when they leave. After all, easy come, easy go. The first thing that you need to do is to determine whether you're going to actually delete the user or just deny him or her access to the database. There is a slight difference.

If you are the database Administrator and you simply want to stop someone from accessing the database, you can do so without having to actually delete that person as a user. You can simply shut off her login privileges (a very simple process).

One of the reasons why you add users to the database is so they can perform various functions, such as scheduling appointments and creating notes. The user's name is also associated with any contact that he may create. Opting to shut off a user's login privileges, rather than delete that user entirely, eliminates the possibility of losing this information. Here's how you shut off a user's access to the database:

1. **Choose Tools⇨Manage Users from any ACT! screen.**

   The Manage Users dialog box opens (refer to Figure 16-1).

2. **Select the name of the user for whom you wish to change the access rights.**

3. **Click Edit User Information.**

4. **Click Next to bypass the Password window.**

   If you're removing a user's ability to log in to the database, he no longer can use a password.

5. **Select Inactive and then click Finish.**

If you're using ACT! 2005 Standard Edition, you are limited to ten *active* users. When someone no longer works for your company — or no longer needs access to the database — make sure you change the user information to reflect his or her inactive status.

Some of you are still determined to permanently erase all traces of past users from both your database and your mind. The only users you can safely remove from your database are those users who never added contacts, activities, notes, or histories. You might also have other users who no longer need to be associated with specific contacts, activities, notes, or histories. ACT!, being the smart program that you've grown to know and love, allows you to delete a user while preserving the information (notes, histories, and so on) associated with him by reassigning those items to another user.

Follow these steps to remove a user from your database:

1. **Choose Tools⇨Manage Users from any ACT! view.**

   The Manage Users dialog box appears (refer to Figure 16-1).

2. **Select the name of the user whom you want to remove from your database.**

3. **Click Delete User.**

   This is where ACT! shows its true colors — and in fact shows off a little. When you choose to delete a user, one of two things happens:

   - *If the user never created any information,* you receive two message windows. The first asks whether you really want to remove the user. If you answer Yes, the contact is no longer a user. The second dialog box asks whether you want to retain this user as a contact. If you answer Yes, the user can no longer be one of the *contacts* in your database.

   - *If the user did enter information into ACT!,* a dialog box pop ups that looks quite a bit like the one you see in Figure 16-3. If you select Delete Records Belonging to This User, you in essence say *adios* to all contact records and associated data including notes and history — no matter who entered that data. You'll also be deleting any notes, and activities created by that user. A safer choice is to choose the Reassign Records to Another User option; you retain all the contacts, notes, histories, and activities created by the user, and the other user's name is now assigned to them.

Figure 16-3:
Deleting a user with attached data.

After you reassign contact records to a new user, you can't reverse the process. From here on, the notes, histories, and contacts that the deleted user created appear to have been created by the new user. However, if you simply delete a user without reassigning his records, you risk losing a lot of contact information. If you don't want that to happen, I recommend simply removing the former user's login privileges.

Rather than deleting a user of your database, you might consider changing the Record Manager field for all contacts that were associated with the old user to reflect the Record Manager they are now associated with. Skip over to Chapter 15 to find out how you can change the field data for a whole bunch of contacts at once.

Contact Access

The Premium edition of ACT! includes a neat little party trick: the ability to assign record level access. Simply, record level access refers to who can see a record. A Database Administrator or Manager can set a record access level preference for contacts, groups, and opportunities.

The three levels of access are

- ✔ **Public:** These records are available for the whole world — or at least the users of your database — to see.
- ✔ **Private:** These records are visible only to the user who created the record.
- ✔ **Limited Access**: Selected users and/or teams of users have the pleasure of viewing these records.

Here are two good reasons why you'd want to limit access to the various records in your database:

- ✔ Users might feel more comfortable working with only their own contacts. By removing access to other contacts, they virtually work in their own little world — or in this case, database.
- ✔ As hard as it may be to imagine, management might feel somewhat protective about the records in their database. They might have nightmares about some of their salespeople walking out the door and into the offices of a competitor with the contents of the company database firmly in hand. By limiting a user to only the contact's that he's developed or working with, you eliminate the chance that the rest of the database could end up in enemy territory.

Creating a team

If you have many users in your database, you'll probably want to divide your users into teams. After you create a team of users, you can assign as many records as you want to that team. The members of the team can access all records that they have been given access to; other database users won't even know that those records exist. Fortunately for you, this isn't as traumatic as choosing sides for the volleyball team back in middle school. Follow these three easy steps to set your teams:

1. **Choose Tools➪Manage Teams from any ACT! screen.**

   The Manage Teams dialog box appears. You'll immediately recognize it because it looks just like Figure 16-4.

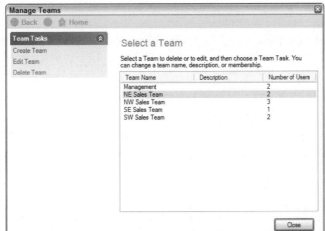

Figure 16-4: Creating a team of users.

2. **Click Create Team from the Team Tasks box.**

   The Manage Teams window pops open. Let the games begin! Here's where you can name the team and assign the players . . . er, users.

   • *To add one or more users:* Select the users in the Available Users list and then click the right arrow button to add the users to the Include These Users in Team list.

   • *To add all available users to the team:* Click the double-right arrow button.

   • *To create a new user:* Click Create User and follow the steps to create a user. The new user is automatically added to the team.

3. **Click Finish when you're finished.**

Assigning access rights

After you assign the players to the teams (access rights; see the preceding section), get ready to rumble! The purpose of the game is to decide who gets to view which contacts. You can do this on a contact-by-contact basis. This works out well if you assign access rights to each new contact as you create it.

1. **Click the Contact Info tab from the Contacts view.**

   In Chapter 4, you can read how to add new contacts to your database and to fill in as many of the fields as possible. One of those fields is the Contact Access field, as shown in Figure 16-5.

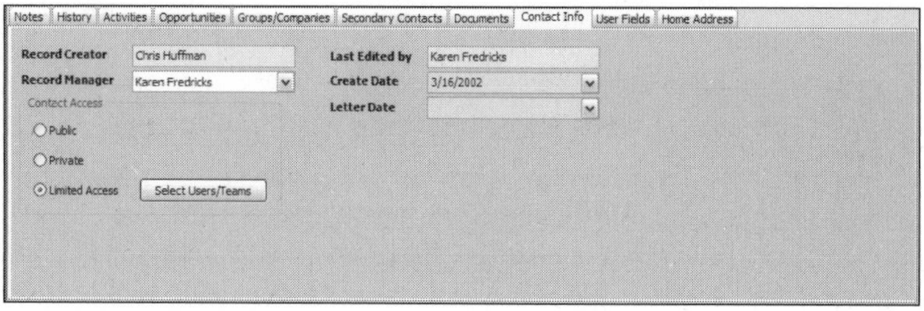

Figure 16-5:
The Contact
Access
field.

2. **Select the Limited Access radio option and then click the Select Users/Team button.**

   The Select Users and Teams window appears, as shown in Figure 16-6.

Figure 16-6:
Select users
and teams
that can
access a
contact
record.

3. **Select the Users and/or the Teams that can access the contact and then click OK.**

   Although this seems pretty straight-forward, just remember that you're indicating who can view the contact as well as denying access to those whom you don't select.

As your database grows, you'll probably find yourself outgrowing the one-by-one method of assigning contact access. You might find yourself worrying about the hundreds of contacts that you have to assign to the Southwestern regional sales manager. In fact, you might start having nightmares about the expanding Northeastern territory and the four new key personnel that were hired to cover the area. Stop fretting! You can change the contact access for multiple contacts just about as easily as you do it for a single contact if you follow these steps.

1. **Create a Lookup of the contacts for whom you'd like to change the Contact Access.**

   I like to think of ACT! as a series of building blocks. Chapter 13 shows you how to create new database fields; Chapter 6 shows you how to create a lookup on any one of those fields. For example, you might be looking for all contacts that have the word *Northeast* in the Territory field. The results of your search appear in the Contact List.

2. **Click Tag All to select all the records.**

3. **Choose Contacts⇨Edit Contact Access⇨Add Users/Teams.**

   You should be feeling a sense of *déjà vu.* The Add Users/Teams dialog box appears. Although the window is slightly different than the one in Figure 16-6, it works in exactly the same way. From here, you can select your teams and/or users just like you did when designating the contact access for a single user.

4. **Click OK after you finish assigning the Users and/or Team that can access the current contact lookup.**

5. **Click Yes in the message prompt that appears.**

   ACT! wants to make really, really sure that you want to change the access rights for your current lookup so it asks you once more to confirm your decision. If you click No, the message prompt closes without changing the user access.

Finding contacts by access level

Life seems good, you're floating in the swimming pool safe in the thought that you've divided all your contacts and assigned them to the appropriate users. Suddenly the thought occurs to you that you might just want to produce a list of the contacts that were assigned to each team. Don't panic — here's an easy way to find contact records assigned to a specific access type.

1. **Choose Lookup⇨Advanced⇨Contact by Access.**

   The Lookup Contacts by Access dialog box appears. Take a gander at Figure 16-7 to see what it looks like.

2. **Select your lookup preferences.**

   • *Select an access type:* Indicate here whether you're hunting for public, private, or limited access contacts.

   • *Select an Accessible To option:* Indicate the user or team that has access to the contacts.

   • *Select the Record Manager:* Variety is the spice of life — or in this case, the lookup. If you're looking to find all of Joe's contacts that the Northwestern sales team has access to, here's your chance.

3. **Click OK to finish.**

Figure 16-7:
The Lookup
Contacts by
Access
dialog box.

Lookup Contacts by Access

Search for

Limited Access Contacts

Accessible to

○ User: Karen Fredricks

● Team: NW Sales Team

For contacts with record manager

Karen Fredricks

☑ Include users

OK   Cancel

Networking 101

Your mother probably taught you to share when you were a little kid. Now that you're grown, it's still a good thing to share — especially when you're talking about a database. This section is designed for those of you who want to place an ACT! database on an existing network of computers.

You achieve optimum performance in ACT! when using a client-server network in which each computer on the network is either a client or a server. *Servers* are powerful computers or processes; their purpose in life is to sit in a back closet and hold all your data. *Clients* are the computers that your individual users actually sit at trying to look busy.

Another type of network — peer-to-peer — is generally simpler but doesn't offer the same performance as a client-server network. A peer-to-peer network doesn't have a dedicated server; the data is stored on various computers. The network performance is directly proportional to the amount of work being done on each computer. If the database is stored on Sally's computer, and Sally happens to be listening to an Internet radio station, downloading a file or two as well as instant-messaging her best friends, you might notice a big decrease in performance.

Getting your network ducks in order

Before you attempt to share a database across a network, digest a few tidbits of information. Feel free to wash these tidbits down with a slice of pizza and a beer if you'd like.

✔ In order to share a database, you must create this database on the computer (server) that will host the shared database.

✔ A copy of ACT! must be installed on the server and on all workstations that will be used to access the database.

✔ All users must have the same version and build of ACT! 2006.

✔ All workstations must have full read/write access to the Database folder and the Supplemental Files folders.

✔ You need to ensure that the database share properties are enabled by choosing Tools➪Database Maintenance➪Share Database from any ACT! screen.

Padding the workstations

After you install ACT! on both the server and the workstations, your job is almost finished. However, you still have one last housekeeping task to accomplish before you can go home for the day. If you are a standalone database user, you'd install both the ACT! program and your database onto your hard drive. In a network installation, however, chances are that the ACT! program is installed on your computer and the database is installed on the server. Enter the PAD file. Not sure what a PAD file is? Keep reading.

If you create an ACT! database called `Mydatabase`, three files magically appear: `mydatabase.adf`, `mydatabase.alf`, and `mydatabase.pad`. The PAD file stands for *pointer to ACT! database* because it is quite simply a pointer to the actual database files. Although this file is small in size, it's big in stature. The PAD file doesn't contain any data per se; its importance lies in the fact that it lets the ACT! program know where to find the database.

In order to have ACT! perform at its very best level, make copies of the PAD file and copy it to the workstation of every one of your ACT! users. The most common method of copying this file to another computer is to use Windows Explorer (or My Computer) to make a copy of the original PAD file and then navigate through the network to paste the file to the hard drive of each remote workstation. You also want to ensure that the remote workstation can access the folder hosting the original PAD file and that the remote user has Full Control Permissions for this location.

Silently Installing ACT!

If you're reading this chapter and really have a vendetta against your IT person, make sure you don't show him this section. If you're an IT person and your salary is directly related to the amount of moaning and complaining you do (more moaning, meaning more money), make sure your boss never reads this section. If you're trying to rollout ACT! on multiple workstations, memorize the following instructions — or at least know where this book is located at all times.

Silent Installation is geek-speak for the ability of network administrators to install ACT! on user workstations from one central location. When the administrator installs ACT!, he uses a command line that records the installation information so that it can be used for subsequent installations. This command includes key preferences and serial number information.

The following steps are not intended for the faint of heart — or the novice computer user. These instructions will make a lot of sense to IT people and other assorted computer geeks. For the rest of us, this section might as well be written in Greek!

Servicing the server

The Administrator has to complete a few steps in order to install ACT! on the server. After all, he's the Administrator, he's being paid the big bucks, and he's got to prove that he's worth it.

1. **Make sure that .NET Framework 1.1 is installed on the server.**

   This is pretty straightforward. If .NET Framework 1.1 has not been installed on the server, you can actually install it by using the following command line:

   ```
   1033dotnetfx.exe
   ```

2. **Install ACT! on the server.**

   To install ACT!, use the following command line:

   ```
   [Drive letter]:\ACTWG\setup.exe /r
           /f1"c:\ISSConfig.iss"
   ```

3. **Start ACT!.**

   The person who starts ACT! the first time must be a local Windows administrator on the machine in order to activate ACT! because you'll be prompted to register and activate ACT!.

4. **Create your new database.**

   If you need help here, feel free to flip back to Chapter 3 for a little help in setting up a new database.

5. **Set the user preferences.**

   The Administrator can set preferences that include the following:

   - The location of personal files associated with ACT!
   - The background colors and fonts for calendars, lists, and other views
   - How contact names display
   - How users are notified of new e-mail messages

6. Copy the appropriate files to the Silent Install folder.

If you installed ACT! as outlined earlier in these steps, an SI folder is created under the ACTWG folder. It should contain the `SilentInst.ini` file. In addition, you want to move a couple of other items into that folder:

- `si.txt` file: This contains the serial number and the error message that displays if a problem occurs during installation. Modify that file to contain your serial number information.

- `ISSConfig.iss` file

- Preferences folder: This contains the preferences that can be deployed to the users' machines. You'll find that folder buried away in

```
C:\Documents and Settings\[User's folder]\Application Data\ACT\
        ACT for Win 8\Preferences
```

Working with the workstations

Here comes the final piece of the puzzle — getting ACT! up and running on the individual work stations. Before you start installing, you want to verify a few things on each workstation:

- ✔ .NET Framework 1.1 must be installed on every workstation prior to installing ACT!.

- ✔ The workstation cannot already have ACT! 2006 installed on it. You can, however, have ACT! 6 or earlier versions installed.

- ✔ Make sure that ACT!, Outlook, Word, Excel, and Internet Explorer are closed.

- ✔ Shut off personal firewall software.

- ✔ LanManServer must be running. To check this, choose Start⇨ Control Panel⇨Administrative Tools⇨Services. In the Name list, click Server and make sure that it's running.

- ✔ SP2 or later must be installed if the operating system is Windows 2000 Professional.

You're ready to run the silent install. All you have to do is use the following command line:

```
[Network Drive letter]:\ ACTWG\setup.exe /s /f1" [Network Drive letter]:\ACTWG
        \SI\ISSConfig.iss" /f2"c:\installation_output.log"
```

If you run into problems or aren't quite sure that the installation worked, check the file named `installation_output.log` at the location specified in the `f2` command line parameter. `Result Code = 0` means that the installation was successful; `Result Code = -3` indicates that the installation failed.

The ACT! Scheduler

As you can see throughout this chapter, the database Administrator and Manager have a lot of responsibility. The ACT! Scheduler feature helps them out with two of these tasks by automating them:

🖊 Database back-up

🖊 Database synchronization of remote databases

Administrators or Managers can access the ACT! Scheduler. Standard users can be given permission to use the ACT! Scheduler for their remote database if they use one. The ACT! Scheduler is actually a program that runs alongside ACT!; if the Scheduler is running, you see an icon in your system tray, as illustrated in Figure 16-8. When a task is created and scheduled for a database, the ACT! Scheduler service lets the task run whether ACT! is running or not.

Figure 16-8:
The ACT!
Scheduler.

Opening the ACT! Scheduler

Like just about everything else, creating a task for the ACT! Scheduler is child's play:

1. Choose Tools➪ACT! Scheduler.

If you already see the ACT! Scheduler icon in your system tray, feel free to right-click it and choose Open ACT! Scheduler. In either case, the ACT! Scheduler opens just like you asked it to do; you can check out its appearance in Figure 16-9.

Figure 16-9:
The ACT!
Scheduler.

2. **Click Create a Task.**

   The first window of the ACT! Scheduler Wizard opens up. Like many of the other setup tasks, ACT! happily steps you through the process. All you have to do is fill in the name and location of your database, user name, and password. Don't forget to click Next to continue.

3. **Select the task you want to schedule and then click Finish.**

   This step is pretty much of a no-brainer — you have a choice of scheduling a backup. If you're working on a remote synchronized database and the Administrator has given you his blessing, you can opt to automate the synchronization process.

Viewing or purging the task log

Although you might just want to "set it and forget it," double-check that your scheduled tasks are indeed being run when scheduled. The ACT! Scheduler creates a log file that you can view. The log file contains details of the automated tasks including the task result and a description of any errors, should they occur. You might want to purge older entries from the log file from time to time as well.

To view the task log:

1. **Choose Tools⇨ACT! Scheduler.**

   By golly, this opens the ACT! Scheduler; refer to Figure 16-9.

2. **Click View Task Log.**

 The View Task Log page appears. Hopefully, you'll see the date and time that the last scheduled activity was run. However, you might also see that one of the following situations caused your backup not to run:

 - *Database locked:* Someone decided to lock the database at the same time that the backup was to run. Chapter 13 mentions how to — and who can — lock a database.

 - *Database schema mismatch:* All databases must be on the same release number. If you schedule the backup of a database that was in a different release version than the one you're currently in, the backup cannot proceed.

 - *An inaccessible path:* If you move the database or change the drive mapping, the backup cannot run.

3. **If desired, purge the task log by clicking Purge Log.**

 The Purge Log dialog box opens.

 a. *Select a date to delete entries occurring on or before.*

 b. *Click OK and wish your Purge Log a fond* adieu.

Importing New Information into ACT!

You might have nothing but time on your hands and decide that the one thing you want to do with all that time is to sit down and enter thousands of new contacts into your database. Or, you might have lots of excess cash in your drawer and decide to hire someone to enter thousands of new contacts into your database. My hat is off to you, and all I can ask is that you send me a postcard in ten years when you finish.

If you're hoping that ACT! has an easier solution — it does! The question you need to ask yourself is where did that data come from? I have great news for you if your data came from any of the following sources:

- ✔ You purchased a list and received it as a download or on a disk.

- ✔ You downloaded a list from an Internet site.

- ✔ You received the list on disk/disc in conjunction with a trade show you attended.

- ✔ Someone in your organization has kept his or her contact information in another (gasp!) program besides ACT!.

- ✔ Another piece of software that you're using — for example, QuickBooks — contains a good portion of the contact information you want to have in ACT!.

All these situations mean that your data is in electronic format, which you can easily import into ACT!. You get to head to the beach rather than head for your keyboard. ACT! can easily import your information if it is currently in one of the following formats:

- ✔ **ACT! in either the current or prior versions**

- ✔ **Outlook**

   If you or someone in your organization is currently using Outlook for contact management, you need to check out Chapter 18 to find out how easily you can import that information into ACT!.

- ✔ **dBase**

- ✔ **Palm Desktop**

- ✔ **Text-delimited**

Most databases have an option to export the data. After you export the data, you need to save the data in text-delimited format. You can easily save data in the correct format using Excel. If you are using a relatively old program that was written for DOS, you might not find an Export option. Not to worry — most DOS programs allow you to print to file, which in essence is creating a text file.

To start importing information and stop spending countless hours hovering over your keyboard, follow these steps:

1. **Open the ACT! database you want to import your information into.**

   If you are importing another ACT! database, perform routine maintenance on that database and back it up *before* attempting to bring in the new data. Not sure how to perform these feats? Chapter 15 explains them in more detail.

   Before you start importing data, be sure to select the Duplicate Checking option. This option is particularly important if you suspect that your current database might include some of the same contacts as the imported information. Duplicate checking merges any duplicate records with existing ACT! records. If you don't have duplicate checking turned on, you might find yourself merging hundreds — or even thousands — of duplicate records *one pair at a time.* Check out Chapter 3 to discover how to turn on this preference setting.

2. **Choose File⇨Import.**

   Only Administrators and Managers have permission to import data into the ACT! database.

   Holy guacamole! A wizard helps you out; if you follow the instructions, you have your data imported in a jiffy.

3. **Click Next to continue.**

   The Specify Source screen of the wizard appears (see Figure 16-10).

4. **Fill in the important information about your import.**

   • *What Type of File Do You Want to Import?:* Choose the file type from the drop-down menu.

   • *File Name and Location:* Click the Browse button to navigate to the file that you're importing.

   • *User Name and Password:* If you're importing an existing ACT! database into the current database, you need to supply this information for the old database. If you're importing data from another format, these options are grayed out.

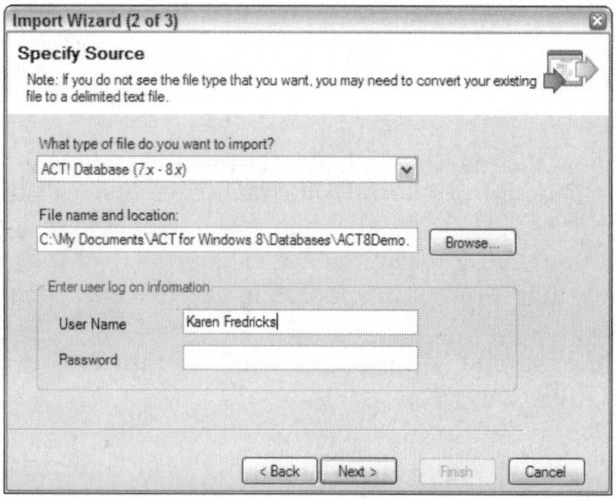

Figure 16-10:
Specifying
the source
file for data
importing.

5. **Click Next to continue.**

6. **Specify the type of records you want to import and then click Next.**

   If you're importing an existing database, you can choose to import contact, group, or company records. If you're importing a text file, you can decide whether you want the imported information to appear as contact, group, or company records.

   The Specify Import Options screen appears, as shown in Figure 16-11.

7. **Specify your import options if importing a text file and then click Next.**

   Here's where you can indicate whether your text file is in tab or comma format and whether you want to include the header row of your import file. The header row is the row that names each of the fields you are importing. If you include it, you end up with a contact record whose company name might be "company."

   The Contact Map screen of the wizard appears, as shown in Figure 16-12.

Figure 16-11:
Text file
import
options.

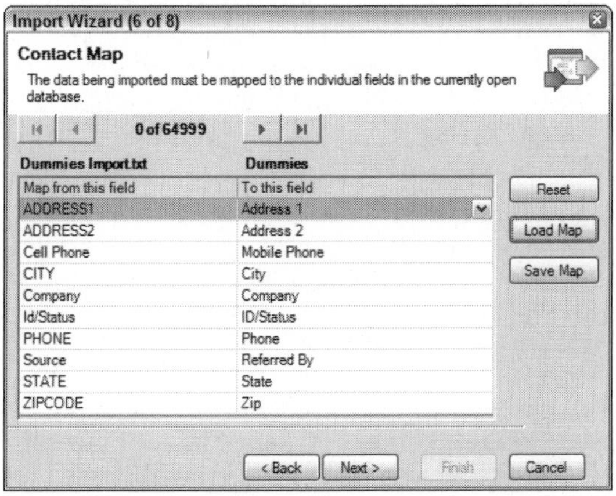

Figure 16-12:
Mapping
fields for a
data import.

8. **Map the fields from the new information to existing fields in the ACT! database and then click Next.**

   Mapping fields allows you to associate field names from the import database to the corresponding fields in your current ACT! database. If the names of the fields in your import database exactly match the names of the fields in your current ACT! database, you're home free. You'll notice in Figure 16-12 that the left side of this screen indicates the field names of the *source* database you are importing; the right side indicates the field names of your current or *target* database.

   Blank fields in the right column are indications that the field in the left column doesn't import. To remedy this situation, you need to click the drop-down arrows for all blank ACT! fields and indicate the name of the ACT! field you want to use to hold this new data. If your ACT! database is missing key fields, you need to add them to your database before you can import information; Chapter 13 tells you how to add fields to your database.

After you map the fields, you can save the mapping by clicking the Save Map button. That way, you can click the Load Map button in the future if you ever import another similar database. It also comes in handy to save a map in case you have to stop the import in order to add in a few missing fields.

You'll notice a few arrow buttons along the top. If you click the right-pointing arrow, you're treated to a sneak preview of what your information looks like after the import completes.

To make life easier on yourself, consider renaming the fields in your import database to exactly match the names of your ACT! fields. For example, ACT!'s main address field is labeled *Address 1*. Renaming the address field in your import database to Address 1 causes the fields in both databases to map automatically.

Don't create new fields that might be lurking *incognito* in your database. You'll want to be very familiar with the structure of your ACT! database before attempting an import. Many users add a Cell Phone field to their ACT! database without realizing that a Mobile Phone field was already in existence. *Postal code, zip,* and *zip code* are pretty much three different ways of saying exactly the same thing.

 9. **Specify the merge options if importing another ACT! database into your current one.**

ACT! asks for a bit of feedback concerning what happens if a contact record in the import database matches a contact record in your current ACT! database. Typically, you want to merge the information together so that the notes you entered for Nancy Wilson in your import database combine with the notes you added for Nancy in your current ACT! database. However, if you prefer, you can change the option so either

   • Duplicated information isn't imported.

   • Information from the import database overrides the information in your current ACT! database.

10. **Click Finish to start your merge.**

You might want to take a quick break after completing the wizard. Depending on the number of contacts you are importing, this step can take a while. Just make sure you keep an eye on your computer because ACT! might run into multiple duplicate contacts and ask you whether you want to merge them.

After importing your contacts, you can tweak them a bit. For example, you might want to change the ID/Status field to Prospect, or the Referred By field to Imported Database. Chapter 6 walks you through creating a lookup based on the contact's Create Date field, and Chapter 15 shows you how to perform a global search and replace.

Chapter 17

ACT!ing with Synchronizations

*I*n past versions of ACT!, synchronization was a very delicate — and technical — operation. If not done correctly, you had a great chance of corrupting your database. The synchronization process is now much more streamlined. Although many steps are involved, they're not difficult or complicated.

Remote users must have a way to connect their computers to the main computer's network in order to synchronize. In some cases, that involves bringing in the remote user's laptop and connecting it to the network. Synchronization can also be done by connecting to the host remotely via a VPN — or if you have the Premium version of ACT!, by the use of an IIS. Creating a VPN or an IIS (Internet Information Services) is beyond the scope of this book; I assume that you already have the correct info structure in place.

What in the World Is Synchronization?

To understand synchronization, you need to know the following terms:

▸ The *master* database is the main database that contains all your data.

▸ The *remote* database is a separate database being used by another user, generally in a different location.

ACT! users commonly confuse backing up and restoring data with a true data synchronization. If you back up your database and restore it on a remote user's computer, the remote user now has a carbon copy of your database. This method works fine if the remote user doesn't want to make any changes to his database. However, if you both make changes to your respective databases, you have no way of merging those changes. If you back up your database and restore it once again to the remote user's computer, you wipe out any changes he made.

Synchronization means that you can make changes from either the master or the remote database. It's the exact same concept that's used when you synchronize your PDA to your computer. After synchronizing, changes made in the master database are seen in the remote database and vice versa.

Why synchronize?

Here are several reasons why you want to synchronize your data:

- ✔ **You want to share your database information with other remote users in your organization and vice versa.**
- ✔ **Your database is located on an office server, but you need to keep your information on a laptop for traveling purposes.**
- ✔ **For security purposes, you want some of your users to have access to only portions of your database.**

  ACT!'s synchronization allows you to send and receive changes based on selected contacts so that your remote user's database contains only a portion of the entire master database.

Chapters 22 and 23 talk about *ACT! Premium for Web,* the Web-based version of ACT!. If your remote user doesn't need to carry his database with him on a laptop computer, consider this alternative method.

The synchronization cycle in a nutshell

Here's what happens during the synchronization cycle:

1. Any changes that you make to your remote database are compiled into a packet and sent back to the master database.

2. When the master database "hears" the remote database, it accepts the changes and sends out any changes that occurred in the master database that affect the remote user.

3. As other remote users sync to the master database, they can also receive any contact changes that affect them, including ones made by other remote users.

Things that change during a synchronization

When you synchronize your data, you merge any changes that you make to your database with changes made by your remote user(s), including the following:

- ✔ **Contact information:** If you change a contact's telephone number and the remote user changes the address, ACT! merges both changes into the original contact record. If you change the same contact's telephone number and the numbers don't match, ACT! applies the most recent change.

- ✔ **Notes and histories:** If you and the remote user add notes, the contact record now reflects all the notes and histories of both the master and remote users.

- ✔ **The Task List:** Any tasks that either you or the remote users create now appear in both the master and the remote databases. You can even schedule an activity for your remote users.

- ✔ **Calendars:** Synchronization allows you to share the calendars of all the users in your organization.

- ✔ **Field definitions:** If the master database has added, removed, or changed fields, these changes are sent to the remote users.

- ✔ **Drop-down lists:** Changes made in the master database to field drop-down lists are sent to remote users.

- ✔ **Layouts:** New or customized contact, company, and group layouts synchronize with remote users.

- ✔ **Templates:** Letters, reports, envelopes, and labels synchronize with to remote users.

- ✔ **Attachments:** All documents attached to the master and remote databases synchronize.

Documents stored in your personal folders don't synchronize.

Performing a Synchronization in Four ACT!s

The synchronization process consists of four parts: understanding the sync process, setting up the master database, setting up the remote database, and the actual sync process.

The synchronization setup must be done directly on the server. Do not attempt to set up a synchronization using one of the workstations.

ACT! 1: Doing your homework

If your knees are shaking, just relax, take a deep breath, and plot your strategy. Before bravely forging ahead and attempting to sync, you can do a little preparation. Here are some tips that make your synchronizations run more smoothly:

- **Enter your data consistently.** I know I sound like a broken record, but this is worth repeating: Enter your data consistently. For example, if you enter a contact's company name as *Tech Benders, Inc.* and someone else enters it as *Tech Benders,* you have duplicate contact records when you synchronize data. To help enter data consistently, rely on drop-down lists whenever possible.

- **Determine which contacts to include in the remote user's database.** This decision might involve setting up a query to identify those contacts. If Joe is to receive all the contacts in the Southwest region, consider adding a region field to your database — or at the very least, identify those states included in the Southwest.

- **Perform a spring-cleaning on your database.** Scan for duplicate records and clean up your database *before* starting the synchronization process. Turn to Chapter 16 to do so.

- **Use the same criteria to search for duplicate records.** ACT! matches contact records using a *Unique ID,* which is an identifier assigned to each record in your database. If you set up the synchronization procedure correctly, identical contacts in all databases have the same Unique ID. If both you and your remote users add the same contact to your databases, each contact is assigned a different Unique ID. If the Unique IDs of two records do not match, ACT! matches duplicate records using the criteria you specify. To ensure that the synchronization process doesn't create duplicate contact records, both databases need to use the same criteria for determining duplicate records.

  You can find out how to modify your duplicate record match criteria in Chapter 16.

- **All users must have the same product and version of ACT!.** You can't synchronize an ACT! 2006 database with an ACT! 6 database. You also can't synchronize an ACT! 2006 database with an ACT! 2006 Premium database. Make sure that all databases have the most recent release update of ACT!:

  - To display your current version, choose Help⇨About ACT!

  - To update your version of ACT!, choose Help⇨ACT! Update.

ACT! 2: Setting up the main database

You must follow a number of steps in order to set up a remote database. Sound like a lot of work? Don't worry; only Administrators and Managers need apply because other users don't have the appropriate rights to set up synchronization. And, if you are an Administrator or a Manager, you can stop hiding under your desk; although there are a lot of steps, they are all very easy to follow. You'll also want to make sure that you are sitting at the server when you set up the synchronization.

Enabling synchronization

The first thing you need to do is to turn on the synchronization. Follow these steps:

1. **From any ACT! screen, choose Tools⇨Synchronization Panel.**

   The Synchronization dialog box opens, as shown in Figure 17-1.

Figure 17-1:
Start
synchron-
ization here.

2. **Click the Enable Synchronization option in the Admin Tasks area and then click Yes in the ACT! message dialog box.**

Defining a sync set

The *sync set* is the main list of contacts that the remote user receives. An Administrator or a Manager of the master database creates the sync set. On the simplest level, the sync set consists of all contacts that the remote user has permission to access. However, the Administrator might set up additional criteria to limit the number of contacts that the remote user can access. After you send the database out to the remote user, he has the opportunity to add additional contacts that he has permission to access to his database. Contacts that are added to the remote database by the remote user automatically become part of the remote user's sync.

Consider these key elements before creating a sync set:

- ✔ A sync set is only a starting point; remote users can add additional contacts to their databases from the master database.

- ✔ A sync set can include only contact records that the remote user has permission to access.

- ✔ A sync set always includes all the master database Record Manager contacts as well as all group and company records. The groups and companies populate only those records that the remote user has access to.

- ✔ Master database Administrators and Managers can create sync sets based on a query.

- ✔ An Administrator or a Manager can copy, edit, or delete sync sets.

- ✔ More than one remote database can use a sync set; however, each remote database has only one sync set.

Follow these simple steps to create a sync set:

1. **From any ACT! screen, choose Tools⇨Synchronization Panel.**

   The Synchronization panel opens (refer to Figure 17-1).

2. **Click the Manage Sync Set option in the Admin Tasks area.**

3. **Click Create New Sync Set.**

   For the purposes of this section, I show you how to create a brand-new sync set. Just remember that you can always go back and copy, edit, or delete your sync set, following these same instructions.

4. **Give your sync set a name, an optional description, and then click Next.**

   What you decide to call the sync set is a big deal because you need to recognize it by name later on. If the sync set consists of the contacts used by the remote sales guys, you might name the sync set something clever like *Remote Sales Guys*.

5. **Select the names of the remote users who will use the sync set, click the right-pointing arrow, and then click Next.**

   The remote user must be an active user of the master database, even if he doesn't have permission to access all records.

6. **Decide on one of the following options:**

   - *To synchronize all the available contacts to the sync users,* select the Synchronize All Available Contacts option, click Next, and then click Finish.

- *To further limit the contacts the remote user sees,* select the Define Sync Set Criteria option, click Next, and then click Create Criteria.

  The Sync Set Criteria window opens, as shown in Figure 17-2.

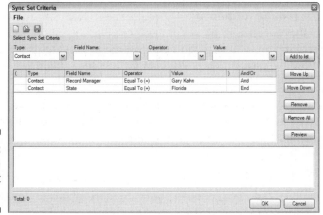

Figure 17-2:
Determine
sync set
criteria.

7. **Choose the criteria you want to set the sync to:**
   - *Field type:* You have only one choice of field type — Contact.
   - *Field Name:* From the Field Name drop-down list, select one of the available contact fields.
   - *Operator:* From the Operator drop-down list, select one of the available items, such as Contains or Equal To (=).
   - *Value:* From the Value drop-down list, select one of the available items that correspond to the selected field name.

8. **Click the Add to List button.**

   As you add a criterion, it appears in the bottom section of the window. Notice in Figure 17-2 that I'm creating my sync set to include all contacts in Florida that are managed by Gary Kahn.

9. **To select more than one criterion, repeat Steps 7 and 8.**

   You might need to use the And/Or column to help you build the query. *And* indicates that a contact must match *all* criteria; *Or* indicates that a contact can match *any one* criterion.

10. **Click the Preview button to see a list of all the contacts that match the criteria you indicated.**

    You even see the total number of records that are included in the sync set.

11. **When you're happy with your results, click OK, click Next to confirm your criteria, and then click Finish.**

    If necessary, you can create or edit additional sync sets or click Home to return to the main Synchronization dialog box.

Creating the remote database

After you enable synchronization and create a sync set, you're ready to create the remote database(s). Depending on the access rights given to them by the master database Administrator, the remote user might not be able to perform various functions, such as backing up their database.

The Administrator can assign a Standard user the right to perform various administrative functions, such as backing up the database and performing routine maintenance. These permissions must be assigned before the creation of the remote database. Chapter 16 shows you how to assign these permissions.

1. **From any ACT! screen, choose Tools⇨Synchronization Panel.**

   The Synchronization dialog box opens (refer to Figure 17-1).

2. **Click Create Remote Database in the Admin Tasks area.**

   Like with most of the other ACT! tasks, you now follow a wizard through the next several steps. Probably the hardest thing you have to do is click Next at each juncture.

3. **Give the remote database a name, click the Browse button to save the new database to a different location if necessary, and then click Next.**

   ACT! database names don't like spaces or symbols.

4. **Select a sync set to use with the database and then click Next.**

   You see the sync set that you created waiting for you.

5. **Indicate the following choices and then click Next.**

   • *Allow database supplemental files to synchronize.*

   • *Allow attachments to synchronize.*

   • *Set the number of days after which the synchronization expires.* This ensures that the remote user synchronizes on a timely basis or risks having the database expire. After a database expires, the remote user can synchronize to the master database one last time, at which point the master database Administrator or Manager has to create a new remote database.

6. **If you're using ACT! Premium for Workgroups, make note of the name of the Master computer and the port assigned to listen for incoming syncs.**

Because the Premium version offers an additional sync option, choose to sync either across the network or over the Internet. If you sync over the Internet, you're prompted for the computer's external IP address. You can find out how to ascertain the server's IP address in Chapter 22.

 7. **Give the database a password (optional) and then click Finish.**

    This might be a good time to wander around the office complaining about how busy you are. ACT! is going to take a moment to create the remote database for you, and you might as well look busy!

 8. **Click the Home button to return to the Synchronization Panel; if necessary, start all over again.**

    If all remote users will use the same sync set, you can skip that part and click Create Remote Database.

 9. **Click Close when you finish creating all the remote databases.**

10. **Choose Tools⇨Synchronize⇨Accept Incoming Syncs.**

    The final step sets the master database in a wait-and-see mode. As the Administrator, your job is almost finished. Time to sit back, pat yourself on the back, and figure out a way to get that database to the remote user.

Delivering the remote data

The only thing you have left to do at this point is to get that new database, along with all the associated files and attachments, out to the remote users. But wouldn't you know it? ACT! has solved that problem for you already. When you create the remote database, you actually create a special backup file; unlike a traditional backup file, this one comes with an .rdb extension. You can simply e-mail the file to the remote user or burn it to CD and send it via snail mail. Just don't forget to send along the password if you used one to create the backup!

ACT! 3: Setting up the remote database

When you set up the remote database and send it off by carrier pigeon to your remote user, the ball is in the other guy's court. Relax and go float in the pool — just make sure to keep the cellphone on in case the remote user has a question. And don't forget the sunscreen!

Restoring the remote database

If you are the remote user, you have a few chores to do. Thankfully, none of them are very hard. The first thing you need to do is restore the remote database that the Administrator of the master database sent. This procedure works pretty much the same way as the restore procedure that I discuss in Chapter 15; the main difference lies in the fact that the remote database has a different backup extension than a traditional database backup file.

Traditional ACT! backup files have a `.zip` extension. Remote database backup files have an `.rdb` extension. Could it be that RDB stands for *Remote Database?* You be the judge!

You, as the remote user, can follow these steps to set up the remote database:

1. **Save the `.rdb` file that you receive from the master database Administrator onto an appropriate spot on your hard drive.**

   My suggestion is that you jot down the location so that you don't have to call the Administrator and ask for help. My experience is that Administrators get very cranky when interrupted in mid-swim.

2. **Open ACT!; from any screen, choose File⇨Restore⇨Database.**

   The Restore Database window appears.

3. **Select the Unpack and Restore Remote Database option and then click OK.**

   The Unpack and Restore an ACT! Remote Database window opens.

4. **Click the Browse button next to the Select the Remote Database File to Restore field to locate the remote database (`.rdb`) backup file that you saved in Step 1.**

5. **Click Browse to select a location to save the restored database.**

   If you're not going to store the database on a network, you'll probably find that the default location, located in your My Documents folder, fills the bill nicely. If you're sharing the database, save it to a place on your network.

6. **Select the Share This Database with Other Users option if you are sharing the database with other users.**

7. **Click OK.**

   If the database you're restoring is password-protected, type your secret password and click OK. Don't know the password? Your Administrator might just have to finish his swim and supply you with it!

After you restore the database, you can open and begin using it just like any other ACT! database. You can also begin to synchronize your data at any time.

ACT! 4: Synchronizing data

The remote user is the keeper of the synchronization key and the only one who can initiate a sync. You'd think that having such a big responsibility would entail a lot of work. Fortunately for you, it doesn't.

1. **From any ACT! screen, choose Tools⇨Synchronize.**

2. **Click the Synchronize Now option.**

   When you synchronize the database, two things happen:

   - Any changes made in the remote database now appear in the master database.

   - Any changes made in the master database associated with contact records included in the remote user's sync set now appear in the remote database.

The synchronization can take a few minutes depending on the number of changes that have been made to both the remote and the master databases. You see an indicator bar roll across your screen and then a congratulatory message celebrating the fact that you performed a successful synchronization. You're also asked to refresh your database so you don't drive yourself crazy looking for changes that might take a moment to appear.

Setting up automatic synchronization

In the standard edition of ACT!, the master database cannot receive sync packets if other users are logged on to a multi-user database. Of course, one way to get around this limitation is to come in at dawn — or stay until midnight — to perform your synchronization. For most of you, this option is not what you have in mind! As the remote user, you might prefer to have ACT! perform your synchronization automatically for you while you're at home snoozing.

Here's how you set up an automatic synchronization:

1. **Open the remote ACT! database.**

2. **Choose Tools⇨Synchronization Panel.**

   The Synchronization dialog box opens (refer to Figure 17-1).

3. **Click Set Sync Schedule in the Users Tasks area.**

   The Sync Schedule window opens, as seen in Figure 17-3.

4. **Indicate your scheduling preferences.**

   - *Occurs:* Indicate the frequency with which you want the synchronization to occur

   - *Occurs At:* Indicate the date and time you want to commence using the automatic synchronization

5. **Click Finish.**

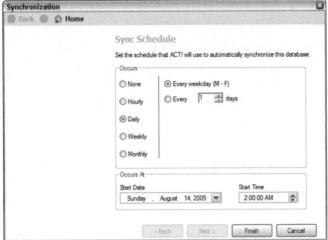

Figure 17-3:
Scheduling
an
automatic
sync.

In the standard ACT! version, you must leave both the master and remote databases open so that synchronization updates are sent and received automatically at the specified times. And only one person can access each database at the time of synchronization.

Chapter 16 talks about the ACT! Scheduler, which is a feature of ACT! Premium. If your organization uses Premium, the remote user(s) can set up the Scheduler and have the synchronization occur even if ACT! isn't open.

Adding contact records to a sync set

Because a sync set is created based on a query and may be used for more than one remote user, you might find that your database is missing some contacts. These contacts represent people that you might have access to but who didn't match the criteria the Administrator used for the sync set. Ironically, these contacts actually reside in the remote database even though you can't access them.

Sound confusing? To put it a little simpler, if you find that you're missing one of your contacts, you can add it to the database:

1. **Choose Tools⇨Synchronization Panel from any ACT! screen.**

   The Synchronization dialog box appears (refer to Figure 17-1).

2. **In the User Tasks area, click Manage Subscription List.**

   You now see a list of all the contacts that you can access. The contacts that are a part of the sync set are indicated with a check mark.

3. **Click Add Contacts to Sync Set in the Subscription Tasks area.**

   The Contacts dialog box opens, as shown in Figure 17-4.

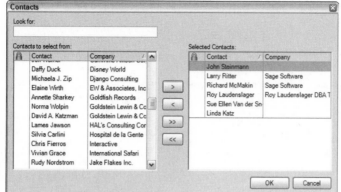

Figure 17-4:
Add contacts to the remote database.

4. **Select the contact(s) from the list on the left, and then click the right arrow button to add them to the remote database.**

5. **When you finish, click OK and then click the Finish button in the Manage Subscription List window.**

The additional contacts appear in your database after your next synchronization.

Maintaining the Synchronization

Wow! The worst is over. Your remote database is synching back to the master database, and life is beautiful. But meanwhile back at the ranch — or at least at the master database — the Administrator's job continues. You might want to check a few minor details from time to time. Or you might decide that the fun is over, and you no longer want to continue syncing.

Viewing the last data synchronized

The synchronization process goes so smoothly that you might be left wondering what, if anything, actually synchronized. Sure enough, you can easily determine that by creating a lookup. Here's all you need to do:

1. **From any ACT! screen, choose Lookup⇨Advanced⇨Last Synchronized.**

   The Last Synchronized window opens, as shown in Figure 17-5.

2. **Specify the Lookup criteria:**

   • *Last Session/Date Range:* You can view either the last contacts synchronized or the contacts that synchronized during a specific date range.

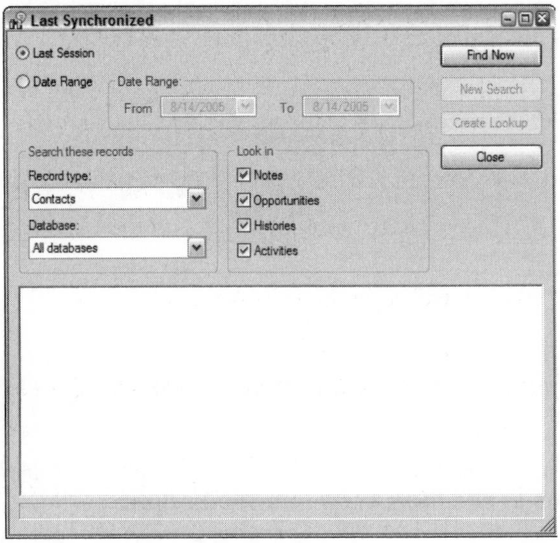

Figure 17-5:
Create a
lookup of
the last
records
synch-
ronized.

- *Record Type:* Indicate whether you want to find contact, company, or group records.

- *Look In:* Specify whether you want to find notes, opportunities, histories, and/or activities that changed during the last synchronization.

3. **Click the Find Now button.**

   The contact records that changed during the last synchronization are shown in the lower section of the Last Synchronized window.

4. **Click the Create Lookup button.**

   The Contact List displays a list of all contacts that changed during the last synchronization.

Although creating a lookup of all the recently synched contacts is generally a job for an Administrator, remote users also have this functionality should they feel an overwhelming desire to find out what changes other users have made to their contacts.

Looking up the sync set lookup

As an Administrator, you probably rush through your day; chances are you occasionally forget something: lunch, your head — or maybe the contacts included in a sync set. You can easily create a list of all the contacts that are part of a sync set by choosing Lookup⇨Advanced⇨Sync Set. The Contact List magically appears, displaying all the contacts included in the sync set. The difficult part is figuring out what to do for lunch!

Viewing and printing sync settings

You might want to review the sync settings of your database that were created for each of the remote databases. Again, this feat is easy to accomplish:

1. **From any ACT! screen, choose Tools⇨Synchronization Panel.**

   The ever-familiar Synchronization dialog box appears (refer to Figure 17-1).

2. **Click Manage Database in the User Tasks area.**

   The Synchronization window opens.

3. **Select the name of your database and click View Settings in the User Tasks area.**

   As you can see from Figure 17-6, you see the names of the master databases and the remote sync set, the sync server port, and the expiration period of the database.

4. **If you want to print the results, click Print and then click Finish.**

Figure 17-6:
Displaying
the sync
settings.

Re-creating a remote database

You might find yourself needing to send out another sync set to a remote user. For example, a remote user might have forgotten to synchronize and finds that his database is about to expire. Or maybe the remote user's computer died a slow and painful death and needs to be replaced. In any case, here is a simple way to re-create a remote database:

1. **From any ACT! screen, choose Tools⇨Synchronization Panel.**

2. **Click Manage Database in the User Tasks area of the Synchronization panel.**

3. **Select the remote database you want to re-create, click Recreate Database, and then click Yes.**

4. **Click the Browse button to specify a location to save the newly re-created database and then click OK.**

   ACT! whirs and hisses as it busily sets up the remote database again. ACT! doesn't complain about having to do this chore a second time. In fact, you're even rewarded with a happy message confirming that you have indeed re-created the remote user's database.

5. **Click OK.**

Stopping the synchronization process

All good things must come to an end, and so it is with your remote database. You can sever the ties that bind the master database to the remote one of three ways. After the synchronization stops, the only way to get it going again is to completely create — or re-create — the remote database. The three ways to sever the ties are

- **Letting the expiration date expire:** Remote databases are assigned an expiration date when they are created. If the remote user fails to synchronize during the allotted time period, the remote database can sync to the master database one last time after the expiration date.

- **From the master database:** The master database can disable synchronization for a remote database and optionally allow one last synchronization before disabling the remote database. The remote database receives a notification that synchronization is disabled and is allowed one last synchronization session.

- **From the remote database:** A user with Administrator rights can disable the remote database so that it no longer synchronizes to the main database. After a remote database is disabled, it is no longer a remote database. However, the database can still be used as a standalone database.

To disable either a master or remote synchronized database, follow these steps:

1. **From any ACT! screen , choose Tools⇨Synchronization Panel.**

2. **In the Admin Tasks area of the Synchronize dialog box, click Disable Synchronization.**

3. **When prompted, click Yes to disable the synchronization.**

Part V
Commonly Overlooked ACT! Features

The 5th Wave   By Rich Tennant

JUST KEEP FOLLOWING THE SIGNS.

In this part . . .

*I*f you aren't content with relying on the basic ACT! functions to keep your life organized and you want to squeeze every last drop of functionality out of ACT!, here's the place to find some of the best-kept secrets of ACT!. Want to teach ACT! to play nicely with your Microsoft products? Interested in keeping a record of your ongoing sales activities? Want the functionality of a high-priced relational database — without mortgaging the farm? ACT! can help you accomplish these goals, and Part V shows you how.

Chapter 18

Integrating ACT! with Microsoft

· ·

· ·

*F*ace it. Microsoft is everywhere. Most likely, you're running more than one of its products on your computer. Like many other software products, ACT! 2006 has taken the "if you can't beat 'em, join 'em" philosophy. ACT! fully integrates with four of the most popular Microsoft products — Outlook, Internet Explorer, Excel, and Word.

Although other Microsoft products don't fully integrate with ACT!, you don't need to stop using them. For example, you can easily store PowerPoint presentations on the Documents tab for easy access.

Changing Your Outlook on Life

A common misconception I hear from potential ACT! users is that they don't need ACT! because they're using Outlook. You might snicker at that suggestion because by now, you realize that Outlook is a PIM (personal information manager) whereas ACT! is a true contact manager. I like to think of ACT! as Outlook on steroids; try doing a mail merge, customize fields, or log in notes in Outlook to see what I mean.

Still, some ACT! users find themselves needing to use Outlook for a variety of reasons:

> ✔ His company uses Outlook to maintain the company calendar.

> ✔ She uses Outlook to keep track of personal addresses and information that don't belong in ACT!

Fortunately, you can use both ACT! and Outlook, but be aware of a few of the ground rules first:

If you read the side of the ACT! box you'll notice that ACT! will work with Outlook versions 2000, 2002 and 2003. If you're using an older version of Outlook, it won't work with any of the versions of ACT! 2006.

- You can import all your Outlook contact information — including appointments, tasks, notes, and journal entries — into ACT!.

- You won't see new Outlook contact information, notes, and journal entries unless you reimport your Outlook data. You can, however, continue to synchronize your ACT! and Outlook calendars.

- Because Outlook appointments and tasks aren't *contact centric* (not tied to a specific contact's record), imported or synchronized data appears in ACT! associated with the My Record of the user who imported or synchronized the information.

- ACT! converts your Outlook notes into one ACT! note.

- You can view all ACT! e-mail addresses in Outlook without synchronizing or importing.

- You can view all Outlook e-mail addresses in ACT! without synchronizing or importing.

- The ACT! e-mail client is a mirror image of the Outlook e-mail client. Inbox folders created in Outlook are visible in ACT! and vice versa.

Importing Outlook contacts into ACT!

ACT! very nicely includes Outlook as one of its import options. After all, more people switch from Outlook to ACT! than from ACT! to Outlook. Here's all you need to do to import the Outlook data:

1. **From any ACT! screen, choose File⇨Import.**

   Backing up your database is a good idea before attempting to try something as tricky as a data import. Chapter 15 explains how to create an ACT! backup.

   The Import Wizard opens with a nice welcoming screen that you can skip by clicking Next.

2. **Select Outlook as the type of data you want to import and click Next.**

   ACT! automatically imports your main Outlook address book. "Sub" address books will not be imported unless you move those contacts into your main address book.

3. **Specify that you want to import contact records and click Next.**

   Your contact records include the good stuff, such as the person's name, company, address, phone number, and shoe size.

4. **Specify your import options and click Next.**

   The Specify Import Options wizard screen opens, as shown in Figure 18-1.

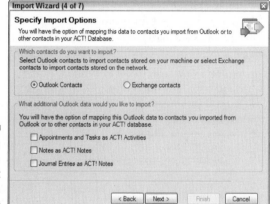

Figure 18-1:
Outlook-to-
ACT! import
options.

- *Outlook Contacts:* Imports your Outlook contacts into ACT!.

- *Exchange Contacts:* Imports your Exchange contacts into ACT! if your company maintains an Outlook Exchange server.

- *Appointments and Tasks as ACT! Activities:* Converts your Outlook appointments and tasks into ACT! activities.

- *Notes as ACT! Notes:* Converts your Outlook notes into ACT! notes.

- *Journal Entries as ACT! Notes:* Imports your Outlook journal entries as ACT! notes.

5. **Confirm the mapping of your Outlook fields to ACT! fields and then click Next.**

   I personally love it when my software does most of my work for me. ACT! has already "translated" the existing Outlook fields into ACT! fields. For example, Outlook's Business Address Postal Code becomes ACT!'s Zip Code field.

6. **Specify your merge options and then click Next.**

   The merge options let you tell ACT! what you'd like to do — replace, ignore, or use the newest contact record (if one of your Outlook contacts matches one of your ACT! contact records).

7. **Click Finish.**

E-mailing Outlook contacts in ACT!

The preceding section describes how to import your Outlook contacts into ACT! and transform them into contact records. However, you can still view all your Outlook e-mail addresses in ACT! even if you don't import your entire Outlook address book into ACT!.

Sending an ACT! e-mail to one of your Outlook contacts is almost too easy. All you need to do is follow these steps:

1. **Generate a new ACT! e-mail message by clicking the E-Mail icon on ACT!'s Navigation bar and then clicking New.**

   The new message window appears.

2. **Click the To button.**

   The Select Recipients dialog box opens, which looks a lot like the Select Recipients dialog box you see in Figure 18-2.

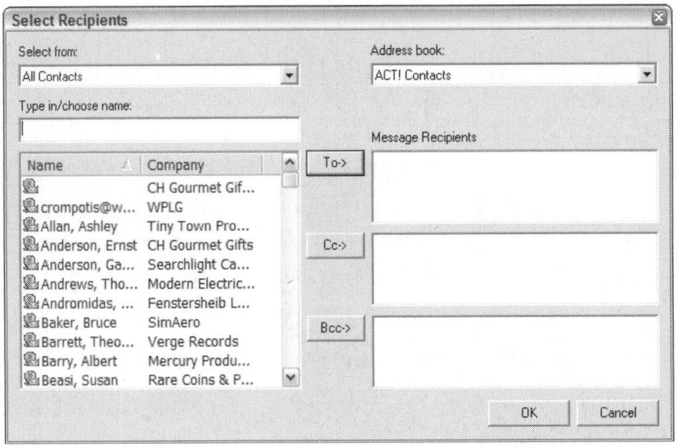

Figure 18-2:
The E-mail
Select
Recipients
dialog box.

3. **Select Microsoft Outlook from the Address Book drop-down list.**

   You now see a list of all your Outlook contacts. To speed up the process, you might consider typing in the first couple of letters of the person's first name in the Type In/Choose Name area.

4. **Select the desired name from the list and then click OK.**

Configuring Outlook to work with ACT!'s Address Book

Although ACT! automatically detects your default Outlook address book(s), Outlook isn't quite that bright. You have to tell Outlook where to find your ACT! data. Follow these steps to do so:

1. **In Outlook, choose Tools➪E-mail Accounts.**

   The E-mail Accounts Wizard opens.

2. **Select the Add a New Directory or Address Book option and then click Next.**

3. **In the Directory or Address Book Type window, select the Additional Address Books option and then click Next.**

4. **Select the ACT! 2006 Address Book option and click Next.**

   The ACT! 2006 Address Book(s) dialog box opens, as shown in Figure 18-3. If you have multiple ACT! databases you can specify three ACT! databases if you like.

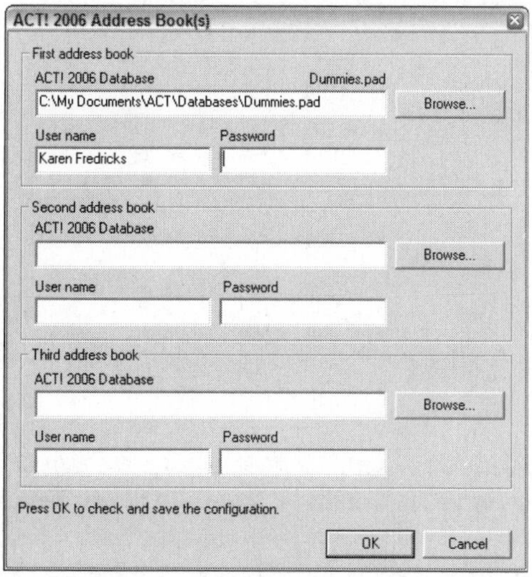

Figure 18-3: Add an ACT! address book to Outlook.

5. **Click Browse to locate and select your ACT! database in the First Address Book section.**

6. **Enter your ACT! user name and password and then click OK.**

   If you have multiple ACT! databases you can specify them in the Second and Third address book sections before closing the ACT! 2006 Address Books) dialog window.

You receive a message telling you to exit Outlook and then reopen it again for your changes to take effect. So. . .

7. **Exit Outlook and reopen it again so your changes take effect.**

E-mailing ACT! contacts in Outlook

After you configure Outlook to play nicely with ACT!, any e-mail addresses that you add to ACT! can be used when sending e-mail using Outlook. You can even create a history of the e-mail sent using Outlook that appears on the contact's History tab in ACT!.

1. **Create a new message in Outlook.**

2. **Fill in the recipient's name.**

   There are a few ways you can accomplish this. If you type in the first couple of letters of the recipient's first name, Outlook catches on and completes the name for you. If you prefer, you can click the To button to open the Select Names dialog box, as shown in Figure 18-4.

Figure 18-4:
Select a
contact to
associate
with a new
Outlook
message.

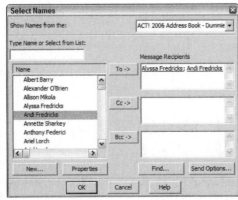

3. **Select the name of your ACT! database from the Show Names from The area.**

4. **Select a contact in the Type Name or Select from List search area and click the right-pointing arrow.**

   To speed up the process, type the first couple of letters of your intended recipient's first name.

5. **Click OK.**

   Your message looks pretty much like what you see in Figure 18-5.

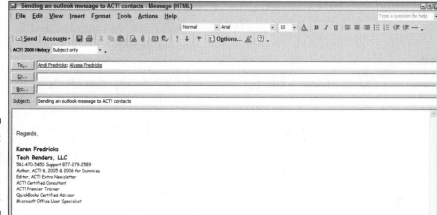

Figure 18-5:
E-mailing an
ACT!
contact in
Outlook

6. **Choose an option from the ACT! History drop-down list.**

   If you need a refresher in ACT!'s e-mail History options head over to Chapter 12.

   Don't see the ACT! History option? Right-click the Outlook toolbar and choose ACT! History.

7. **Fill in your message and Click Send.**

   Once again, you get to sit around twiddling your thumbs while ACT! slaves away, creating a history of the sent e-mail on the contact's History tab.

Creating ACT! history from an e-mail received in Outlook

If you want to attach an e-mail message received in Outlook to a contact's History tab in ACT!, follow these steps:

1. **In Outlook, open the message you want to attach to the ACT! History tab.**

2. **Choose an option from the ACT! History drop-down list.**

   Don't see the ACT! History option? Right-click the Outlook toolbar and choose ACT! History.

3. **Click the Attach to ACT! 2006 Contact(s) button on the Outlook toolbar.**

   Not sure what the button looks like? There should be a vaguely familiar button on the right end of the toolbar — it's the graphic associated with ACT!. If you added more than one ACT! address book to Outlook, you're prompted to select the database in which the contact is stored.

290 Part V: Commonly Overlooked ACT! Features

4. **Select a contact in the Attach E-mail to Contact window and click OK.**

   A link to the e-mail message appears on the contact's ACT! History tab.

Sharing ACT! and Outlook calendars

After you bring your Outlook data into ACT! including your activities — you'll want to keep both your ACT! and Outlook calendars up to date by synchronizing your calendars. (See the section "Importing Outlook contacts into ACT!," earlier in this chapter, if you still need to import your Outlook data.)

Synchronizing your ACT! and Outlook calendars

To keep your ACT! and Outlook calendars the same, follow these steps:

1. **From any ACT! screen, choose Tools⇨Outlook Activities⇨Update Activities.**

   The Update Calendars dialog box opens. Figure 18-6 shows you the various options from which you can choose.

Figure 18-6: Synchronize your ACT! and Outlook calendars.

2. **In the Update area, select the type of update you want to perform — ACT!-to-Outlook, Outlook-to-ACT!, or a two-way sync.**

3. **Select a date option in the For These Dates area.**

   If you chose the Date Range option, select a starting and ending date. Choosing the Today and Future option is always a good idea.

4. **Click Update.**

If you are using ACT!, Outlook, and a PDA, you need to make a decision as to which program to use in order to sync your handheld device. If you attempt to synchronize both ACT! and Outlook to your PDA, chances are quite high that you end up with duplication of your contacts and activities. You're safer synchronizing ACT! and Outlook through ACT! and then synchronizing your PDA to just one of your databases.

Removing Outlook activities from ACT!

After you synchronize your Outlook and ACT! activities, you might want to remove them. If you realize immediately that your synchronization didn't work entirely as planned, you can always restore an ACT! backup. You can also simply remove any synchronized activities.

1. **From any ACT! screen, choose Tools⊃Outlook Activities⊃Remove Activities.**

   The Remote Activities dialog box appears.

2. **Select the appropriate option:**

   • *To remove ACT! activities from Outlook,* select the ACT! Activities from Outlook check box.

   • *To remove Outlook activities from ACT!,* select the Outlook Activities from ACT! check box.

   • *To remove both types of activities,* select both check boxes.

3. **Click OK.**

Choosing to remove Outlook activities from ACT! will remove only those activities that have been added through the synchronization process. It has no effect on Outlook activities imported to your database through importing.

Displaying Outlook activities in ACT!

You can view — or not view — your Outlook activities in ACT! in a number of ways. Your Outlook activities appear on your Activities tab, Task List, and even on the calendars.

Viewing Outlook activities on the ACT! Activities tab

A major difference between ACT! and Outlook is in how the two programs schedule activities. I consider Outlook to be somewhat of a free-for-all; scheduled activities are not generally associated with a specific contact. Not so with ACT!; Chapter 8 shows you how every activity *must* be associated with a contact record.

Because of this difference in scheduling procedures, you don't find your Outlook activities on the Activities tab of an individual contact. You do, however, see all your Outlook activities on the Activities tab of your own My Record contact. Here's how you do it:

1. **Display your My Record contact by choosing Lookup⇨My Record.**

2. **Click the Activities tab.**

   Your Outlook activities show up as To-Do's.

Now, here comes the really cool part: You can edit every one of those synchronized activities. For example, even though all the Outlook activities appear on the Activities tab of your own My Record, you can edit the activity with a simple double-click and change the Schedule With person to any one of your contacts. By doing that, the activity disappears from your own record and reappears on the Schedule With contact's record as though the activity had been originally created in ACT!.

Viewing Outlook activities from ACT!'s Task List

Viewing your Outlook activities in your Task List requires some additional fiddling, but I know you're up to the (Task List) task. Please, no groaning!

1. **Click the Task List icon on ACT!'s Navigation bar.**

   The Task List opens in all its glory.

2. **Click the Options button on the Task List toolbar and select Show Outlook Tasks.**

   If you don't see the Task List toolbar, just click the Show Filters button (and read all about list filters in Chapter 5).

Viewing Outlook activities in ACT! calendars

By now, it probably comes as no surprise to you that your Outlook activities appear magically on all your ACT! calendars. In fact, it would probably have been a surprise if I had said that you can't see them. Because your Outlook activities appear on all your ACT! calendars, feel free to select Work Week, Weekly, or Monthly from the Calendar toolbar.

Viewing ACT! activities from Outlook

All your ACT! activities that you synchronize to Outlook are now accessible — and editable — in Outlook. Because ACT! and Outlook activities are created differently, your ACT! activities look a bit different when you view them in Outlook. The main difference lies in the association between activity and contact that Outlook doesn't have — you can't view an Outlook contact and see all of his or her associated activities like you can in ACT!. However, an ACT! activity opened in Outlook displays all the associated contacts in the Details area, as you can see in Figure 18-7.

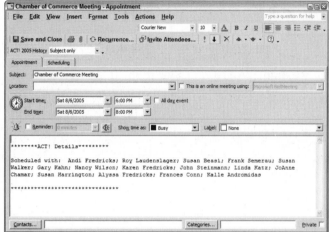

Figure 18-7:
An ACT!
activity
displayed in
Outlook.

Exploring the Internet

The Internet Services button sits on the bottom of the Navigation bar. When you click the Internet Services button, Internet Explorer opens, albeit with a different home page than you're used to seeing because it opens to www. act.com. You'll notice that all your favorites are intact and that you can navigate through the Web until the cows come home.

Viewing a contact's Web site

Because ACT! is all about contacts, it seems only logical that you might want to view a contact's Web site. Accomplish this feat of daring by following these steps:

1. **Click the Web site address that you entered into the contact record.**

   You probably already noticed that the Web site address is blue and that when you hover the mouse over the field, your cursor turns into a pointing hand — indicating that this is a hot (hyper-) link. If you click the link, you're hurled into the exciting world of the Internet.

2. **Internet Explorer launches and displays the contact's Web site.**

3. **After you peruse the site and are ready to continue working in ACT!, close the browser.**

Taking advantage of Internet Links

If you're like me, you like to take advantage of the abundance of information on the Internet. Even more important to me — and probably to you, too — is the ability to find information about contacts. As its name implies, ACT!'s Internet Links links your contact information to a site on the Internet. Among the most frequently used informational sites are the various Yahoo! pages that help you find information on anything from a local weather report to driving directions and maps. By using an Internet Link in ACT!, you can access these sites in a new, unique way: Yahoo! searches for your information based on the information in the current contact record.

If one of your contacts is located in Boca Raton, Florida, you can go to that contact's record and click the Yahoo! Weather link to find the local Boca Raton weather report. If your My Record has you listed in the city of Miami and you're currently on the record of a contact located in Fort Lauderdale, the Yahoo! Driving Directions link supplies you with the driving directions to get from Miami to Fort Lauderdale.

To use one of those links:

1. **In ACT!, display the contact record containing the information that you want to use.**

2. **Choose View⇨Internet Services⇨Internet Links.**

   You see a menu featuring the Internet Links installed on your computer.

3. **Choose the site that you want to link to.**

   Depending on the site that you're linking to, you might be asked to confirm the information that you've selected in ACT!. Internet Explorer then displays the results; for example, if you're looking for driving directions, the My Record information appears on the left side of the screen, and the contact's information is on the right.

   Internet sites are extremely volatile — here today, gone tomorrow. If an Internet Link fails to function, maybe the site has changed its content information or disappeared from the scene altogether.

Attaching a Web page to a contact

ACT! works in mysterious ways. After you install it, you might start to notice remnants of it — or at least ACT! icons — sprinkled throughout your other programs. If you look carefully on the Internet Explorer icon bar, you'll notice a new kid — er, icon — on the block. The ACT! icon will attach the current site that you're viewing to a contact's history tab. Here are a few more details:

1. **Open the Web page you want to attach to an ACT! contact.**

2. **Click the Attach Web page to ACT! Contact icon.**

If you prefer, you can also choose Tools⇨Attach Web page to ACT! contact. In either case, the Attach Web page to the following Contacts dialog box opens. To make life even easier, the contact that you were viewing in ACT! also appears, as shown in Figure 18-8.

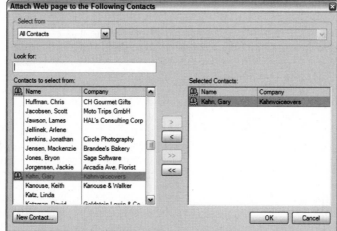

Figure 18-8:
Attaching a
Web page
to a contact
record.

3. **Click OK.**

   In the event that you wish to associate a different contact with the Web page, select one or more contacts from the Contacts to Select from area, and then click the right arrow to move the contact name(s) into the Selected Contacts list before clicking OK.

   The details of the attached Web page display on the History tab for the selected contact(s). You can double-click the attachment icon to open the Web page.

Excelling in Excel

At the risk of sounding like a nerd, my accounting background has turned me into an Excel junkie. Apparently I'm not alone because ACT! supplies you with numerous opportunities to interface with Excel.

Exporting a list to Excel

Very often, ACT! users want to export a part of their database to Excel. Perhaps they need to get information to a non-ACT! user. Or maybe they want to manipulate the data in a different way. It could be that they need to import their ACT! information into another program, and Excel is the vehicle of choice.

If you look closely, you find hints of Excel throughout ACT! 2006. Specifically, if you look really close to the Contact List, Group List, Company List, and Opportunity List icon bars, you see an icon that looks like a mini-spreadsheet. If you hover your mouse over it for a second, you see that the button is called Export to Excel.

Excel, the Opportunities List, and pivot tables

Because the Opportunities List deals with numbers and dollar amounts, it's probably the list that you'll most often want to see in Excel. And, just like with the Contact, Group, and Company lists, one click is all it takes.

Remember: You can list only one product in the Product Name column of the opportunity in either ACT! or Excel. Opportunities with multiple products list the first product name followed by an ellipsis (...).

Now here comes the cool part: When you export the Opportunities List to Excel, your information is automatically translated into a pivot

table and chart. According to Microsoft, "... in a pivot table, each column or field in your source data becomes a pivot table field that summarizes multiple rows of information." What that means is that you get some neat-looking charts like the one you see in the figure here — that you can manipulate to your heart's content.

After Excel opens with your Opportunities List, just click the Opportunities pivot table or the Opportunities Pivot tab to introduce yourself to the exciting world of pivot tables! Read more about how useful mining data with pivot tables and charts can be in *Excel Data Analysis For Dummies* by Stephen L. Nelson, Wiley.

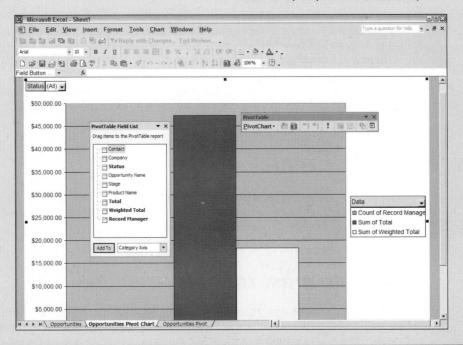

Funnily enough, the button works exactly as you would suspect. Click it, and Excel opens, displaying the list view that you're currently in. Don't see the field you're looking for? Does Excel show you a field you don't want? No problemo. If you customize the list to show just the fields you want (find out how to do that in Chapter 5), Excel displays those very same fields.

Because other programs can easily use Excel data, only Standard, Manager, and Administrator ACT! users can export list data to Excel. An Administrator can also remove this privilege from standard users if he gets mad at them.

Importing a product or drop-down list into ACT!

I've never figured out whether I'm lazy or smart — or a little of each. Whatever, I love to use shortcuts to save myself valuable time. If you're a new user of ACT!, you might have already developed a rather lengthy Product List in another piece of software. For example, you might have created a Price List using Excel or created an Inventory List in your accounting software. If I didn't like you so much, I'd tell you to start typing, but instead I tell you how to export that list from Excel into ACT!.

To import data into ACT!, follow these steps:

1. **Save the Excel file as a tab or comma-delimited file.**

2. **In ACT!, choose Tools⇨Define Fields⇨Manage Drop-Down Lists.**

3. **Select the drop-down list into which you want to import the data, click Edit Drop-Down List, and click Next.**

4. **Choose the Import Drop-Down List Items option.**

   From here, browse to the place where you save the Excel file and watch while ACT! brings in your list of information — and saves you a lot of typing.

Mapping ACT! fields to Excel

Another excellent ACT! feature (pun intended) is the ability to map specific ACT! contact, group, or company fields to Excel cells. After they're mapped, the spreadsheet cells automatically update with the corresponding field information when the document opens. Sound too cool to be true? Just try following these steps:

1. **Add an Excel spreadsheet to a contact by clicking the Add Document button on the contact's Documents tab.**

You'll find the Documents tab located on the Contact view screen; you'll get the 411 on the topic in Chapter 5. Hopefully, you'll pick a spreadsheet that you routinely have to type boring information into such a name, address, and phone numbers.

2. **Click the Documents tab, select the spreadsheet, and then click Edit Document.**

   The spreadsheet opens. You'll notice that after you install ACT!, Excel is now the proud owner of a new ACT! menu, just like the one in Figure 18-9.

Figure 18-9:
The ACT!
menu in
Excel.

ACT!	Help
📎	Attach to ACT!
	Map to Contact...
	Map to Company...
	Map to Group...
	Refresh

If you prefer, you can attach a spreadsheet to ACT! while you're in Excel by choosing ACT!⇨Attach to ACT!.

3. **In Excel, select the Excel cell you want to map to an ACT! field.**

4. **Choose ACT!⇨Map to Contact (or Company or Group).**

   The Map Fields dialog box opens. As you scroll through the list, notice that all the ACT! fields are in it.

5. **Select the ACT! field you want to map to the selected Excel field and then click Add.**

   You can easily add as many fields as you want by selecting an Excel cell, choosing an ACT! field, and then clicking the Add button to "map" the two together. Each ACT! field name appears in angle brackets in the Excel cell.

6. **Save and close the spreadsheet when you finish.**

7. **In ACT!, select the spreadsheet on the Documents tab and then click the Map to Excel button.**

   Sit back in wonder and amazement as your spreadsheet appears. But wait, if you look carefully — or not even too carefully — you'll see that the contact's information has been filled into all the right places.

What's in a Word

ACT! can use Word as the default word processor (see Chapter 3 to appoint Word as your default word processor), and you can attach Word documents to the Documents tab (see Chapter 5). What you might not have noticed, however, is that when you install ACT!, it adds an ACT! menu to Word (as shown in Figure 18-10).

Figure 18-10:
The ACT!
menu that
appears in
Word.

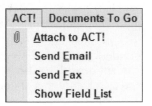

ACT!	Documents To Go
📎	**Attach to ACT!**
	Send Email
	Send Fax
	Show Field List

You can use Word's ACT! menu to help you with several tasks.

Attaching a document to a contact record

Follow these steps to attach a Word document to a contact's Document tab:

1. **Open or create a document in Word.**

2. **From Word, choose ACT!⇨Attach to ACT!.**

   The Select Contacts window opens.

3. **Select the contact you want to attach the document to and then click OK.**

   In essence, you create a link to your document. If you look carefully, you'll notice something new on the Documents tab — an icon that matches the type of document you just added. So, if you add a Word document, you see the familiar-looking Word icon smack dab in the middle of your Documents tab as well as the name and path of the attached file. Go ahead, make my day: Double-click the icon. The attached document miraculously opens in all its glory.

Sending a document as an e-mail

In this age of viruses, you're probably hesitant to send too many attachments knowing that the recipient might not even open it. If you're using Word to create your documents, here's a simple way to convert the document into the body of an e-mail or send it as an attachment:

1. **Open or create a document in Word.**

2. **From Word, choose ACT!⇨Send Email.**

ACT! asks whether you want to send the Word document as an attachment or use it as the body of your e-mail.

3. **Chose your poison and click OK.**

   The Select Contacts window opens.

4. **Select the contact you want to send the e-mail message to, click the right-arrow button, and then click OK.**

   The New Message window appears. Wonder of wonders, it's all set to go with either a Word document attachment or with the body of the e-mail showing an amazing resemblance to the contents of your Word document.

5. **Type the subject and then click Send.**

   Through the wonders of modern science — or at least the wonders of ACT! — a history of your sent e-mail appears on the contact's History tab.

Sending a document in a fax

If you want to fax a Word document, follow these steps:

1. **Open or create a document in Word.**

2. **From Word, choose ACT!⇨Send Fax.**

   The Select Contacts window opens.

3. **Select the contact you want to send the fax message to, click the right arrow button, and then click OK.**

   Your fax software now opens. At this point, you need to follow the instructions of your fax software with one big difference — ACT! creates a history of your fax.

The ability to fax using ACT! is dependent on having access to fax software and a phone line. The various options for sending a fax depend on the fax software installed on your computer. If the fax option is grayed out, you can't fax because your machine lacks the proper software.

Showing ACT!'s mail merge fields

Sometimes in your zealousness, you might close the list of mail merge fields that opens when you edit or create a template. (See Chapter 11 to find out how to create a template.) Not to worry — getting them back is easy enough.

In Word, choose ACT!⇨Show Field List. The Add Mail Merge Fields dialog box reappears — and you can continue adding fields to your template.

Chapter 19

ACT!ing on Your Opportunities

- -

- -

*I*n this chapter, I lead you through the entire sales process using ACT!. I show you how to create an initial opportunity, make changes to it as a sale makes its way through the sales funnel, and view your opportunities by using the Opportunity List and various ACT! reports.

Creating Opportunities

ACT! was originally created by a salesperson for salespeople. Ironically, many users of the earlier versions of ACT! found the program a bit lacking when it came to tracking sales opportunities. Happily, that is no longer the case in ACT! 2006.

In ACT!, an *opportunity* is a potential sale to a contact. Each opportunity must be associated with a contact. All sales information for a contact appears on the Opportunities tab of the contact record. (Figure 19-1 shows an example of the Opportunities tab.) When you create an opportunity, you can list the names of your products or services, specify a sales stage and forecasted close date, and even make use of eight customizable fields. Click a button, and ACT! generates a quote. You can even schedule a follow-up activity for the opportunity.

By automating the sales process using ACT!, you have a better chance of closing more sales. First of all, if you follow up on your activities as I show you in Chapter 8, you have significantly fewer contacts falling through the cracks of your database. Secondly, you can adjust your predictions as the opportunity moves through the sales stages. Most importantly, you can generate reports based on your projected sales, allowing you to focus on the deals that you think you have the best chance of closing.

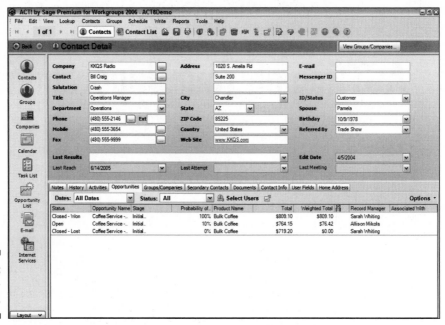

Figure 19-1:
The Oppor-
tunities tab.

Initiating the opportunity

So why are you sitting around reading a book? It's time for you to go out there and make some money. Here's how you're going to make your first million:

1. **Perform a lookup to find the contact for whom you're creating an opportunity.**

   What? A little rusty on those lookups? Fear not — and head to Chapter 6 for a quick refresher.

2. **Create a new opportunity by clicking the Opportunities tab and then clicking the New Opportunity icon.**

   If you have a bit of trouble locating the New Opportunity icon, it's under-standable; it's the icon on the Opportunities tab that looks like a graph. You also know you're on the right track when you hover your cursor over the button; a ToolTip proclaiming New Opportunity shows up.

   The Opportunity dialog box opens, as shown in Figure 19-2.

3. **Give the opportunity a name.**

   After you create the opportunity, you can track it down by doing a Name lookup, so consider assigning a name that starts with the company name that you're doing business with or the Purchase Order number. If you don't give the opportunity a name, ACT! assigns one for you auto-matically: New Opportunity.

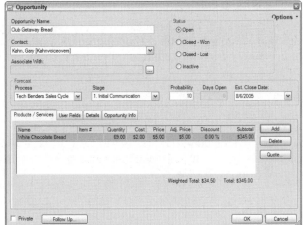

Figure 19-2:
The
Opportunity
dialog box.

4. **Assign a sales status.**

   This option is a fairly simple one. All new opportunities are assigned the Open status.

   For more on the other choices here, see the upcoming section, "Closing the deal."

5. **Assign a sales process.**

   Here's where ACT! really forces you to get organized. Although not necessary, you possibly have more than one Process List with your opportunities. You might use one for the pre-sales steps that you want everyone in your organization to follow and another for the steps that you need to follow after you land that large deal.

   Each process comes with its own list of stages. Your homework is to verbalize your sales processes and translate them into ACT! (see Chapter 13). Doing so keeps you organized, lets you know where you stand in the scheme of things, and allows you to generate some useful sales reports later on.

6. **Assign a sales stage.**

   If you're hearing a nagging voice in the back of your head, it's because I'm nagging you. An important concept in computing is Garbage In, Garbage Out (GIGO). You want to set the sales stage so you know where this opportunity lies in your sales pipeline and so this opportunity doesn't fall by the wayside. Too, you'll want to change the stage as the opportunity progresses through your sales cycle. For more information see the following section, "Modifying the opportunity."

7. **Enter a probability of closing.**

   This step could be rather easy because you can assign probabilities to each sales stage when you set up the sales process. Feel free to overwrite the probability percentage based on your own hunches for each opportunity.

8. **Enter the estimated close date.**

   You use this information for sorting and reporting later.

All that's left for you to do is fill in the Product/Services, User Fields, Details, and Opportunity Info tabs — a little time consuming, but you reap the rewards later for all your hard work now.

Product/Services tab

If you're like most people, this part is fun. Here's where you get to count the cash, bill for the beans, dream of the dollars. . . . In any event, the Products/Services tab is where you get to add all the line items for your opportunity and sit back while ACT! crunches the numbers for you.

Although the process of adding products or services to an opportunity is pretty straightforward, I walk you through it, just in case:

1. **Choose a product or service name from the Name drop-down list.**

2. **Click the Add button if you'd like to add additional products.**

   If you're selling a new item, scroll to the bottom of the list and click Edit List to add it.

   Chapter 13 gives you the full lowdown on creating a Product List.

3. **Add an item number.**

   If you fill in all the appropriate item numbers when creating your Product List, this step isn't necessary. Or, if you don't use item numbers, this step isn't necessary.

4. **Enter the quantity.**

5. **Double-check the cost and price.**

   This information fills in automatically from your Product List. If the information is incorrect, head back to the Product List to correct it.

6. **(Optional) Adjust either the adjusted price or the discount percentage.**

   If you're giving this customer a special price, feel free to overwrite the default price. If you lower (or raise!) a price, ACT! automatically calculates the discount percentage. If you prefer to tinker with the percentage, ACT! automatically adjusts the price.

7. **Repeat Steps 1–6 as many times as necessary until your opportunity includes all the necessary line items and then click OK.**

Giving 'em a discount

You can create discounts on an item-by-item basis by either changing the adjusted price or the discount percentage. That works pretty well for most situations, but you might prefer to add the discount rate as a totally separate line item. In order to do this, you need to add a Discount Item entry to your Product List. Because the discount amount varies, you need to manually insert the amount of the discount each time you create a new opportunity.

To create a discount item, follow these steps:

1. **From any ACT! screen, choose Tools⇨ Define Fields⇨Manage Product List⇨Add.**

2. **Type a name for the discount, such as Discount.**

To use the discount item

1. **From the Opportunities tab, add or edit an opportunity.**

2. **Add a new item and choose Discount from the Name list. If you want to make this the bottom item, you probably want to choose Discount as your last item.**

3. **In the Adjusted Price field, type in a hyphen (–) followed by the dollar discount amount for the order.**

User Fields tab

The User Fields tab consists of eight customizable fields. Chapter 13 explains how you can customize those eight fields by renaming them. Maybe you're a manufacturer's rep and want to indicate your eight major lines. Or you might want to indicate the eight manufacturers you deal with. Don't forget that you can query and generate reports with these fields, so use them wisely. You can check out the Opportunity dialog box's User Fields tab in Figure 19-3.

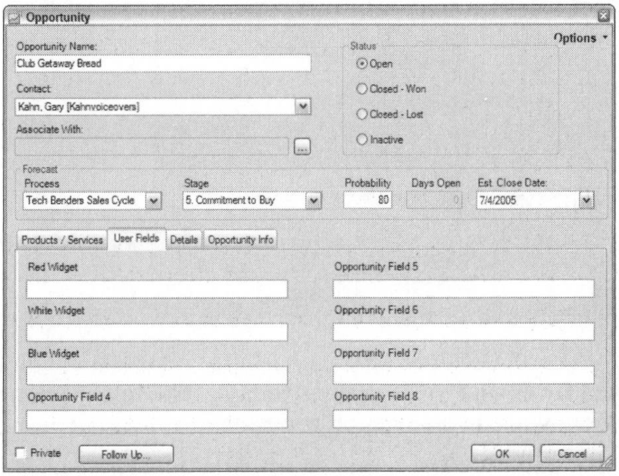

Figure 19-3: The User Fields tab.

Chapter 1 details several of the differences between ACT! 2006 and ACT! 2006 Premium for Workgroups. One of those differences is Premium's ability to customize the Opportunity field's data type so that they can include drop-down lists or be formatted for numbers and currency.

Details tab

In general, a database consists of many fields with each containing a single piece of information. But people are people, and sometimes storing all your important information into a bunch of teeny, tiny fields isn't possible. That said, you can use the Details tab to write The Great American Novel — or at least a few important tidbits of additional info — about your opportunity.

If the information that you want to include with the opportunity is in a document, such as a word processing file, you can copy the text in the other application and paste it on the Details tab.

Opportunity Info tab

By now, your mind is probably fogging over from all the information that you're inputting. The information on the User Fields, Details, and Opportunity Info tabs are purely optional, albeit helpful. If your poor fingers are wearing down to little stubs, you can always go back and complete the rest of this information later. Figure 19-4 shows the Opportunity Info tab.

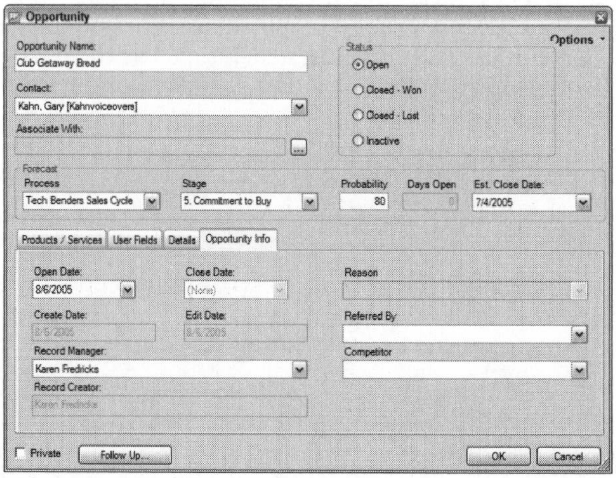

Figure 19-4: The Opportunity Info tab.

✔ **Open Date:** By default, ACT! assigns today's date to a new opportunity. This is where you can change it if necessary.

✔ **Record Manager:** By default, the name of the logged-on user appears as the opportunity's Record Manager. Feel free to change it if necessary.

✔ **Referred By:** If you go by the positive reward theory — the big guys get big thank-you gifts, and the little guys get a pat on the back — you might just want to attribute each of your opportunities to the appropriate source.

✔ **Competitor:** If you keep one eye on the competition, here's where you can do it.

Getting all your information into a sales opportunity is only half the fun. The other half consists of sticking to your original course of action. Click the Follow Up button. You get to set up your follow-up activity in the Schedule Activity dialog box. You'll notice in Figure 19-5 that ACT! inserts the opportunity name and stage into the Regarding field. Then click OK. You've just gotta love a program that does so much of your work for you!

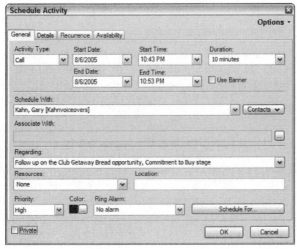

Figure 19-5:
Schedule a
follow-up
activity for
a sales
opportunity.

At this point, you're essentially done with creating the opportunity. Sit back and relax a moment while ACT! does one more thing for you: create a history of the big sales event on the contact's History tab.

Modifying the opportunity

As your opportunity progresses, going back and modifying the sales stage is often necessary. Again, this information appears in your various reports, so updating your opportunities is vitally important. This process is painless and short:

1. **Find the opportunity that you want to update and open it.**

   You have several choices here:

- *Create a lookup:* Create a lookup for the contact associated with the opportunity and then click the Opportunities tab. On the Opportunities tab, double-click the opportunity.

- *Modify an opportunity:* From the Opportunity List, double-click the opportunity that you want to modify.

- *Search an opportunity:* From any of the ACT! screens, choose Lookup⇨Opportunities and then select one of the field choices. For example, you can search by opportunity name, product, or status. ACT! then scurries through your database and opens the Opportunity List, which presents you with all opportunities that met your search criteria. Double-click the opportunity you want to modify.

The Opportunity dialog box opens (refer to Figure 19-2).

2. **Change the information in the Stage field as necessary.**

The purpose of ACT!'s opportunities is to allow you to track a potential sale from its inception to its final outcome. You'll probably find editing your opportunities useful as they progress through the various sales stages. This allows you to view any of your opportunities to assess exactly where you stand.

3. **Schedule another follow-up if necessary by clicking the Follow Up button.**

4. **Click OK when you finish editing the opportunity.**

The biggest challenge for many busy people is remembering to take care of all those nagging little details. Chapter 8 focuses on the activity series. You might consider creating a sales activity series and including "updating sales stage" as one of the steps.

Closing the deal

When you close a sale, you can record the outcome and the closing date. ACT! records a history on the contact's History tab — and if you associate the opportunity with a group or company, on the History tab for the group or company as well.

1. **Find the contact for whom you're recording the outcome of an opportunity.**

Step 1 in the preceding section shows you several ways to meet this goal.

2. **On the Opportunities tab, double-click the opportunity that you want to complete.**

3. **Change the status to indicate the current state of the opportunity in the Opportunity dialog box.**

    - Closed-Won

    - Closed-Lost

    - Inactive

    As usual, ACT! scurries around trying to make life easier for you. If you select one of the close options, the Opportunity Info tab pops up so you can add a few final details.

4. **Click OK.**

    The opportunity remains on the Opportunities tab. The status changes to Won, Lost, or Inactive depending on the choice you made. The Actual Close Date updates to reflect today's date.

You Can Quote Me on That

After you create an opportunity, ACT! can convert it into a written quote for you. The quote template actually consists of two pieces:

✔ quote.adt file: Word creates this. You can edit the template by changing the fonts, graphics, and wording. Typically, the .adt file contains information about both you and your contact and can also contain disclaimer information.

✔ quote.xlt file: This Excel-created file is embedded into the .adt file. It appears as a table in the center of a quote and contains numeric data, such as quantity, pricing, and totals. Because of how the .xlt file is created, you probably don't want to make any changes to the file; doing so can run the risk of leaving the quote generator inoperable.

Only one quote template works directly from the Opportunity dialog box. If you create other quote templates, you can use them like a regular template (see Chapter 11); contact information flows into them but not opportunity information.

Because the quote template consists of both a Word document and an embedded Excel table, you must have both programs installed on your computer in order to generate quotes using ACT!. You can see a quote in Figure 19-6.

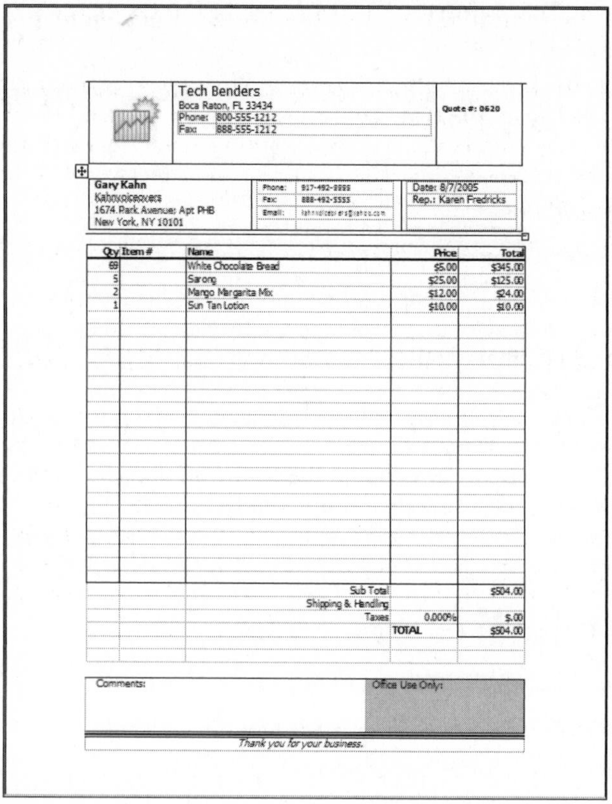

Tech Benders
Boca Raton, FL 33434
Phone: 800-555-1212
Fax: 888-555-1212

Quote #: 0620

Gary Kahn
Kahnwiceoxecs
1674 Park Avenue Apt PHB
New York, NY 10101

Phone: 917-492-9999
Fax: 888-492-5555
Email: kahnwiceoxers@sehoo.com

Date: 8/7/2005
Rep.: Karen Fredricks

Qty	Item #	Name	Price	Total
69		White Chocolate Bread	$5.00	$345.00
5		Sarong	$25.00	$125.00
2		Mango Margarita Mix	$12.00	$24.00
1		Sun Tan Lotion	$10.00	$10.00

Sub Total		$504.00
Shipping & Handling		
Taxes	0.000%	$.00
TOTAL		$504.00

Comments:

Office Use Only:

Thank you for your business.

Figure 19-6:
Sample
quote
created
using ACT!.

Creating a quote for an opportunity

You can literally create a quote at the click of a button. And here's how you find the button:

1. **Open an existing opportunity.**

2. **Click the Quote button on the Products/Services tab.**

3. **If you set your preferences to prompt you for a quote number, type in the number in the Enter Quote Number dialog window that appears and click OK.**

   After a moment or so of whirring and hissing, Word opens, revealing the quote, which is all filled out and ready to go.

Chapter 3 focuses on the various ACT! preferences settings. Buried away in those settings is one that determines whether you're prompted to supply a quote number every time you generate a quote. At the same time, you can indicate the numbers and/or letters that you want to include in the beginning of each quote number. You find those settings by choosing Tools⇨Preferences and clicking the Quote Preferences button of the General tab.

To change the order in which your products appear on your quote, simply click the appropriate column heading on the Products/Services tab of the Opportunity dialog box. To sort the products alphabetically, click the Name column heading. Want them sorted by price? Click the Subtotal column heading.

4. **Print and save the quote as you do any other Word document.**

Editing the opportunity quote template

As I mention earlier, you can't do much fiddling with the Excel portion of the quote template; doing so could cause your calculations to not calculate. You can, however, modify the font if you'd like. The Word portion of the quote can also be modified to your exacting specifications. Chapter 11 goes into greater detail about the exciting world of template modifications, but for now, here's a quick refresher course. You also need to set your word processor preference to Word in order to edit the `quote.adt` template; Chapter 3 shows you how to do that.

1. **From any ACT! screen, choose Write⇨Edit Template.**

2. **Choose quote.adt and then click Open.**

3. **Edit the template as necessary and then save it.**

When you click the Quote button in the Opportunity dialog box, ACT! automatically looks for the `quote.adt` template file. Although I advocate saving templates and reports as other, unique names when attempting to modify them, the same theory does not hold true for the quote template. If you change the name, you can't access it from the Opportunity dialog box — and your product information doesn't magically pour into it. Do not change the name of the opportunity quote!

Viewing the Opportunity List

The Opportunity List provides you with a way to view all your opportunities for all of your contacts. You can filter the Opportunity List to display only those opportunities that match your specifications. You can then print the Opportunity List. Or, if you're really ambitious, you can export the Opportunity List to Excel where you find pivot tables waiting patiently for you. Not sure what a pivot table is? Head to Chapter 18 for more details.

Getting to the Opportunity List is almost too easy: Just click the Opportunity List icon on the Navigation bar. A list of opportunities appears, as you can see in Figure 19-7. The Opportunity List even comes equipped with a status bar running across the bottom that displays the total number of opportunities, and the weighted and grand totals of all the opportunities. You'll also notice that the Opportunity List comes equipped with its very own toolbar containing icons pertaining specifically to the Opportunity List.

Filtering the Opportunity List

If you hate to make a decision at the ice cream store, you might not appreciate the Opportunity List filters. But if you're the kind of person who loves to have things, well, exactly the way *you* want them, you're going to love the Opportunity List!

The various filter options are located at the top of the Opportunity List window. As you change filter options, the Opportunity List changes to include the options you select. After this is set, you can click the Hide Filters button in the upper-right corner of the Opportunity List. Don't see any filters? Click the Show Filters button that appears instead.

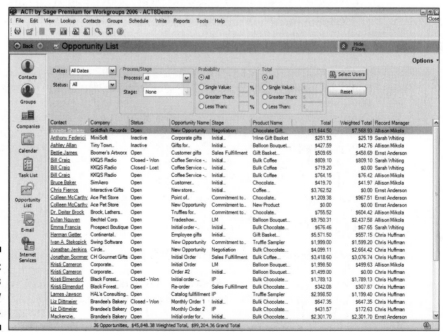

Figure 19-7: ACT!'s Opportunity List.

Feel free to choose from the following Opportunity List filters:

- **Dates:** Limits the opportunities to those matching the estimated closing date that you indicate.

- **Status:** Indicates whether you want to view Open, Closed-Won, Closed-Lost, Inactive, or all opportunities. You can also choose None, which frankly doesn't make a whole lot of sense because then you don't see any of your opportunities!

- **Process/Stage:** If you set up more than one series of sales processes, here's where you indicate which one you like to see and what stage(s) you'd like to focus on.

- **Probability:** Type the percent you want to use; you can find opportunities that match only a specific percentage or those that are greater than or less than a given percentage.

- **Total:** Type the amount of the opportunity you want to use or choose whether to view opportunities that are greater than or less than a given amount.

- **Select Users:** Selects the names of the Record Managers associated with the opportunities you want to view.

- **Options:** Actually, you have only one true filtering option here; select Show Private to display your private opportunities. You'll also notice the Customize Columns option that lets you add, remove, and change the order of your columns.

Resetting the Opportunity List filters

After you diligently work to set all your filters, you probably need to reset them again sooner or later. You can accomplish that task in either of the following two ways:

- Click the Reset button from the Opportunity List.
- Choose Lookup⇨Opportunities⇨All Opportunities.

Printing the Opportunity List

Now comes the exciting part. Okay, it might not be your exact idea of excitement, but seeing all your hard work translated onto a piece of white paper can at least give you a nice sense of accomplishment. Remember all those numerous opportunity fields that you so painstakingly filled? Here's where you get to display them in all their glory.

1. **Click Quick Print (the printer icon) from the Opportunity List toolbar.**

2. **From the Print dialog box, click OK.**

Customize your columns before printing out a copy of your Opportunity List. I tell you how in Chapter 5.

Many of you will find the ability to transfer your Opportunity List data into Excel at the click of a button one of the coolest of the ACT! features. You can read more about it by flipping back to Chapter 18.

Working with Opportunity History

Chapter 7 talks about the nifty histories created by ACT! when you change certain key pieces of contact information. You create a history for an opportunity when you create, change the status or stage, generate a quote, or change the estimated close date. You can view the opportunity history from the contact's History tab. If the opportunity is associated with a group or company, you can view the opportunity from those History tabs as well.

ACT!'s Premium version lets you customize the eight opportunity user fields. You can also modify them to become History fields so that whatever information you put into them is forever recorded on the History tab, even if you change the content of one of those fields.

Okay, do you want the good news or the bad news? Well, I can't hear your response — and don't you feel silly responding to an inanimate object? — so I give you the bad news first. You might find the histories that ACT! creates are a bit terse. The good news is that you can edit them as much as you like by simply double-clicking the history. The Edit History dialog box opens, as shown in Figure 19-8. Edit away to your heart's content — after all, who said you couldn't change history?

Figure 19-8: Editing an opportunity history.

Reporting on Opportunities

You poor reader, you! You work so hard in filling out the numerous opportunity fields. Knowing that you need a little break, ACT! rewards you with an abundance of sales reports and charts. Whether you need to report on a single customer or all your current opportunities, ACT! has a way of giving you the information.

You can monitor the opportunities that you have at each stage of the sales development cycle and display this information in a report or graphically in a sales funnel or sales graph.

If you feel an overwhelming desire to chop down a few more trees in the rain forest, ACT! can help. ACT! comes equipped with a dozen opportunity reports to suit most of your reporting needs. Chapter 9 gives you a synopsis on all those reports. If you don't find a report that suits you, a few options are available to you such as printing the Opportunity List or the contact's Opportunities tab.

Reporting on a single contact

The Opportunities tab provides you with the sales information on any given contact. The columns on the Opportunities tab work just like the columns in other ACT! areas, such as the History tab and the Contact List. You can change their order, sort by any column, and add new columns. You can filter the list by date and status.

You can use the information contained on the Opportunities tab to create a quick-and-dirty report the same way that you create a report based on the Contact List. ACT! prints the report in the exact same order as it appears onscreen — that is, what you see onscreen is what you see on paper. To print a report on a single opportunity, follow these steps:

1. **Go to the contact record of the person for whom you like to track opportunities.**

2. **Right-click the Opportunities tab or click the Options button.**

   You can use a lot of informational fields when you enter a new opportunity. You can portray each of these fields as a column on the Opportunities tab. You can customize the tab in any one of the following ways:

   • *Add a column.* Select a field from the Available Fields area and click the right-pointing arrow.

   • *Change the order of the columns.* Select a field from the Show as Columns in This Order area and then click the Move Up or Move Down button.

    • *Remove a column.* Select a field from the Show as Columns in This Order area and click the left-pointing arrow.

  3. Click OK when you finish adding columns.

  4. Choose File⇨Quick Print Current Window.

Creating an opportunities graph

An opportunities graph can show your sales forecast or your closed sales for a month, a quarter, or any period of time you choose. Many sales organizations prefer to see sales information in the form of a graph. As usual, ACT! is up to the task and can create one for you in the blink of an eye — or at least in the click of the mouse.

Here's all you need to do to see all your opportunities translated through the wonder of modern technology into a graph:

  1. Create a lookup of contacts to include in the graph.

    Need a warm-up on performing lookups? Head to Chapter 6.

  2. Choose Reports⇨Opportunity Reports⇨Opportunity Graph.

    The Graph Options dialog box appears, as shown in Figure 19-9.

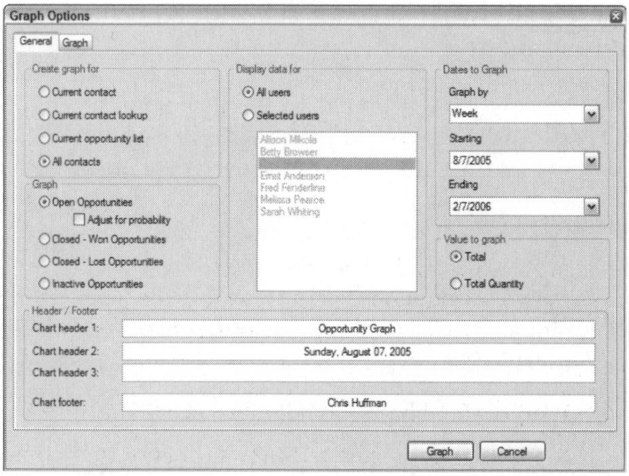

Figure 19-9:
The Graph
Options
dialog box.

  3. On the General tab, indicate the information you to want include in your graph:

    • *In the Create Graph For area,* select the Current Contact, Current Contact Lookup, Current Opportunity List, or All Contacts radio button.

- *In the Graph area,* select the type of opportunities to appear in the graph.

- *In the Display Data For area,* choose the Record Managers of the contacts you're including in your graph.

- *Enter header and footer information* to appear on your graph.

- *In the Dates to Graph area,* fill in the date range and intervals.

- *In the Value to Graph area,* fill in values to use in your graph.

4. **On the Graph tab, make a few more graph-specific choices.**

   You can make decisions about whether you want a bar or line graph, the graph size, gridlines, the colors used in the graph, or the scaling used in your graph (see Figure 19-10).

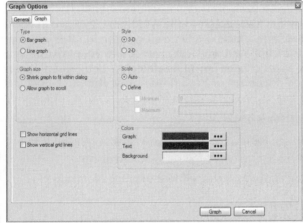

Figure 19-10:
More graph
options.

5. **Click the Graph button.**

   Voilà! Your graph appears before your eyes. Try not to look too surprised. If the boss walks by, you might want to make little grunting noises indicating how studiously you're working on your graph. You can see a sample graph in Figure 19-11.

6. **In the Opportunities Forecast Graph dialog box, you can**

   - *Lookup:* Change the criteria for the contacts that appear in the opportunity graph.

   - *Save:* Save your graph as a bitmap (.bmp) or JPEG (.jpg) file to preserve your artwork for future generations — or for insertion into another document.

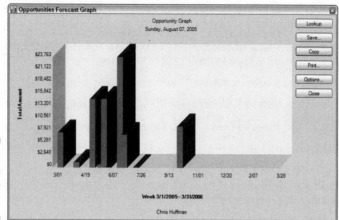

Figure 19-11:
A sample
opportunity
graph.

- *Copy:* Save the graph to the Windows Clipboard in case you want to perform a little cosmetic surgery on it. After you copy the graph to the Clipboard, you can paste it into your favorite graphics program and change any of its elements. You can also paste it into a Word document or PowerPoint presentation to really impress the natives.

- *Print:* Does just that.

- *Options:* Return to the options you first tangled with in Steps 3 and 4.

- *Close:* Exit the graph without printing or saving it.

Viewing the opportunity pipeline

A picture is worth a thousand words — or in this case, it might be worth thousands of dollars! Most large sales organizations are already familiar with the concept of a sales pipeline. The ACT! pipeline graphic represents the number of opportunities at each stage of the sales development process. Each section of an opportunity pipeline represents one of your pre-determined sales stages. Opportunities that are marked as closed, or those that are missing a sales stage, are excluded.

1. **Perform a lookup to find the contacts that you want to include in the opportunity pipeline.**

   Although you don't have to assign a sales stage to an opportunity, only opportunities with assigned stages are included in the opportunity pipeline.

2. **Choose Reports➪Opportunity Reports➪Opportunity Pipeline.**

   The Opportunity Pipeline Options dialog box opens, as shown in Figure 19-12. Modify any of the pipeline options to reflect how they will appear in your opportunity pipeline:

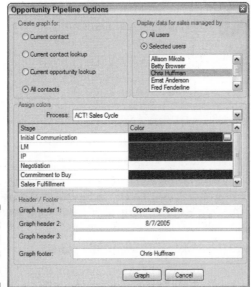

Figure 19-12:
Set pipeline
options
here.

- *Select the contacts* you want to include in your pipeline from the Create Graph For area.

- *Select the Record Managers* whose data you want to include from the Display Data for Sales Managed By area.

- *Select the process* that you want to track.

- *Color-coordinate your opportunity pipeline* by assigning colors to each of your sales stages in the Assign Colors area. If you want to change a color, click the ellipsis button to the right of the color and select another color.

- *Fill in the header and footer information* that you would like to include with your pipeline.

3. **Click the Graph button.**

   You are now the proud owner of a beautiful opportunity pipeline (similar to what's shown in Figure 19-13), guaranteed to impress the heck out of your boss and other members of your sales team.

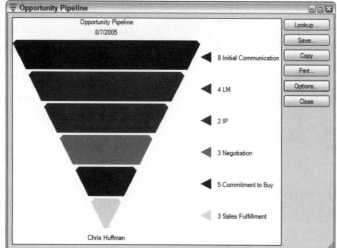

Figure 19-13:
A sales
pipeline.

4. **In the Opportunity Pipeline dialog box, you have options similar to those available in the Opportunity Forecast Graph window (see the preceding section).**

   • *Lookup:* Change the lookup criteria for the pipeline.

   • *Save:* Save your pipeline as a bitmap (.bmp) or JPEG (.jpg) file to preserve your artwork for future generations or for inclusion in another document.

   • *Copy:* Copy it to the Windows Clipboard and later paste it into a graphics program for modifications.

   • *Print:* It doesn't get any more self-explanatory than this!

   • *Options:* Modify the pipeline.

   • *Close:* Exit without saving or printing the pipeline.

As neat as the Opportunity Pipeline appears at first glance, closer examination uncovers a rather annoying fact. The graphic used in the Opportunity Pipeline is just that — a graphic. Unlike the Opportunity Graph discussed earlier, the graphic does not change to reflect the information on which the pipeline is based.

Chapter 20

Grouping Your Contacts

. . . .

In This Chapter

▶ Understanding groups

▶ Creating groups

▶ Establishing group rules

▶ Putting groups to work

▶ Utilizing group notes and activities

. . . .

*I*n this chapter, I focus on a very commonly overlooked ACT! feature: the ACT! group. What exactly is a group? Generally speaking, a group is a collection of something. In ACT!, however, a *group* is a collection of contacts. More specifically, a group is a semi-permanent lookup whose contact records you assign to the group by any criteria that you want.

The contact record helps you to keep track of all activities as they relate to an individual; the group allows you to track activities as they relate to an entire group of contacts. Thus, when used correctly, ACT! groups provide you with the potential to increase the overall power and efficiency of the ACT! program.

Throughout this chapter, after explaining all the ins and outs of groups, I show you how to create a group. I then show you how to put groups to work so that you can enjoy all the benefits that groups have to offer. After reading this chapter, you'll become a real group pro — knowing when to use them (and when not to) and how to use them to their greatest potential.

A Few Good Reasons to Create a Group

You shouldn't just create groups willy-nilly without putting some thought into them. If you do that, you're liable to end up with bad groups, which consume your time without offering any real benefits. (See the sidebar "Don't create bad groups!" to see what I mean.) So what exactly makes a good group, you ask? Here are a few examples of when groups can really make life easy for you:

✔ **Managing large projects:** Groups are particularly well suited for those of you who work on large projects. For example, if you're building a home, you're involved with any number of people from building inspectors and city officials to subcontractors, your own personnel, and the new home-owner. Assigning all these contacts to a group allows you to easily zero in on only those contacts involved in the project.

✔ **Tracking real estate listings:** If you're a real estate agent or broker, set-ting up a group for each listing allows you to track all clients that see a particular property and to list all properties that you show to a particu-lar client.

✔ **Organizing your classes and seminars:** If you teach classes and semi-nars, you can set up groups to track all the attendees for each of your classes. Then, when the time comes, you can print out class lists to ensure that you contact all class members. You also have a clear listing as to what classes an individual contact has taken with you.

✔ **Focusing on a specific group of contacts:** Say you went to a trade show and came back with 75 good, solid leads — all of which you are deter-mined to call. Your first step is to put all those leads into a group. On Monday, you might call 20 of those leads, moving each one out of the group as you make the call. On Tuesday, your list is down to 55 but maybe you have the chance to call only 5 people. Wednesday finds you putting out fires around your business, and you don't have a chance to continue phoning until Friday; you can easily access those remaining 50 contacts and take up where you left off.

In previous versions of ACT!, you might have relied on groups to track mem-bers of a large company or account. If you're using groups to track your companies, you can convert them into companies with a few clicks of your mouse. Chapter 21 shows you the various ins and outs of this company feature.

Don't create bad groups!

Here's an example of a bad group: I once worked with an ACT! user who had exactly 50 groups — one for each state. He had then subdivided each group into subgroups representing each ZIP code within the state. This user had overlooked the obvious — his database already contained fields for both state and ZIP code. His groups provided him with no more information than he already had — and after he had put all that time and effort into creating them.

Many ACT! users create groups to track con-tacts for their newsletter or holiday card mail-ings. Unfortunately, this situation is another poor use of a group; although the user sees who will receive the mailing, he doesn't find out who is *not* to receive the mailing. More importantly, he doesn't find out who fell through the cracks and was just overlooked. Setting up a Mailing field allows you to track all three things.

What All Groups Have in Common

In the preceding section, I provide examples of using groups that surely give you an idea of how you can use groups for a wide range of tasks. Despite the flexibility of groups, however, all groups share a few common elements:

- ✔ **Volatility:** In general, groups and the contacts within them don't have to be permanent. A contractor, for example, replaces subcontractors he works with if they do a poor job. And, after that contractor completes a house, he might no longer need to use the group that he created for the project and may choose to delete it. Removing a contact from a group doesn't in turn remove the contact from the database.

- ✔ **No limit to the number of groups:** You're allowed to create as many groups as you want; your only limitation is self imposed. Working with thousands of groups, however, is probably rather cumbersome.

- ✔ **There is no limit to the number of contacts that belong to a group.** Add as many contacts to a group as you'd like.

- ✔ **No limit to the number of groups a contact can belong to:** Depending on the type of groups that you set up, you might find that a contact needs to belong to more than one group. For example, if you use groups to help with project management, you might need to include the same subcontractor in several groups.

- ✔ **Relational cross-referencing:** By creating a group, you can easily move between the group as a whole and the individual members within the group. From the Group Detail window, you can see a list of all the contacts that belong to that group; from the Contacts Detail window, you can see all the groups that a contact belongs to.

- ✔ **Fifteen levels of subgroups:** You might be working on a huge project that requires a greater amount of micro-management and consequently more subgroups. Maybe you're working with the Federal Government and want to have a group for each major governmental department subdivided into Agencies subdivided into Districts subdivided into customers subdivided into . . . you get the drift!

Creating a Group

Like most of the other ACT! commands, creating groups is as easy as pie. Just remember that planning is always the first step: If you work in a shared database, all users need to agree on how to use groups *before* creating groups and adding contact records to them.

A group isn't meant to be a replacement for the ID/Status field (or any other existing field for that matter; see the sidebar "Don't create bad groups!"). The ID/Status field serves to categorize each contact. For example, you might categorize each contact as a vendor, customer, or prospect using the ID/Status field. Limit your groups to help you accomplish something that can't be done through the use of fields.

To create a group, simply follow these steps:

1. **Display the Group Detail window by clicking the Groups icon on the Navigation bar.**

   The Group Detail window should look vaguely familiar — in fact, it's nearly identical to the Contact Detail window. Just like the Contact Detail window, the Group Detail window features tabs along the middle of the screen. And, just like the Contact Detail window, the Group Detail window allows you to choose the layout of your choice. As shown in Figure 20-1, the only differences between the Group and Contact Detail windows are the list of Subgroups appearing in the Subgroups field and the Hierarchy field. If you're creating your very first group, the screen is blank.

2. **Choose Groups⇨New Group.**

   If you prefer, you can right-click in the Group Detail window and choose New Group. Or, feel free to click the New Group icon on the toolbar (the third icon on the left). You can even click the Insert key on your keyboard. We aim to please!

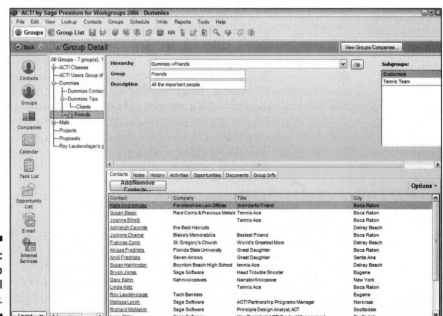

Figure 20-1:
The Group
Detail
window.

A new group appears, which is blank and naked as the day it was born.

3. **In the Group field, enter a name for the new group.**

When you move to another field, the group list automatically updates and your group is saved.

4. **(Optional) Create a subgroup by right-clicking the primary group in the Group List tree to the left of the Group Detail window, choosing New Subgroup, and then filling in the name of the subgroup.**

You can have as many subgroups per group as you like. And, you can have up to 15 levels of subgroups; in other words, you can further divide your subgroups into sub-subgroups. And, after you create a group, you can go back to the scene of the crime and add a subgroup at any time. After it's created, you can drag a group into position under an existing group to transform it into a subgroup or drag a subgroup to the top of the Group List tree to make it a full-fledged group.

Understanding Group Membership

Just like there are membership levels at most clubs, groups can also have two distinct levels of membership:

✔ **Static:** A *static* member is one that is more or less handpicked to go into a group. You might think of these members as having VIP memberships. These members receive a lifetime membership and are never be removed from a group unless you specifically remove them. By default, you can see all your static group members displayed on the Groups/Companies tab of a contact's Contact Detail window.

✔ **Dynamic:** A *dynamic* member is one that is added to a group through a query. As long as the contact meets the query requirements, he remains a part of the group; if he no longer matches the query, he is automatically removed from the Group. The Groups/Companies tab doesn't display dynamic group membership; you have to click the Display Dynamic Group Membership button to see a listing of a contact's dynamic group membership.

Adding static group members

Here are the two ways you can add static members to a group: from the Groups view or from the Contact Detail view. You'll probably find the Groups view method to be more convenient if you're adding a whole lot of members at one time. The Contact Detail method is best used for the stragglers that you want to add on a contact-by-contact basis.

Adding multiple contacts to a group

To add a whole bunch of special, static members to a group, follow these simple steps.

1. **If possible, create a lookup of the potential members.**

   You might want to look for all contacts that you just added to your database, or you can go to the Contact List and handpick those VIMs (Very Important Members).

2. **Switch to the Groups view and select the group to which you'd like to add the new members.**

3. **Choose Groups➪Group Membership➪Add/Remove Contacts and then click the Contacts button to add some contact records to your group.**

   If you prefer, you can also click the Add/Remove Contacts button on the Contacts tab of the Group Detail window — or even right-click in the Group Detail window and choose Group Membership➪Add/Remove Contacts.

   In any case, the Add/Remove Contacts dialog box appears (see Figure 20-2).

4. **Choose Current Lookup from the Select From drop-down list.**

5. **Click the double right-pointing arrows to add the current lookup to your group and then click OK.**

Need to remove contacts from your group? Follow the same procedure you follow to add a contact to a group — except that you click the left-pointing arrow in the Add/Remove Contacts dialog box! To add a few more people to the group, choose All Contacts from the Select From drop-down list and hunt for those additional folks.

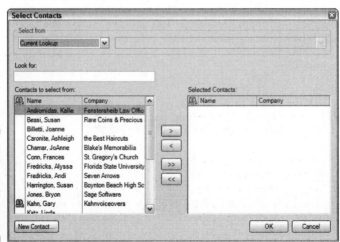

Figure 20-2: Add or remove contacts from a group.

Adding new contacts to a group does not *remove* existing members of the group — it just adds additional members.

Adding a single contact to a group

In addition to adding or removing several contacts at a time to/from your group, you might want to do it on a contact-by-contact basis. This is easy to do as well.

1. **If necessary, create a lookup for the contact that you want to add to a group.**

2. **Click the Contacts icon on the Navigation bar to make sure you are in the Contact Detail window.**

3. **Click the Groups/Companies tab.**

   The Groups/Companies tab is the home to both group and company information. To make sure that you are viewing group information, make sure that the Show Membership For drop-down list is displaying Groups and Subgroups.

4. **Click the Add Contact to Group button.**

   The Add Contact to Group dialog box opens.

5. **Select the group to which you want to add the current contact, click the right-arrow button to add him/her to that group and then click OK.**

   Because a contact can belong to more than one group, you can add the contact to as many groups as you like. The contact's Groups/Companies tab displays the groups the contact is a member of. If you want to remove the contact from a group, click the group name and then click the left arrow button.

Creating dynamic group members

In the preceding sections of this chapter, I show you how using groups in ACT! is a good thing. I show you how to add contacts to and remove them from groups. By now, you're probably an old group pro, qualified to receive an Official ACT! Groupie certificate. But, like the best-laid plans of mice and keyboards, there is one small hitch to your otherwise perfect world. What happens if you forget to add a contact to a group?

For some of you, forgetting to add a contact to a group isn't a life-threatening event. In other circumstances, however, it might be absolutely crucial that all appropriate contacts are added to the proper group. For example, what if you send a notification to all members of a group about an important meeting, but the CEO isn't included in the group?

Step away from the aspirin — this problem is easily licked with the simple creation of a group definition *query.* A definition query is ACT!'s way of automatically adding contacts to a group based on information in specific fields. Your group rules can be as simple as adding all contacts created by Joe Blow to the Joe Blow Group, or they can be based on much more complex criteria, such as *All customers in the Southwest region managed by Joe, Sue, or Steve belong in the Widgets Group.*

A query runs every time you look at the Group Detail window. You create a query based on specific field values. For example, you might set up a group rule to find all the *prospects* in *New York* for whom *Mike* is the sales rep; base your rule on the ID/Status, State, and Record Manager fields.

To set up a group definition query, follow these steps:

1. **Choose View⇨Group List from any ACT! window.**

2. **Select the group to which you want to add a query, right-click it, and then choose Group Membership⇨Add/Remove Contacts⇨ Edit Criteria.**

   The opening screen of the Group Criteria dialog box opens, as shown in Figure 20-3.

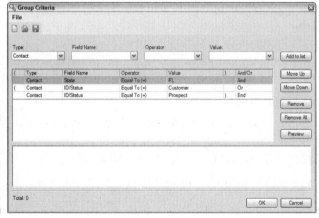

Figure 20-3:
Create a
group
membership
query.

3. **Fill in the criteria to use to establish group membership.**

   • *Type:* You can query on either Contact or Opportunity fields.

   • *Field Name:* All the fields in your database are included in the Contact or Opportunity field drop-down lists. Select the field that determines the membership into your group.

- *Operator:* Pick an operator from the drop-down list. The choices are fairly self explanatory with options like Equals, Contains, and Ends With. It might even make you feel like you're playing charades!

- *Value:* Type in the field value you're looking to match. If you select the State field name, for example, the value might be FL.

4. Click the Add to List button.

Your entry now appears in the table portion of the Group Criteria dialog box, and ACT! is ready and waiting for you to add another criterion.

5. Repeat the process until you select all the values.

For example, if you want the contact record to be in one of a series of states and have an ID/Status of Customer, you can add a second condition.

6. Change the And/Or indicator as needed.

By default, ACT! inserts an And in the And/Or column. That means that a contact must match both criteria in order to become a member of the group. The And/Or indicator is actually a drop-down with two choices: *And* and *Or.* In Figure 20-3, I changed the value to Or, indicating that I was searching for either Customers or Prospects.

If you add a second condition, the contact must match both conditions, not one or the other. For example, if you specify values for both the City and ID/Status fields, all members of the group have to reside in the same city and have identical ID/Status values. The only way to avoid this scenario is to change the And/Or value to Or.

The parentheses help you to group your criteria. In Figure 20-3, I'm looking for contacts who are prospects or customers and reside in Florida.

7. Click the Preview button.

After a few seconds of contemplation, ACT! presents you with a list of the contacts that match your criteria.

8. Click OK.

Take a look at the Group Detail window Contacts tab to see that all the contacts that appeared in the preview are now members of the group. And those contacts that didn't meet the specifications were sent out in the cold — or at least removed from the group.

Groups consist of both dynamic (based on a query rule) and static (manually selected) members. When you run a group rule to establish dynamic membership, your static members will remain in the group even if they don't match the group query criteria.

Working with Groups

You can customize groups in the exact same way that you can customize the Contact Detail window. You can add new fields, change the layout, and add tabs. You can even do a special Group lookup to search for a group based on the information in any one of the group fields that you create. For a crash course in adding new fields, scurry to Chapter 13. For a refresher course in customizing layouts, scamper over to Chapter 14.

After you create a group and stick a few unsuspecting contacts into it, things really get exciting. I love to use the phrase "unleash the power of ACT!" — I have this vision of Mr. Clean roaring out of my monitor. Okay, maybe I need to get a life, but I feel that by correctly using groups, you can really get a lot of bang for your buck with the ACT! program. This is how you can fool ACT! into believing it's a relational database. Try not to let too many people in on the secret — it might just raise the price of the software.

Think of your groups as a program within a program. You have nearly the same functionality that you do with the contact portion of ACT! — with one big difference: The notes, histories, activities and opportunities you create while in the Group Detail window affect the entire group. After you set up a group, you can add group notes, histories, activities, and opportunities for the group in exactly the same way you set them up for a contact. You can even attach a group-specific file to the group Documents tab. This is a great timesaver because information that you input belongs to the group and doesn't have to be duplicated on the contact level. You also won't have to rack your brain trying to remember which of the contacts in your group you attached a note to.

Using groups to schedule activities

One of the most powerful aspects of ACT! is its ability to associate a contact with an activity. (See Chapter 8 to read more about activities in ACT!.) Many scheduling programs allow you to design beautiful calendars; the problem is that these calendars aren't tied to a particular contact record. For example, if you schedule an appointment to visit Jane Smith and forget the date of the appointment, your only recourse is to flip through your calendar until you find the appointment. After you met with Jane, you have no history of the appointment unless you once again search through your previous appointments.

To take this analogy one step further, suppose that you chair a special committee for your local Chamber of Commerce and need to schedule a meeting. Scheduling the same appointment with each of the twenty-odd participants is very time consuming. Trying to fit each committee member's name on your calendar isn't very practical either. By scheduling the meeting with the group, however, you achieve your goal without the hassle.

Here's how it works:

1. **Click the Groups icon on the Navigation bar.**

2. **Select the group with which you want to schedule a meeting by clicking it on the Groups tree.**

3. **Click the Schedule Meeting icon on the toolbar.**

   The Schedule Activity dialog box pops open (see Figure 20-4). The name of the group that you select magically appears in the Associate With field and you can enter in all the pertinent activity information. At this point, you can click OK to schedule the meeting. However, if you'd like to have the activity scheduled for each and every member of your group, keep reading.

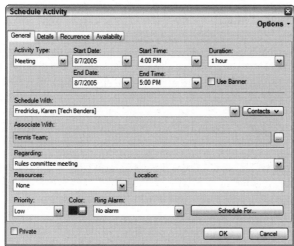

Figure 20-4: Scheduling a group activity.

4. **Select Groups from the Select From drop-down list and then choose the name of the group you are scheduling the activity with.**

5. **Click the Contacts button and then click Select Contacts.**

   In the Select Contacts window that opens you can add any individual contacts that you might want to include in your meeting. When you schedule an activity with multiple people, the activity appears on each and every contact's individual Activities tabs.

6. **Click the double-pointing right arrows.**

   Whoosh! All your group members suddenly show up in the Selected Contacts dialog box.

7. **Click OK to close the Contacts dialog box and OK again to close the Schedule Activity dialog box.**

8. **Flip over to the Group Detail window by clicking the Groups icon on the Navigation bar.**

   Okay, I know I get overly excited about the little things in life, but to me this is way cool. You'll notice from Figure 20-5 that when you schedule an activity with an entire group, your friend the hyperlink shows up in the Schedule With column. By clicking the word *multiple* — which shows up when you schedule a group activity — you're sent to the Contact List where you're rewarded with all the contacts invited to the festivities. Or, if you prefer, look on the Activities tab of any of the individual attendees; once again, you'll notice that *multiple* appears in the Scheduled With column; click it to go to the Contact List to see the list of attendees.

Using notes with groups

If you're wondering about the benefits of a group note, here are two good reasons. First, say that your contact, Larry Lawyer, is involved in many of your projects. You created a group for each of these projects like the good ACT! groupie that you are. Throughout the course of several weeks, you continually converse with Larry about the various projects. Over a period of time, as you create more and more notes for Larry, it becomes harder and harder to determine which notes belong to which project. By assigning a note to a group, you can keep all of the individual project notes together.

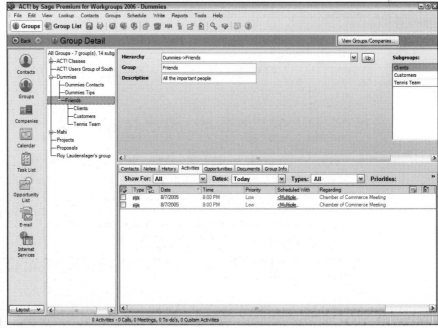

Figure 20-5:
The Group Detail window's Activities tab.

Another group note benefit is laziness — which in this case, is a good thing! If you assign a note to a group, you won't have to create the note separately for each of your group members. You also won't have to scratch your head trying to figure out which contact record you recorded the note on.

You can create a note and assign it to a specific group in three different ways. I describe each of these ways in the following subsections.

Entering a note directly from the Group Detail window

By far, the easiest way to enter a Group note is via the Group Detail window. Use this method when all you need to do is add a note that pertains to the group as a whole.

1. **Choose View⇨Group List from any of the ACT! windows.**

2. **Select the name of the group for which you want to enter a note and give it a double-click.**

3. **On the Notes tab, click the Insert Note icon.**

   If you don't remember the drill on adding a note, you might want to read Chapter 7.

Entering a note from the Contact Detail window and assigning it to the group

You can also add a group note using the Contact Detail window as your starting point. The drill is just about the same as for adding a regular note, with one extra step.

1. **From the Contact Detail window, create a lookup for the contact record of the group member for whom you want to create a new note.**

   Scratching your head as to how you're going to find that contact? You find the answers to all your lookup questions in Chapter 6.

2. **On the Notes tab, click the Insert Note icon.**

   The Insert Note window pops open. If you want to see a real, live picture of this window, stroll over to Chapter 7 for a better look. To edit an existing note, give the note a double-click.

3. **Click the ellipsis button in the Associate With area.**

   For those of you who might not be acquainted with an ellipsis, it's the button decorated with the three little dots.

4. **Select the appropriate group name, click the right-pointing arrow, and then click OK.**

Creating a group history

Another method of adding a group note is slightly more complicated than the other methods. So why, you might be wondering, am I including this in a *For Dummies* book? The reason is that you might find yourself in a situation where you need to designate a note as belonging to a group after you have had some sort of interaction with the group as a whole. Besides, by now you know that nothing in ACT! is hard once you learn the trick. Here's how you do it:

1. **Choose View➪Group List to see a list of all your groups.**

2. **Select the group you want, give it a right-click, and choose Create Lookup.**

3. **From the Contact List that appears, click the Tag All button.**

4. **Press Ctrl+H.**

   The Record History window opens. You can see what it looks like in Figure 20-6.

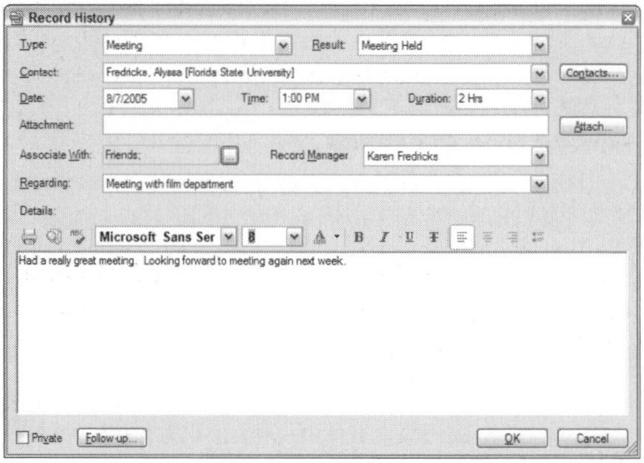

Figure 20-6:
Record a
history for a
group.

5. **Fill in your information, making sure that you include the group name in the Associate With field.**

   ACT! grabs a pen and paper and starts jotting that note down for all of the contacts in your group. Well, maybe no pen is involved but you get the idea!

Chapter 21

Joining a Company

· ·

· ·

*T*he first portion of this book focuses mainly on the contact aspect of ACT!; after all, ACT! is considered to be a contact manager. In Chapter 20, you can find out about groups, which (as the name implies) allows you to group your contacts into more manageably sized pieces. The company portion of ACT! is one that (quite frankly) not all of you will need to use. However, those of you who work with larger companies and organizations will find this feature invaluable.

In this chapter, I lead you through setting up a company — and if necessary, a division. I show you how to add (or remove) members of a company and how to use the various company features. You even find out about the company reports before all is said and done.

The 411 on Companies

Face it: Bureaucracy is alive and well and living in most civilized countries. Actually, it probably lives in *un*civilized ones as well. Your database might contain the names of the head guy (also know as The Decision Maker), your main point of contact, the guy who signs the checks, and the person who actually does all the work (the Administrative Assistant). Seems easy at first, until the head guy gets fired, the check-signer takes off for Brazil, and new people replace them both.

In really large companies (generally those that have their own cafeteria and a lot of cubicles), various divisions within the company often compound this hierarchy. Fortunately, ACT! can accommodate your need to track contacts, companies, and even divisions.

Just like navigating your way through a maze of cubicles can be intimidating, you might be a little hesitant about learning yet another piece of the software puzzle. Relax! A lot of similarities exist between the contact and company portions of ACT!; you can apply most of the concepts that you know about contacts to companies as well. For example

- ✔ You can add your own unique company fields and associated drop-down lists (see Chapter 13).
- ✔ Companies come with a variety of modifiable layouts (see Chapter 14).
- ✔ You can add company-specific documents, notes, activities, and opportunities (see Chapters 5, 7, 8, and 19).
- ✔ ACT! provides you with various customizable company-specific reports (see Chapters 9 and 10).
- ✔ You can view, modify, and print a list of all your companies.
- ✔ You can create company-based lookups (see Chapter 6).
- ✔ You can create a mail merge to a specific company (see Chapter 11).

Hey Dude, Where's My Company?

Just like with contacts and groups, ACT! provides you with a whole series of windows that help you manage your companies. Although most of these windows parallel the contact and group windows, you'll soon see that the correct usage of companies can transform ACT! into a highly effective relational database. Although you might find navigating this maze of windows a bit confusing, read on and you'll soon navigate around your companies like a seasoned veteran.

The Companies tab

Sorry to disappoint you, but in ACT!, the *Companies tab* doesn't refer to the boss's decision to pick up the check for Friday night's beer bash! The Companies tab actually refers to one part of the Groups/Companies tab in the Contact Detail window. When you click the tab, you have a choice of seeing the membership information for either the groups or the companies that a contact is associated with. The Company List works in much the same way in that it flips you back and forth between your groups and companies; guess you can consider that you're getting two tabs for the price of one!

In ACT!, you can hyperlink a contact's company to a single company record; you'll learn how to do this later in the chapter. The Company tab works a bit differently because a single contact can be a member of multiple companies. Sound confusing? Think about it. I am linked to Tech Benders because that's the name of my company. But what if I were a sales rep and assigned to several companies, all of which I like to cross-reference on my contact page? Or what if you have a contractor in your database who works with more than one company? Enter the Groups/Companies tab, as shown in Figure 21-1.

The Company List

The Company Detail and Contact Detail windows provide two ways you can see company information. The Company List lets you view a list of all your companies at one time. As with all lists, you can change the sorting order, add or remove columns, filter the information, and print the list; feel free to review Chapter 5 if you need a refresher course in how to do any of that.

You can access the Company List (see Figure 21-2) in a number of ways:

✔ **Choose View⇨Company List from any of the ACT! screens.**

✔ **Click the Companies icon on the Navigation bar and then click the Company List button.**

✔ **Create a Company lookup by choosing Lookup⇨Companies⇨All Companies.**

   If you create a lookup based on any of the individual company fields, the resulting Company List includes only those companies that match your search criteria.

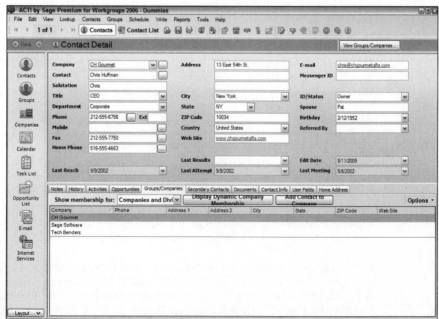

Figure 21-1:
The Groups/
Companies
tab.

Figure 21-2:
ACT!'s
Company
List.

Okay, you have three possible ways to get to the Company List, but I actually use a fourth method. Chapter 3 shows you how to customize the Navigation bar. Consider removing the Company icon from the Nav bar, which simply takes you to the Company Detail screen of the first company as it appears alphabetically in the Company List. Add the Company List icon, and you're one click away from accessing a list of your companies.

In addition to allowing you to see a list of all your companies, the Company List allows you to accomplish various company chores, all of which you can access by right-clicking your way to the shortcut menu. As you can see from the shortcut menu in Figure 21-3, your options include

- ✔ Create or deleting companies and divisions

- ✔ Create a lookup on any of the company fields

- ✔ Attach notes, histories, and files to a company

- ✔ Move, which means you can demote a company to a division or promote a division to a separate company

- ✔ Add or remove members from a company

- ✔ Export the Company List to Excel

- ✔ Customize the columns that appear in the Company List

- ✔ Print the Company List

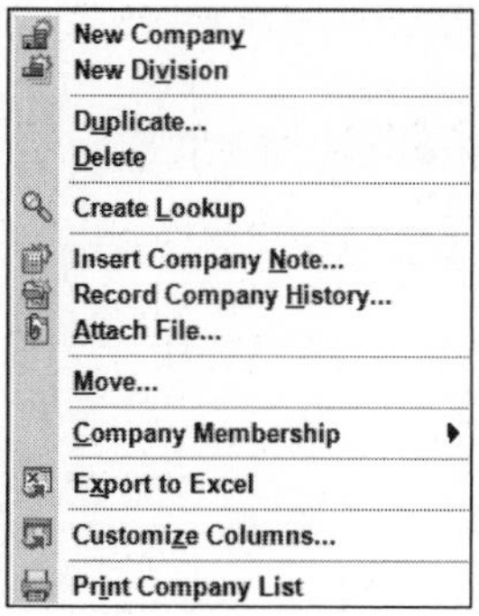

| New Company |
| New Division |
| Duplicate... |
| Delete |
| Create Lookup |
| Insert Company Note... |
| Record Company History... |
| Attach File... |
| Move... |
| Company Membership ▶ |
| Export to Excel |
| Customize Columns... |
| Print Company List |

Figure 21-3:
The
Company
List shortcut
menu.

After you arrive at the Company List, you might find that your visit is some-what short-lived because you want to zoom in on one of the companies for more details. Not a problem — just double-click the company you want to focus on, and you're transported lickety-split to the Company Detail window.

Knowing the juicy company details

The Company Detail window has many of the same features as the Contact Detail window, such as its own definable fields and layouts as well as system tabs for inserting or viewing notes, histories, activities, opportunities, and documents. You even have a few user-defined tabs to house additional company information.

You create and manage companies in the Company Detail window. Not sure how to get there? Just click the Companies icon on the Navigation bar or double-click one of the company names from the Company List. If you look at Figure 21-4, the Company Detail window looks almost exactly like the Contact Detail window.

Because the Company Detail window is so similar to the Contact Detail window, you might find yourself wandering dazed and confused into the wrong window by mistake. You might think that you're entering new con-tacts, contact details, or contact notes when you're actually entering new companies, company details, and company notes. Just like checking the title bar to assure that you are in the correct database is important, remember to sneak a peak at the Back and Forward bar to make sure you're in the correct view. Believe me, the only thing worse than entering lots and lots of data is deleting it all — and then starting all over again!

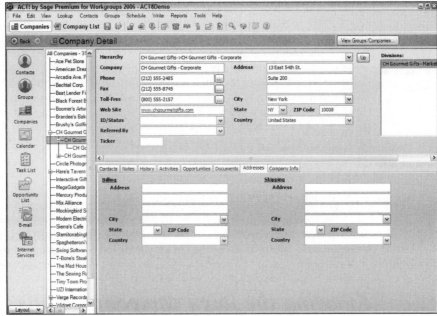

Figure 21-4:
The
Company
Detail
window.

At first glance, the Company Detail window looks like a clone of the Contact Detail window. A couple of major differences, however, are

- **Division and Hierarchy fields:** You can subdivide companies into divisions; the Division field allows you to see all the divisions within a company. You can zoom into a division by double-clicking it. The Hierarchy field indicates that you're viewing a division; clicking the Up button returns you to the main company.

- **The Companies Tree:** The Companies tree (on the left side of the screen) displays the hierarchy of all available companies and divisions in your database. If a plus sign appears next to a company, you can click it to display the company's divisions.

- **The Contacts tab:** There is a certain symmetry here. In the Contact Detail window, you have a Groups/Companies tab; in the Company Detail window, you have a Contacts tab. This Contacts tab lists all the contacts that are associated with the current company or division. The neat thing about the Contacts tab is that you can zoom to any individual contact by clicking the hyperlink attached to the name.

Hyperlinks

The company feature you'll probably like the best is the ability to quickly flip back and forth between a company and the contacts that "belong" to that company. This is done through a series of hyperlinks. When you indicate that a contact is associated with a company, the company name turns to blue on the Contact Detail window and on the Contact List; click this name, and you arrive at the Company Detail window. From the Company Detail window, you see a series of tabs running across the middle of the screen. You'll be learning how to create those hyperlinks later on in this chapter. Click the Contacts tab, and you see a list of the contacts associated with the company. Guess what? All the contact names appear in blue, which isn't a decorative font treatment. Venture forth and click a contact name; the hyperlink returns you safely to the Contact Detail window of the contact you clicked.

Company Housekeeping

The Company portion of ACT! is at the same time both surprisingly powerful and surprisingly easy to use. Like anything else in life, your companies function best when you give a little thought to their care and feeding. Here are a few of the routine tasks you need to know about.

Forming a new company

When you create a company in real life, you have to hire an attorney and sign a bunch of papers. In ACT!, the procedure is a bit simpler, thank heavens! You can add a new company from either the Company List or Company Detail window.

1. **Click the New Company icon on the toolbar of the Company Detail window or the Company List.**

   A blank Company Detail window appears.

   Adding a new company works in pretty much the same way as adding a new contact. When that blank screen appears, you are the proud owner of a new, albeit blank, company. You need to start entering some information.

2. **Fill all the necessary information into the various company fields.**

3. **Click the Contacts tab, click the Add/Remove Contacts button, and then click the Contacts button in the Add/Remove Contacts dialog box.**

   Whew! I agree, that seems like a lot of steps, but you safely arrive at your destination — the Select Contacts dialog box, as shown in Figure 21-5. Type in the first several letters of the last name of the contact you want to associate with this company.

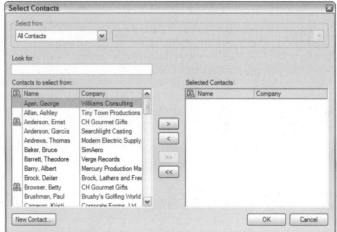

Figure 21-5:
Adding
contacts to
a company.

4. **Click the right-pointing arrow.**

   Add as many names as you like to the company.

5. **Click OK when you finish.**

Creating a division (or subdivision)

You might find yourself dealing with companies that vary in size from the sole proprietor who runs his business from his backyard tree house to the Fortune 500 company with locations all around North America — or the world for that matter. You might even find yourself working with a really super-sized corporation — like the federal government. ACT! allows you to create 15 division levels, so you can have divisions of a company as well as divisions of your divisions. Sound confusing? It is, but then so is the structure of many mega corporations.

To create a new division, subdivision, sub-subdivision, or whatever, follow these steps:

1. **Display the company to which you want to add a division.**

   You can find a list of the companies from either the Company Detail window or the Company List.

2. **Click the New Division icon on the toolbar.**

   You right-clickers in the crowd can also right-click and choose New Division from the shortcut menu. Either way, a blank Company Detail window appears.

3. **Enter the pertinent info for the division that you are creating.**

   The next time you display the original company, you see the division you added in the Divisions field. Double-click it to land in the new division. To add members to the division, click the Add/Remove Contacts button on the Contacts tab and add division members just like you add company members.

After creating a division (or subdivision), the Company Detail window is probably your best source for navigating through the corporate maze. In the main company window, all the divisions listed in the Divisions field along the right side (refer to Figure 21-4). If you want to hone in on a division, just double-click the division name; the company name and path now appear in the Hierarchy field, and any additional subdivisions appear in the Divisions field. You can keep drilling down through the divisions until you reach the final subdivision or oil — whichever comes first.

Notice the Include Subdivisions option at the top of the Company List. As the name implies, clicking it shows you all the divisions and subdivisions. However, the list appears in alphabetical order, so you'll find it pretty impossible to figure out which divisions belong to what company. Although you can perform most of these housekeeping tasks from the Company List, chances are pretty good that you'll eventually end up with a muddled mix of company, divisions and subdivisions.

Deleting a company

I almost hesitate to tell you about this feature because you could easily delete a company by accident. The good news is that even if you delete a company, the contacts associated with the company are still alive and well and living in your database. The bad news is that all the information from the company fields is lost forever — unless, of course, you have a backup! If you don't have a backup, Chapter 15 will show you how to get one.

1. **Select the company you want to delete in one of the following ways:**

   - Highlight the company or division from the Company List.

   - View the company from the Company Detail window.

2. **Right-click and select Delete Company.**

3. **Click Yes to confirm that you want to delete the selected company.**

If you delete a company that contains divisions, the divisions don't get deleted — they get promoted to their very own companies. If your intention is to delete a company and all its divisions, you need to delete the various divisions before deleting the company itself.

Converting a group to a company

You might already be an ACT! fanatic and have recently converted from ACT! 6 to ACT! 2006. ACT! 6 users had to be content with groups because the concept of companies was nonexistent at that time. You might have set up a group that in actuality is a company. New users in the crowd might set up a group from time to time and find that the group miraculously transformed itself into a full-scale company. By now, you know that ACT! thinks of everything, and this is just one more instance. You can easily convert a group into a company at the click (or two) of a button by following these steps:

1. **From any ACT! screen, choose View⇨Group List.**

2. **From the Group List, choose the group you want to convert to a company.**

3. **Right-click and choose Convert to Company.**

   If you prefer, you can also head up to the menu bar and choose Group⇨ Convert to Company. In any case, the Convert Groups to Companies Wizard appears.

4. **Continue clicking Next until you arrive at the last screen; then click Finish.**

   If you like, I can try to make these instructions a bit more difficult. Basically the wizard is confirming that yes, you want to convert the group into a company. By default, the group name becomes the company name, the group address now is the company address, and so on. Feel free to muddle in there if you want, but don't blame me if your muddling efforts are successful!

After the conversion is complete, you might want to race over to the Company List to have a look at the company you just worked so hard to create! You'll also notice that the original group has disappeared — or at least been replaced by the new company.

Following the company rules

Nothing is worse than letting things slip through the cracks, and ACT! works like a demon to prevent this from happening. Companies are only as good as the contacts associated with them — so what happens when you forget to link a contact to a company? Never fear, once again ACT! is here with a solution. Setting up company rules helps automate the process. That way, whenever you add a new contact to an existing company, the contact is automatically linked to that company.

To set up a company rule, follow these steps:

1. **Click the Add/Remove Contacts button on the Contacts tab of the company for which you'd like to create a rule.**

2. **Choose Edit Criteria from the Add/Remove Contacts window.**

   The Company Criteria dialog box, as shown in Figure 21-6, opens.

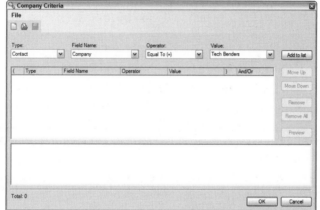

Figure 21-6: Creating company rules in ACT!.

3. **Indicate the criteria that you're using to determine how the new contacts are automatically linked to an existing company.**

   Nine times out of ten, you base the criteria on the company name, so you fill in your criteria exactly as you see it in Figure 21-6. If you're working with a large company with multiple offices, you might need to indicate the city as well. For those of you who always prefer multiple-choice to fill-in-the-blank exams, you can choose all the values from drop-down lists so that you can simply select the criteria you want:

   - *Type:* Indicate whether you want to match a Contact or an Opportunity field.

   - *Field Name:* Indicate the field you want to use.

   - *Operator:* Typically, you use something like Equal To or Contains.

   - *Value:* Indicate the name of the company or the exact verbiage you want to match.

   If this window looks vaguely familiar, you could be having flashbacks — or remembering the Advanced Query window. Chapter 6 discusses the Advanced Query window in full detail and will give you additional help in creating a Company query.

4. **Click the Add to List button.**

In general, you only add one criterion — the company's name. However, if you need to have more than one criterion, go ahead and add as many as you like. The criteria that you select display in the center pane.

5. Click the Preview button to preview the contacts linked to the company.

6. Click OK when you finish.

The next time you add a new contact and indicate that he works at an old company — or at least one of your existing ones — ACT! automatically links the contact to the company.

Joining the Company Association

The beginning of this chapter concentrates on the company side of things; you can read how to create a company and associate contacts with that company. This section looks at the individual contact and his association with a company. As I mention earlier, there are two ways that a contact can be associated with a company:

- ✔ Through the use of a hyperlink in the contact's company field
- ✔ By association with a company or companies on the contact's Groups/Companies tab

A contact can be *linked* to only one company. However, a contact can be a *member* of more than one company.

Hyperlinking a contact to a company

You have two important concepts to remember before linking a contact to a company:

- ✔ You can hyperlink a contact to only one company.
- ✔ Linking a contact to a company creates a hyperlink from the contact to the corresponding company.

Sound a bit confusing? It is, but here's a way to simplify things. Linking a contact to a company is done using the Company field on the Contact Detail window. In general, the contact is linked to his own company.

With those concepts in hand, follow these steps to link a contact to a company:

1. Create a lookup of the contact that you want to link to a company.

2. **Click the Browse button (with the ellipsis) next to the Company field in the Contact Detail window.**

   The Link to Company dialog box appears, as shown in Figure 21-7.

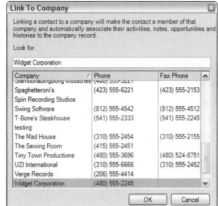

Figure 21-7:
Create a
hyperlink
between a
contact and
a company.

3. **Select the company to which you want to link the contact and then click OK.**

   If the company name on the Contact Detail window is an identical match to one of the companies that you created, ACT! will match them up automatically. If the name isn't identical, you can type the first few letter of the company name in the Look For field so that ACT! will automatically scroll down the list of companies and find it for you.

   The company name appears in blue, indicating that a hyperlink is created between the contact and the company.

   If you find that you no longer want the link, simply click the Browse button again. ACT! asks you whether it's okay to disable the link. Click OK, and it's history.

Adding or removing company members

Just because a contact is *linked* to a company doesn't mean that he is a *member* of that company. I know this seems like fuzzy logic, but this concept ties in to the fact that a contact can be linked to only one company but can be a member of several. You saw earlier in this chapter how you could associate a contact with a company from the Company Detail window. Here you can see how to associate a contact to one or more companies from the Contact Detail window.

Don't worry — gaining membership to a company is easy and doesn't require a membership application or initiation fee. You can add new members to the club, er, company from either the Company Detail or the Contact Detail windows. After you associate contacts with a company using the Company Detail window, start with an individual contact and sign him up as a member of the company:

1. **Create a lookup on the contact that you want to add as a member to the company.**

2. **Click the Groups/Companies tab and show membership for Companies and Divisions.**

    You'll probably find that last step a bit unnecessary; I do, too. Just remember that Groups and Companies are forced to share the same tab, so you have to specify that you're interested in using the Company portion of the tab.

3. **Click the Add Contacts to Company button.**

    The Add Contacts to Company window shows up, as shown in Figure 21-8.

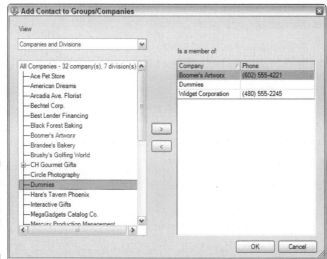

Figure 21-8:
Adding a
contact to
Groups/
Companies.

4. **Select the company you wish to link to the current contact, click the right pointing arrow, and then click OK.**

Working with a Company

You might want to think of a company as a mini database within a database. The Company Detail window includes the same tabs as other views do — Notes, History, Activities, Opportunities, and Documents. However, it has one major difference: You can filter the Notes, History, Activities, and Opportunities tabs to show just the information that pertains directly to the contact. This feature is very useful and powerful and gives ACT! a whole new dimension.

Jotting down a company note

The concept of company notes is a powerful but confusing one. Say you have 12 contacts, all associated with one company. Also assume that each of those contacts has an average of 20 notes that you've entered. If my math is correct — and it doesn't hurt to double-check me here — the combined total notes for all the company members is 240. Now imagine having to sift through all those notes looking for the one important one. Yikes! That might take a while. Conversely, imagine your company just closed a major deal with the other company; you'd probably find having to enter the same note 20 times, once for each member of the company, repetitious and a huge waste of your time. Enter the company note.

Entering a note from the Company Detail window solves both of these dilemmas: You don't have to enter the note repeatedly, and you don't have to search through a mountain of notes to find it.

Entering a company note is as easy as 1-2-3:

1. **Click the Notes tab in the Company Detail window.**

2. **Click the Insert Note button.**

3. **Fill in the details of the note and click OK.**

Now comes the fun part. If you look at Figure 21-9, you'll notice the Show For drop-down list. Here's where you can filter the notes to show only company-specific notes. You have three choices from which to choose:

 ✔ **All:** Shows both company-specific and contact-specific notes

 ✔ **Company:** Shows only company-specific notes

 ✔ **Company Contact:** Shows only contact-specific notes

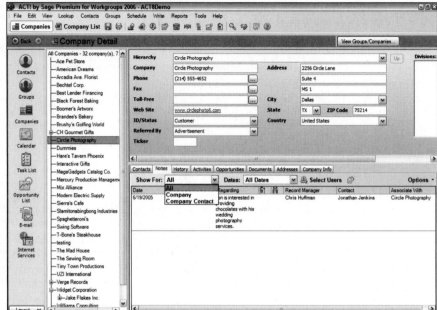

When you enter a note from the Company Detail window, you can access it only from the Company Detail window. If you enter a note from the Contact Detail window of a company member, you can view the note from both the Contact Detail and Company Detail windows.

Associating a note, history, activity, or opportunity with a company

The final piece of the company puzzle occurs when you want to create a note, history, activity, or opportunity with a specific member of a company and you want to make sure that it's easily accessible from the Company Detail window. And, of course, you don't want to have to plow through numerous items just to find the specific note, history, activity, or opportunity for which you're looking. If you were dealing with another contact management program, I might just tell you to take a hike; however, you're dealing with ACT!, so of course, I have a solution for you.

Actually, the solution is pretty easy. Any time you create a note, history, activity, or opportunity, ACT! allows you to associate it with a company. By doing that, you take advantage of the Company filter on the appropriate Groups/Companies tab so that you can view just the pertinent information that you want. I show you how to do it for an opportunity, but you can use the same methodology when creating a note, history, or activity.

1. **Create a lookup for the contact with whom you want to create a sales opportunity.**

2. **Click the Opportunities tab and then click the New Opportunity icon.**

   Fill in all the appropriate Opportunity information. If you need a little help, flip over to Chapter 19.

3. **Click the ellipsis button next to the Associate With field.**

   The Associate with Group/Company dialog box appears, as shown in Figure 21-10.

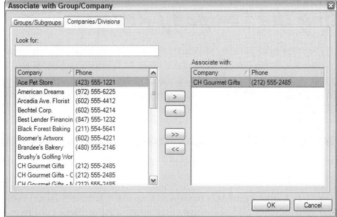

Figure 21-10:
Associate a note, history, activity or opportunity with a company.

4. **Click the Companies/Divisions tab.**

5. **Locate the company from the list on the left, and click the right-pointing arrow to select it.**

   The company name appears in the Associate With list.

6. **Click OK.**

After you associate a note, history, activity, or opportunity with a company, you can view them from the Company Detail window. Filter the History, Activities, and Opportunities tabs exactly the same way as the Notes tab by clicking the Show For drop-down list and selecting your desired filtering option. And, when you quickly find just the item you're looking for in the filtered list, think of me before heading out to the pool!

Accessing the company files

Unlike the other systems tabs, you can't filter the Documents tab. Rather, it sits there like a giant bank vault, just waiting for your deposit. Okay, maybe all this talk about companies has left me with dreams of *Monopoly,* but you can attach as many documents as you like to the Documents tab of the Company Detail window. This saves you having to hunt through the various company contacts looking for the contact to whom you attached an important file.

Getting the Company Reports

Although ACT! might not be submitting reports to the SEC for you, at times, it seems like it comes pretty darned close. ACT! comes out of the box with five reports, all of which you can clone and then customize to fit your needs. If you haven't done so already, you can read about customizing your reports in Chapter 10.

- ✔ **Company Membership:** Lists all your companies and their members.

- ✔ **Company Summary:** Shows the notes, histories, activities, and opportunities for all companies.

- ✔ **Company Comprehensive:** Gives you the complete lowdown on a company. It includes all field information as well as notes, histories, activities, and opportunities.

- ✔ **Company List:** Provides you with a list of all your companies including the description, phone, and toll-free numbers.

- ✔ **Company Directory:** Lists the regular and shipping addresses as well as phone and toll-free numbers for each of your companies.

Chapter 22

Working with ACT! Premium for Web

. . . .

In This Chapter

▶ Configuring your hardware and software

▶ Making changes to Windows

▶ Installing the Web-based version of ACT!

▶ Sharing the database with others

. . . .

Using an online product allows you to access, update, and share ACT! information via the Internet. Best of all, the information is in real time. You can perform lookups, run reports, and work on the Web-based version of ACT! just as if you're working back in the main office. However, you need to make sure that your hardware — and systems administrator — are up to the task. You'll need to tweak Windows and then make sure your users know where to find the database on the 'Net.

Looking Before You Leap

On paper — or at least on the side of the software box — placing a database on the Web sounds easy. All you need in order to put your database on the Internet for all the world (or at least your company) to see is a Web server with Internet Information Services (IIS) installed, a licensed copy of ACT!, and a Web site. And configuring ACT! Premium for Web is simple if you know all about IIS. However, for those of you who think IIS is simply a misspelling of *is,* you might want to read on.

Handling the hardware

Before you install the ACT! Premium for Web software, you need to ensure that your hardware is up to the task. You need a server with the following specs:

- ✔ A Pentium 4 processor
- ✔ 300MB of free hard drive space for the software and additional space for the actual ACT! databases and related files
- ✔ At least 1GB of RAM

  If you over ten people are coming to the party — or Web site — you want at least 1.5GB of RAM and extra pigs-in-blankets. Accommodating over 25 attendees requires at least 2GB of RAM and shrimp cocktail.

- ✔ A CD drive
- ✔ A high-speed Internet connection

Going on a Windows fact-finding mission

All versions of Windows are not created equal, at least when they pertain to hosting a Web site. Some of the lesser versions — like Windows Millennium Edition (Me) or XP Home Edition just won't cut the mustard here. You need one of the big guns to do the job:

- ✔ Windows 2000 Server or Small Business Server
- ✔ Windows 2003 Standard, Web or Enterprise

In addition, if you are going to have a maximum of ten *concurrent* (at the same time), users you can also use

- ✔ Windows XP Professional
- ✔ Windows 2000 Professional

Installing IIS

After you have your hardware (check) and the proper operating system, you need to start transforming your computer into a full-fledged Web server. This is actually easier done than said if you follow these directions:

1. **Choose Start➪Control Panel➪Add or Remove Programs➪Add/ Remove Windows Components➪Internet Information Services (IIS) and then click Next.**

   The cool thing here is that Windows takes the guesswork out of everything — and even tells you what those IIS initials stand for. You can see the Windows Components setup screen in Figure 22-1.Your computer will buzz along for a minute.

Figure 22-1:
The
Windows
Components
setup
screen.

2. **Pop in your original Windows installation disc when prompted and then click Next.**

   What I like about this is that you can accomplish a very high-tech feat with a fairly low-tech skill level.

What's in an IP name?

Although you and I might name our computers with endearing names such as *Hal* or *Son of a Pitchfork,* programmers think in terms of numbers and name their computers with names such as 192.168.2.38. Guess that has a ring to it — if you're a computer. This name/number is a computer's *internal IP address.* A computer's internal IP address identifies it from the other computers in your internal network; hence, the modifier *internal.* Within your network, you can assign IP addresses at random as long as each one is unique.

When you connect to the outside world, you have an external IP address. This number identifies you to the outside world — the great big world outside your internal network. Your external IP also has a cute name such as 67.87.243.62.

External IP addresses come in two flavors: dynamic and static. A *dynamic* IP address is like a cute little toddler — it bounces around all over the place. Your external IP address is assigned to you by your ISP (Internet service provider) on a round-robin, first-come-first-served basis. Consequently, one day, your name is 67.87.243.62; the next day, it's 1.160.10.240.

Your remote users log on to your Web server using your Web server's external IP address. The trouble is that remote users might feel like they're playing a giant game of "keep away" if they have to use a different IP address every time they want to get into ACT!. Enter the static IP address. A *static* IP address doesn't change, making life much easier for your remote users.

Stop the IP, I want to get on

If you have a dynamic IP address, you have to get a static one or risk having your remote users not being able to access the database. There are various methods of obtaining a static IP:

- ✔ **Check with your ISP.** Surprisingly enough, if you pay your ISP a little extra money each month, it will be most happy to accommodate you.

- ✔ **Use any one of the many services** that can provide you with a static IP address for a very reasonable price — if not for free. Check out

  - **DynIP.com:** `http://dynip.com`

  - **No-IP.com:** `www.no-ip.com`

  - **DNS2Go:** `http://dns2go.com`

  Each can transform your magical number into something along the lines of *yoursite.theirsite.com*.

- ✔ **Register a domain** if you really want to get fancy. You can substitute it for your external IP address number so that you can go to your Web site by using either 12.34.567.89 or `mywebsite.com`.

There are a number of ways to determine the external IP address of your Web server. The easiest is to pull up your Web browser, go to one of these sites, and jot down the number provided there:

- ✔ **WhatIsMyIP.com:** `http://whatismyip.com`
- ✔ **ConfirmIP.com:** `www.confirmip.com`

Giving Windows an Internet Makeover

After you gather all your supplies — pencils, paper, Web server, operating system — now's the time to put them all together. The following steps aren't hard, but there sure are a lot of them. Just remember that paying attention to the details will ensure that your installation proceeds without a hitch.

Confirming that IIS is alive and well

In the preceding section, you can read how to install IIS. However, just like the light switch, you'll need to turn it on if you expect it to work.

1. **Right-click the My Computer icon on your desktop and choose Manage.**

   The Computer Management window opens, as shown in Figure 22-2.

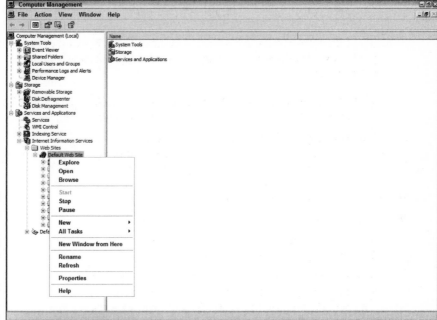

Figure 22-2:
The
Windows
Computer
Manage-
ment
window.

2. **Expand the Services and Applications area by clicking its plus sign.**

3. **Expand Internet Information Services by clicking its plus sign.**

4. **Expand the Web Site item by clicking its plus sign.**

5. **Right-click Default Web Site.**

   If this service isn't running, the word `Start` shows up after the Default
   Web Site item; right-clicking it gives you the choice of Start to start it
   again. If the contextual menu includes Stop, you're already started and
   you should close the Computer Management Window.

Inviting an Internet Guest Account

An *Internet Guest Account* (IUSR) is a special account that you create in
Windows. The IUSR can access your Web site but not the rest of your server.
ACT! Premium for Web needs to have an IUSR set up so that it can be secure
in the knowledge that the outside world can access your database — and
only your database. The IUSR account is generally created when you install
IIS, but it's always a good idea to check for its presence. If it's missing, you
need to go back to the drawing board and reinstall IIS.

1. **Right-click the My Computer icon on your desktop and choose Manage.**

2. **Expand the Local Users and Groups area by clicking its plus sign; click
   the Users folder.**

Usually, the IUSR is named after his father — which, in this case, happens to be the name of your computer. In Figure 22-3, you can see that my Internet Guest Account is named IUSR_KSFLAPTOP.

 3. **Close the Computer Management window.**

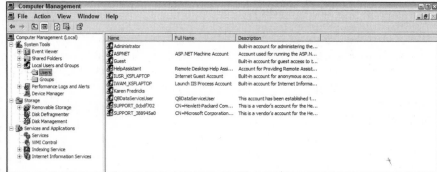

Figure 22-3:
Verifying the
Internet
Guest
Account.

Making an ASP.NET of yourself

In a nutshell, ASP.NET is used to create Web pages and Web services. ASP
.NET impersonation allows outside users to access an application — in this
case, your ACT! database. With ASP.NET impersonation, IIS becomes responsible for who is let into the party and who is denied admission.

 1. **Right-click the My Computer icon on your desktop and choose
    Manage.**

 2. **Expand the Services and Applications area by clicking its plus sign;
    then click the Services folder.**

 3. **Confirm that ASP.NET is listed as one of the services by right-clicking it.**

    This works exactly like the IIS service that you verify in the earlier section, "Confirming that IIS is alive and well." If this service isn't running,
    the word `Start` shows up on your right-click menu. If the contextual
    menu includes Stop, you are already started, and you should close the
    Computer Management Window.

Just call me APFW

The final thing you want to do is to create your own Windows user. The
bottom line is that the IUSR you create earlier in this chapter has access
to all your Web files; the Windows user you are about to create has access
to only the ACT! Web files.

To create the Windows user, return once more to the scene of the crime —
the Computer Management window.

1. **Right-click the My Computer icon on your desktop and choose
   Manage.**

2. **Expand the Local Users and Groups area by clicking its plus sign; then
   click the Users folder.**

3. **Click the Actions menu and choose New User.**

   The screen shown in Figure 22-4 appears. Although you can name the
   user name anything your little heart desires, I would stick to something
   simple and relatively nonconfusing like APFW — which is an acronym
   for ACT! Premium for Web.

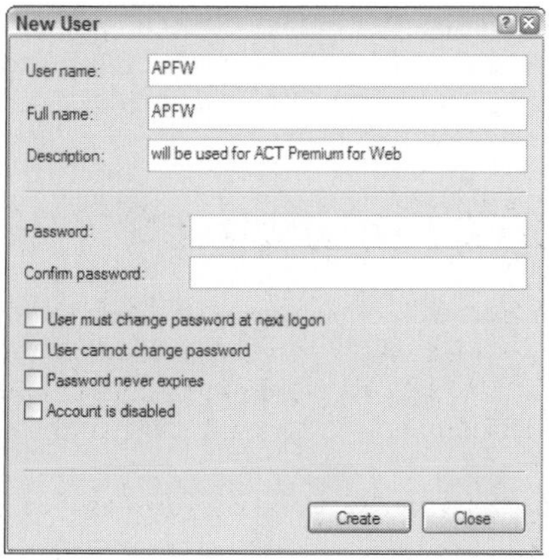

Figure 22-4:
Creating a
Windows
user.

4. **Clear the User Must Change Password at Next Logon option.**

5. **Assign a password to the user.**

   Think of a good password — just make sure you remember it again later!
   To jog your memory, you have to type it in twice.

6. **Click Create to create the new user.**

   The New User dialog window snaps shut — or at least closes with a
   quiet click. You once again find yourself in the Computer Management
   window, which is a good thing because you have a little more tweaking
   to do.

7. **Expand the Local Users and Groups area by clicking its plus sign; then
   click the Groups folder.**

8. **Right-click the Administrators group and choose Add to Group.**

   The Administration Properties window opens. As the name implies, here you add the newly crowned ACT! Premium for Web user to the Administrators group so that the remote has full access to all the database files and folders.

9. **Click the Add button.**

   The Select Users window opens, as shown in Figure 22-5.

10. **Click the Advanced button and then click Find Now.**

11. **Select APFW from the name list and click OK.**

    At this point, you are probably so excited you can hardly contain yourself. Take a deep breath and think of that mango margarita you're going to be treating yourself to.

12. **Click OK two more times to close the Select Users and the Administrators Group windows and then close the Computer Management window.**

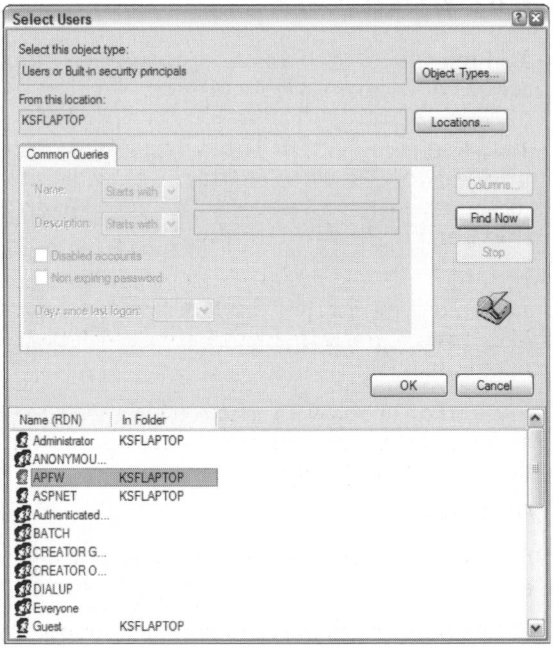

Figure 22-5:
Adding the APFW to the Administrators Group.

Installing ACT! Premium for Web

After you make Windows willing and able to host your database online, you need to install ACT! Premium for Web on your Web server. This requires that you stick the CD in the CD drive and follow the directions. If you already have an older version of ACT! (version 6 or earlier) or version 1.0 of ACT! Premium for Web installed on your computer, the installation wizard will mention it to you but let you carry on anyway. If you have ACT! 2005 or 2006 installed on your computer, ACT! won't let you continue until you uninstall the product.

This chapter is designed to go in a very sequential order. If you haven't already configured Windows as described earlier in this chapter, ACT! Premium for Web will point out the error of your ways and prevent you from continuing.

After the installation is complete, you have 30 days to register the product. After that, you have a choice of registering or not using the product.

Opening your database

After you install ACT! Premium for Web, you need to specify the database(s) that you want to access. You have a few options here:

- ✔ **Create a new database.** You'll find this an extremely easy option because the installation wizard asks you whether that's what your intentions are. A simple click of the Yes button when prompted, followed by the several clicks of Next, Next, and Next will do the deed.

- ✔ **Use an existing 2005 or 2006 database.** Your easiest route here is to first create a backup of your database and then restore it in ACT! Premium for Web. If you're not sure how to accomplish that feat, you can read up on it in Chapter 15.

- ✔ **Use an ACT! 6 or earlier database:** This option is a bit trickier but doable. You want to move the ACT! database on to the server and then open it using the following instructions:

     a. *Choose File⇨Open.*

      Here's where you navigate to the place where you've moved your database.

     b. *Chose ACT! 3-6 Database from the Files of Type drop-down list.*

     c. *Select your database and click Open.*

      Just relax and put your feet up on your desk for a moment while ACT! cheerfully converts your database for you.

In most cases, the ASP.NET user is automatically given full rights to the folder that houses both your ACT! database and all the supplemental folders. However, it never hurts to double-check that the ASP.NET user does indeed have full access rights to all of these folders.

Web Site Administration tool

If you're familiar with ACT!, you're familiar with ACT! Premium for Web. For the Administrator accessing the database from the Web server, everything seems to be safely in the correct place. But wait — those administrators with sharp powers of observation might notice something new that's been added to the Tools menu: Web Site Administration. The database administrator will be making use of this tool to specify the database that can be accessed over the Internet and the name of the Windows account that will be used by the remote users when they first log in to the server.

1. **Choose Tools⇨Web Site Administration.**

   The Web Site Administration tool opens, as shown in Figure 22-6.

2. **Click the User Account tab and then click the Edit button.**

   The Edit User Account window appears. You're asked to supply three key pieces of information:

- *Windows Domain:* You can use the drop-down arrow here to select the domain or workgroup that hosts your ACT! database. By default, the name of the domain or workgroup that you're logged into appears.

- *Windows User Name:* Type in the name of your ASP.NET impersonation user that you set up. See the earlier section, "Making an ASP.NET of yourself."

- *Password:* Type in the password that you assigned to that user.

3. Click OK to close the Edit User Account dialog box.

4. Click the Add/Remove Database tab.

You now have to tell ACT! which database should be added to the Virtual Directory. Don't be scared of all the high tech language; ACT! Premium for Web has already created the virtual directory and will be more than happy to move any database(s) into it that you'd like. On the Add/Remove Database tab, click the Add button to navigate to the location of your database. After you select the database, you're asked to supply the database user's name and password. When you get by the gatekeeper with the correct credentials, the Add/Remove Database tab looks just like Figure 22-7 — with the name of your database appearing in the database area.

Figure 22-7:
Adding a database to the virtual directory.

5. Click the Test button and hold your breath.

Okay, you don't really have to hold your breath to proceed, but you might consider crossing your fingers. You've worked really hard to get to this point, and now is your chance to see whether your database is going to fly on the Internet. If the test is successful, your browser opens up to the ACT! Premium for Web login screen, as shown in Figure 22-8. If the test proves to be unsuccessful you'll need to replicate all the steps you've covered earlier to see if you missed one of them.

6. **Close your Web browser and then close the Web Site Administration window.**

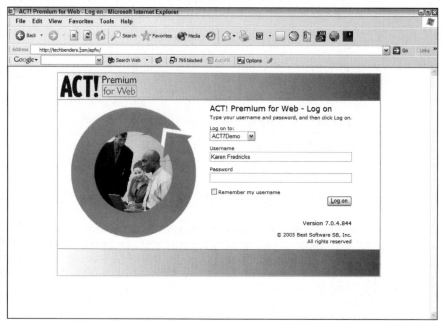

Figure 22-8:
The ACT!
Premium for
Web login
screen.

Inviting Others to the Party

If you've followed this chapter to this point, you've done a really great job configuring your Web server to house ACT! Premium for Web — or at least hiring the right person to configure your Web site. Now you get to reap your rewards, harvest your fruit, and introduce your Web-based database to your remote users.

The hardware configuration isn't as important for the remote users as they are for the Web server. Remote users can even be using older operating systems such as Windows 98 or Windows Me. They can even access the database with an old-fashioned, dial-up connection although a higher connection speed would certainly prove to be much faster and less frustrating.

Remote users do not have to install any software on their machines because they will be accessing ACT! via their Web browsers. They do, however, need to be using either version 5.5 or 6 of Internet Explorer.

The remote users might also have to change a few of their security settings:

- ✔ Accepting cookies (the Web type, not chocolate chip) must be enabled in Internet Explorer.
- ✔ ACT! Premium for Web's site should be added to the Trusted Sites Zone so that pop-ups won't be blocked when accessing the database.
- ✔ Two Active X security controls must be installed to use the word processing function: TX Text and Common Dialog.

Remote users also have to make sure the following software is installed on their machines:

- ✔ Internet Explorer 5.5 or higher
- ✔ Adobe Reader 5.0 or later

You can't drive without a license

You need a license for every one of your remote access users. Although the Administrator can set up as many new users as he'd like, those users can't log in to the database unless there are sufficient licenses to go around. If a user is going to access the database both from the office network and over the Internet, he needs only one license.

Logging in to ACT! Premium for Web

Remote users access ACT! Premium for Web using the external static IP address that you determine earlier in this chapter, followed by the name of the Virtual Directory that houses your ACT! database. A virtual directory is a folder that houses all your Web site data; ACT! Premium for Web creates one called APFW when you install the program. If you purchased a domain, they might log in to `http://mywebsitedomain.com/APFW`, assuming that you named your Virtual Directory APFW. Alternatively, they might log in with something a bit more cryptic, such as `http://12.34.567.89/APFW`.

After you access the Web site, you'll see the ACT! Premium for Web log in screen, as shown in Figure 22-8.

As in all versions of ACT!, you need to provide your correct user name to continue. You might also request that your Administrator assign you a password (show him Chapter 16 if he needs a little extra help) to give you a bit more security.

Feeling a sense of déjà vu

Some of you cynics in the crowd will dive into ACT! just looking for some minute little differences. I'll go ahead and make life easy for you by highlighting a few of the minor distinctions between the two products:

- **Administrative functions need to be done on the server.** Therefore, the File and Edit menus are missing in ACT! Premium for Web, and the Tools menu is abbreviated.

- **The Lookup menu is also missing.** However, notice the Quick Lookup feature at the top of the Navigation bar. Click the Lookup field to see a list of all your fields to make life easier should you want to query any one of your fields. You'll also notice an Advanced Query option directly under it.

- **Companies is now its very own menu** instead of being a submenu under the Groups menu.

- **Opportunities is now its very own menu** instead of being a submenu under the Contacts menu.

- **Your top menus belong to Internet Explorer** and not to ACT! — because you're viewing your database using IE. Double-clicking won't work, and a right-click brings up an IE menu and not the ACT! menus.

- **Reports run in HTML format.**

- **Word processing uses the ACT! word processor** — Word is not an option. Templates will use the .tpw extension.

- **Synchronization isn't necessary for ACT! Premium for Web users** but is still available if desired.

- **The monthly calendar is not available.**

Part VI
The Part of Tens

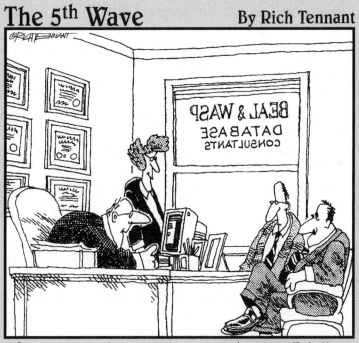

The 5th Wave   By Rich Tennant

"Your database is beyond repair, but before I tell you our backup recommendation, let me ask you a question. How many index cards do you think will fit on the walls of your computer room?"

In this part . . .

Every *For Dummies* book has a Part of Tens. By golly, this book is no exception to that rule. Think of this as the icing on your ACT! cake. Here's where I've put some ways to make a good program like ACT! work even better:

- ✔ First, I give you a rundown of the benefits of using ACT! for Web.

- ✔ Second, I show you some nifty add-on products and gizmos that can improve ACT!'s functionality.

Chapter 23

Ten Reasons to Use ACT! Premium for Web

● ●

In This Chapter

▶ Increasing your options for how you share your data

▶ Understanding the monetary benefits of using ACT! Premium for Web

▶ Increasing your database security

▶ Sparing your IT department several big headaches

● ●

*F*or the past 15 years, ACT! users everywhere have relied on ACT! to take care of their contact management needs. During that same time, reliance on the Internet has increased dramatically. Maybe you've contemplated using an online calendaring system, such as the one that Yahoo! provides, just so that you could access your calendar while away from the office. If you choose that solution, however, you lose some of the functionality that makes ACT! so appealing in the first place. Keeping your calendar in an online program other than ACT! essentially cripples your power.

In this chapter, I show you some of the reasons why you might want to consider the ACT! Premium for Web program. There are several huge benefits to having your ACT! database on the Web.

ACT! Premium for Web is a totally separate version of ACT!. If you are considering using this product for your organization, you'll want to purchase it instead of ACT! 2006 or ACT! 2006 Premium for Workgroups.

Sharing Real-time Information with Users

One of the greatest strengths of ACT! is how easily you can enter notes and other pertinent data into a database. Better still, if your database is located on a network drive, you can share all that information with the other members of your staff. However, many salespeople aren't in the office on a regular basis yet want to share updates with the home office. One way to share information is by using a Web-based product.

Synchronization, which I discuss in detail in Chapter 17, allows you to send and receive updated information to and from your remote users. However, the data is only as current as when the remote user last synchronized. There is no need to synchronize with the ACT! Premium for Web product; users always have the latest and greatest information available to them if they have Internet access.

You might wonder exactly what data is shared in ACT! Premium for Web. That's a pretty easy question to answer — all of it! You can see your core data, such as contact information, appointments and tasks, notes, histories, and sales opportunity information. You can also run a report, create a mail merge, and print labels. And if headquarters decides to make changes to the layout, you'll see those changes the next time you log into the database or refresh your browser. Worried about the customized templates that you created and want to share with your remote users? Don't worry, they're all included in ACT! Premium for Web.

Accessing Your Information Anywhere, Anytime

ACT! Premium for Web is particularly suitable for those who spend a good deal of time away from the office because you can see your database from wherever your travels take you. You'll have the luxury of accessing your database from home, a hotel room, a client site, or even an airport computer kiosk. Addicted to café macchiato grandes? You can hippety-hop to the coffee shop and work away as you feed your caffeine addiction.

Not only does ACT! Premium for Web allow you to work *where* you want to, but it also allows you to work *when* you want to. If insomnia sets in at 2 a.m. from all that coffee, you *could* jump in your car and zip over to your office — or you can save yourself a trip and simply fire up your home computer and work away. (Consider setting your alarm for 3 a.m., hopping on to ACT! Premium for Web, and adding a few strategic notes. You'll find that this strategy goes over very well with your boss, who will be impressed to see that you are working all hours of the day and night. The possibilities are endless!)

Viewing Data from a Network or the Internet

Throughout this book, you might find yourself repeatedly humming the "Have it Your Way" theme song made popular by one of those fast-food places a few years back. ACT! Premium for Web will help bring that song to your lips because it allows you the best of both worlds. Unlike a competing product that's designed exclusively for Web access, ACT! Premium for Web takes ACT! to the next level by allowing you to access your database across your company's network, remotely via the Internet, or by a combination of both methods.

Here's how it works. ACT! Premium for Web is installed on a server configured for Internet Information Services (IIS). IIS, by the way, comes free with Windows XP Professional. After installation, any member of your organization who works from the office can access that data over your company's network. However, that same data can also be accessed over the Internet so that your remote users can happily work away at the same time as your local users.

Lowering the Cost of Deployment and Upkeep

If you're anything like me, you'll want to get the most bang for your buck that you can. This is especially true of software. The cost of a software deployment is directly proportional to the number of users in a company. And typically the CFO, CEO, and any other character running around your office with a similar title wants to keep software and hardware expenditures to a minimum.

The cool thing about ACT! Premium for Web is that after you pay for your software and any hardware that you might need to run a Web site, you're done. Finished. You're completely through with paying for your database. And you can continue to use the software year after year without additional cost. With other online database solutions, you pay a monthly charge to keep your database afloat. And those charges are per user, per database, per month. Ouch.

Avoiding Additional Costs as Your Database Grows

Shopping for an online database program is kind of like shopping for a car — you'd better read the fine print! With ACT! Premium for Web, after you pay for the software, your expenses are final. This is particularly important if your database is going to grow. And believe me, as you add contacts, notes, attached documents, and customized fields, your database is going to grow. If you're using ACT! Premium for Web, the only increase in size you'll have to worry about is your waistline. This isn't the case with other Web-based database programs. Typically, you're charged by the size of your database — the bigger your database, the more you pay.

Utilizing Older Computers

Many of you live by the motto, "If it ain't broke, don't fix it" — particularly when it comes to your computers. Over the years, your trusty computer has chugged away; you've become comfortable with your current software and know all the intricacies of your current hardware. Besides, the thought of transferring all your data to a new machine is a daunting — not to mention an expensive — proposition. However, technology will eventually catch up with you, and you'll find yourself lusting over that sexy new software with all those great new features. Here's where your pain sets in. While drooling over that new software in the local computer store, you glance at the system requirements and realize that your hardware just isn't up to the task.

Although ACT! Premium for Web won't magically replace your dog-eared computer with the latest and greatest computer, it does allow you to access all the great new ACT! features from your very own browser. As long as your old clunker can access the Internet, you can access the latest version of ACT!.

Increasing Your Security

ACT! 2005 Premium introduced contact-level security, which means that the database administrator can decide which contacts a particular user can (and cannot) access. ACT! Premium for Web takes that notion a few steps further by limiting the fields that a user can — and cannot — access. For example, perhaps you store credit card information in your database, but you don't want to allow your remote users to see this information. You can provide remote users with specific layouts that limit the fields that they can access.

Some of you might be worried about having your data on the Web. Don't worry — your data is perfectly secure. First of all, as I mention earlier, ACT! Premium for Web is installed on an IIS server, which includes all kinds of neat security devices. Secondly, access to your data is further protected by your firewall, which sits in front of your server. Obviously, users need to know the URL of the database to even get close to it. And finally, any intruders have to ascertain both a user name and password in order to access the database.

Keeping Possession of Your Information

Many of you feel extremely protective about your data. Some of you might have purchased your contacts; for others, those contacts represent months — or even years — of cultivating potential customers. In either event, you don't want your data to walk out the door.

 If you're considering using another contact management program that's available only online, consider this: All your hard-earned data will now reside on someone else's computer. And, in the event that you want to start housing your information internally again, you might find it difficult — and costly — to get your own information back into your fat little fists.

ACT! Premium for Web offers more benefits than that other online service without forcing you to house your data offsite (which might be why the competitor uses the word *force* in its name!). Your data is safe and secure, living inside one of your own computers.

Sparing Your IT Department

Pity the poor IT person. When something goes wrong with your hardware, you blame him. When something goes wrong with your software, you blame him. And then, when he dons his white cape and pocket protector and rushes to your rescue, you spew all your pent-up frustration directly upon his head. It's only natural that he's not going to be particularly thrilled when you casually mention that you want all your remote salespeople to have access to your database. He's going to think that he has to administer a whole new database. And that he somehow has to get that database — or databases — shipped to the remote users. And, after those remote users get their new databases, he has to figure out how to install software on their machines remotely. And of course, the fact that those remote users are in a different time zone, are constantly on the move, and barely a notch above computer-illiterate doesn't increase his anticipation of the project.

But wait — before your IT person jumps from the nearest window, you might be able to talk him back in from the ledge with a couple of words of reassurance. First of all, he has to administer only one database. Secondly, he doesn't have to ship anything by snail mail, e-mail, or carrier pigeon. He doesn't have to walk those remote users through any sort of software installation. In fact, all he needs to do is send those remote users the Web site address for the database, along with their user names and passwords.

Back at the ranch — or company headquarters — Mr. IT can do all kinds of fun stuff, like set up passwords and user preferences, without having to deal with his remote users. He can customize the database in exactly the same way he is used to customizing the traditional versions of ACT!. In fact, he'll probably love the fact that he's in complete control of the database and won't have to spend his time "fixing" menus that users inadvertently lost or modified. And, best of all, he can send those remote users a copy of this book so they'll know how to use the database.

Working with Familiar Software

I don't know whether it's true that you can't teach old dogs new tricks, but I do know that many of us don't like to wander too far out of our comfort zones. For many of us, the introduction of Windows represented a giant leap for mankind in that it introduced standardization into common computer tasks. Switching software is a similar phenomenon; we grow accustomed to having the software look — and act — in a certain way.

You might feel that one of the greatest ACT! Premium for Web benefits is that if you know ACT!, you know ACT! Premium for Web. From the moment you log on, you'll be in familiar territory: The menus, icons, and various views look exactly like what you've grown accustomed to seeing. You'll find that you already know how to accomplish the routine tasks because you do them in the same way that you do in the non-Web versions of ACT!.

And guess what, folks? Almost all the information that you'll find in this book regarding ACT! 2006 is also applicable to ACT! Premium for Web!

Chapter 24

Ten Tips to Make ACT! Work Better

*I*f you've read this book to this point, you know about the various powerful and timesaving features that you find in the ACT! program. But I believe that you can never have too much of a good thing. With that thought in mind, I give you ten suggestions that allow ACT! to work even better — if that's possible. Some of my suggestions include products that are available for purchase; other suggestions are free to one and all. If you're looking for more information about any of the items I list in this chapter, please visit my Web site at http://techbenders.com/addons.htm.

Hiring an Expert

I like to say that ACT! is kind of a "good news, bad news" product. The good news is that ACT!'s MSRP is fairly inexpensive; the bad news is that ACT!'s retail price is fairly inexpensive. Thus, you might assume that because this software's price is low, it's a fairly easy product to master.

ACT! Certified Consultants like myself are continuously honing their ACT! skills. An ACT! Certified Consultant (ACC) helps ACT! users discover the full power of the program. In addition to showing you various tips and tricks, consultants can help clients use the program to its fullest potential. You can find a local consultant by choosing Help➪Service and Support➪ACT! Consulting from any ACT! screen.

Some ACT! consultants also have an additional certification. An ACT! Premier Trainer (APT) can not only help you customize your database but also help you learn how to use it. You can find a list of ACT! Premier Trainers by going to www.act.com/partners/apt.

Joining a User Group

John Kaufman of the CRM Connection is an ACC who runs the South Denver ACT! User Group. Regular attendees find the information that they learn there about ACT! and ACT! add-on software invaluable. They also get tips and tricks from other ACT! software users. Attendees find John's User Group to be a really great way to stay updated on new and innovative ways to use the ACT! software for their businesses and to test-drive some of the add-ons before actually purchasing them.

Don't live in Denver? I run the ACT! User Group of South Florida where 75 ACT! fanACTics regularly hang out to learn more about ACT!. Don't live in Colorado or Florida? Don't worry; User Groups are in virtually every state of the union. To find a local User Group, go to http://act.com/community/usergroups/find.

Linking Your PDA

Who doesn't use a handheld these days? They're great for people on the go — and ACT! lets you take your database along with you. And, if you believe that the best things in life are free, you'll be happy to know that ACT! 2006 includes both the ACT! Link for Palm OS and the ACT! Link for Pocket PC right on the installation CD.

These links allow you to sync your ACT! information (including notes and history) with your handheld device in just seconds. Your ACT! information synchronizes to the basic fields that are included with the Palm or Pocket PC such as phone numbers and address information.

ACT! links allow you to

- Map basic ACT! Contact fields including phone numbers, snail mail, e-mail addresses, several custom ACT! fields, and the ID/Status field.
- Synchronize ACT! contact notes and histories for each ACT! contact.
- Synchronize a select group of contacts when you use the Group feature in ACT!.

In addition, mini-versions of ACT! are available for Palm, Pocket PC, and BlackBerry handheld devices. These mini-versions of ACT! allow you to view your customized ACT! fields. You can schedule activities and create notes exactly as you do in the full-blown version of ACT!.

Linking Your Accounting Software

Most of you business owners out there need at least two pieces of software to run your business: database software to keep track of customers and to market to potential customers, and accounting software to help you keep an eye on your bottom line. Unfortunately, a piece of software that does it all often comes with a whopping price tag and a very steep learning curve. As a result, maybe you chose to use ACT! for your contact management and something else — like Peachtree or QuickBooks — for your accounting. If you have larger accounting needs, you might be using BusinessWorks or MAS 90, 200, or 500.

Accounting links can be purchased to link accounting software such as Peachtree, QuickBooks, and MAS 90 to ACT!. These products eliminate the need to enter your contact information into both applications. You can enter the contact information into either ACT! or the accounting software and then synchronize the information between the two. The link inserts a new accounting tab into ACT!, showing all the pertinent accounts receivable/payable information for any linked contact in ACT!. This feature allows your sales team access to invoice and payment history without sharing the rest of your confidential accounting information.

Reporting Software

For many of you, entering data into ACT! is only half the fun; the other half is getting that data back out again in a usable format. The typical way that most users want to view their data is in a *report*.

ACT! comes with an amazing array of reports right out of the box. In Chapter 10, you can read just how easily you can tweak those basic reports. Because variety is the spice of life, you might find yourself wandering "outside the box" and hankering for a different report. ACT!'s Report Designer is both powerful and very complex. Some of the more complex reports that involve multiple levels of grouping, filtering, and sorting are beyond the scope of this book because they require a certain level of programming skill. Consequently you might spend a lot of time trying to develop the report of your dreams and come up empty-handed and frustrated.

Don't fret. Roy Laudenslager, who just happens to be the technical editor of this book, has come to be known as the ACT! report guru. From years on the frontline as a technical support specialist for ACT!, he has a good idea of the types of reports that the typical user looks for. This experience led him to develop *Royel's Reports,* a collection of over 40 customized reports, labels, and templates. You can find it at `http://techbenders.com/addons.htm`.

SwiftPage Email

In Chapter 12, I talk about mail merging and also mention some of the pitfalls you might encounter when attempting an e-mail blast. A common problem is not knowing how to create cool-looking HTML (HyperText Markup Language) templates. Well, worry not, my friends. One of my favorite products, Swift-Page Email, can help speed you on your way — or to at least speed your e-mail blast to your customers.

I highly recommend using SwiftPage Email to help you with large-scale e-blasting. Although SwiftPage is fully integrated with ACT!, your actual e-mail is sent via the SwiftPage servers. Large companies like this concept because their internal e-mail servers don't have to handle a large amount of e-mail running through them. Small office users like this concept because of the restrictions that are sometimes placed on them by their Internet service providers (ISPs). SwiftPage is sold on a monthly basis. Pricing is determined by the amount of e-mail that you send and is generally a great bargain. Find out more about the product at `http://techbenders.com/act4 dummies.htm`.

Northwoods Software

Some of you might feel that there is no such thing as a free lunch. Well, for many years now, the nice folks at Northwoods Software have been providing ACT! users with free ACT! add-ons. These add-ons consist of various free enhancements to ACT!. At the Northwoods Web site (`www.nwoods.com`), you can sign up to be placed on its list to receive notification each time a new freebie is released.

Northwoods also produces several fee-based products:

- **Sales Automation Mania (SAM):** Think of this as the Activity Series on steroids. The Activity Series reminds you that certain tasks need to be completed on specific dates. SAM literally does your work for you by automatically printing your mail merges, sending your birthday greetings, or e-mailing your newsletters in the middle of the night.

- **Mail Merge Mania:** ACT! is great if your e-mail marketing consists of 100 or fewer contacts. When you decide to send hundreds — or thousands — of e-mails a day, you'll start running into all sorts of problems, including duplicate or inaccurate e-mail addresses, bounces, unsubscribes, and even limitations on the number of e-mails that your ISP lets you send. This product is an inexpensive way to help you overcome those barriers.

✔ **Web Prospect:** If you receive lots of response from your Web site, you'll want to check out this product. Web Prospect reads the mail you receive from your Web site registration forms and creates contacts in ACT!, saving you hours of retyping. It also works with SAM (see the earlier bullet) to really automate your responses to Web prospects.

Exponenciel

With all the great ACT! add-on products that are available, I can't keep up with them all. However, I do mention several companies by name because of their long-standing love for the ACT! community. Exponenciel (www.exponenciel.com) offers some great free add-ons that you might want to check out, as well as a couple of really cool fee-based products.

✔ **Advanced Field Protection** is designed to give you control over which user may enter data in your ACT! fields. Each user may be assigned a protection scheme. Each protection scheme comprises a list of

- Fully protected fields
- Fields that are protected if not blank (therefore allowing the user to initialize them but not to modify them after initialization)
- Tabs that are to be hidden (including system tabs)

✔ **Excel Templates with Quote/Invoice Maker** makes the generation of quotes and invoices a snap. You'll be able to merge sales/opportunities data in your Excel spreadsheets.

✔ **AutoNumbers For ACT! Records** automatically gives your contacts, companies, and/or groups a unique account number and your opportunities a unique quote number. A manual mode lets you set up a numbering system for the current contact, current lookup, or all contacts.

The ACT! Add-On Store

The ACT! Add-On Store is run by Sharon Randall, a real ACT! fanatic. Her knowledge of the product has helped her to put together the largest assortment of ACT! add-ons that you'll find anywhere. There are literally hundreds of add-on products that work with ACT! 2006. These products were all designed to fill a gap in ACT!. They range from free to hundreds of dollars, depending on their functionality.

Some of products are one-size-fits-all products, like the $49 Field Calculator from The New Hampton Group. Others are geared for specific industries, like the B.E.A.T. program, that's aimed at the mortgage crowd. I like to think of it this way: Over four million estimated ACT! users roam this Earth. Chances are pretty good that several of them needed ACT! to do the very same thing that you need it to do. If you're wrestling with a unique situation that you think ACT! just can't conquer, you might want to check out the Add-On Store.

Playing with Gadgets

My friends always laugh about the fact that if they look in my handbag they'll find an assortment of Universal Serial Bus (USB) devices rather than make-up. I confess — I'm addicted to cool gadgets. I have so many that I hardly know where to begin, but here are three of my favorites:

- **USB storage thumb drives:** I mention USB storage drives as one of the media choices for a backup in Chapter 15. I'd like to explain further why I've fallen in love with these little guys. First of all, they're tiny; hence the nickname *thumb drive.* Secondly, they are powerful; storage on a 512MB drive is roughly equivalent to that of 400 floppy disks. Third, they're inexpensive; you can typically expect to pay around $30 for a 512MB drive. Finally, they're easy to use; just stick one into your USB port, and you're ready to back up the entire contents of your database.

- **Card Scanner:** I am of the opinion that anyone with a pile of business cards sitting on his or her desk needs to have a card scanner. These devices are the approximate size of a radar detector and can easily sit on a corner of your desk formerly reserved for that mountain of cards. You simply feed the cards into the scanner, double-check the results (I find they scan with about 95 percent accuracy), and then import them into ACT!.

- **Logitech Digital Writing System (IO2):** This is my latest play toy and quickly becoming one of my favorites. The writing system consists of a special pen and paper; you write down notes when conferring with a customer, and then plug your pen into a USB port when you arrive back at your office. The pen magically transforms into a scanner, at which point your handwritten notes can be sent to Word — or into an ACT! note. For you disbelievers in the crowd: I have probably the worst hand-writing known to mankind, yet this miracle device was able to decipher my scribbling without a hitch.

Index

• *G* •